LABOUR'S ECONOMIC IDEOLOGY SINCE 1900

Developed through Crises

Christopher Kirkland

D1612565

BRISTOL
UNIVERSITY
PRESS

First published in Great Britain in 2022 by

Bristol University Press
University of Bristol
1–9 Old Park Hill
Bristol
BS2 8BB
UK
t: +44 (0)117 374 6645
e: bup-info@bristol.ac.uk

Details of international sales and distribution partners are available at bristoluniversitypress.co.uk

British Library Cataloguing in Publication Data
A catalogue record for this book is available from the British Library

ISBN 978-1-5292-0424-7 hardcover
ISBN 978-1-5292-0431-5 paperback
ISBN 978-1-5292-0432-2 ePub
ISBN 978-1-5292-0430-8 ePdf

Cover design: Nicky Boroweic
Front cover image: adobeStock
Bristol University Press use environmentally responsible print partners.
Printed and bound in Great Britain by CMP, Poole

Contents

Acknowledgements   vi

1   **Introduction: The Labour Party's Economic Policy**   **1**
     and Crises
     Understanding crises   9
     Outline of the book   12

2   **Taff Vale and the First World War**   **14**
     Introduction   14
     The early Labour Party   14
     Taff Vale, 1900–1901   17
     The First World War   20
     Labour's ideology   23
     Labour's responses to the crises   26
     Labour's understanding of socialism   27
     The Labour Party and the trade unions   30
     Conclusion   34

3   **Governing in Hard Times: The Second Labour**   **36**
     Government and Need for a Coherent Economic Policy
     Introduction   36
     The General Strike of 1926   36
     The Great Slump of 1931   39
     Labour's ideology   42
     Labour's responses to the crises   49
     Labour's understanding of socialism   51
     The Labour Party and the trade unions   54
     Conclusion   56

4   **The Second World War, Reconstruction and Revisionism**   **59**
     Introduction   59
     The Second World War and the immediate post-war period   59
     The sterling crisis of 1947   62

Labour's ideology   64
Labour's responses to the crises   68
Labour's understanding of socialism   70
The Labour Party and the trade unions   75
Conclusion   78

5   **Testing the Labour–Unions Relationship**   **80**
    Introduction   80
    The devaluation of sterling in 1967   81
    Labour, the IMF crisis and the Winter of Discontent   85
    Labour's ideology   90
    Labour's responses to the crises   92
    Labour's understanding of socialism   94
    The Labour Party and the trade unions   96
    Conclusion   99

6   **The Advent of New Labour**   **101**
    Introduction   101
    From government to opposition: an electoral crisis   102
    Labour's ideology   108
    Labour's responses to the crisis   111
    Labour's understanding of socialism   114
    The Labour Party and the trade unions   117
    Conclusion   119

7   **New Labour and the Global Financial Crisis**   **121**
    Introduction   121
    The crisis of 2007/2008   123
    Labour's ideology   125
    Labour's responses to the crisis   129
    Labour's understanding of socialism   132
    Labour and the trade unions   135
    Conclusion   137

8   **Electoral Revision**   **139**
    Introduction   139
    (More) wilderness years   140
    The 2016 Brexit referendum   144
    Labour's ideology   147
    Labour's responses to the crisis   152
    Labour's understanding of socialism   154
    The Labour Party and the trade unions   157
    Conclusion   158

CONTENTS

9   **Conclusion**   **161**

Understanding Labour's crises in a historical context   161

Labour's socialism   162

Labour in government and opposition   166

(How) can Labour win again?   168

References   171

Index   195

Acknowledgements

Like many other publications, this book has taken a significant amount of time to compile and is the product of much labour, not all of which has been mine.

I would like to thank first and foremost the editor, Stephen Wenham. When we first discussed this book in summer 2017, I did not envisage still writing it some four and a half years later. The delays in production have been my fault and mine alone, but the patience the editorial team has shown is much appreciated.

One reason for the delay was the onset of the COVID-19 crisis, which proved to be a rupture to traditional working patterns, encompassing both teaching and research. This undoubtedly impacted on the book, although its impact would have been much more severe without the support of staff at the library services at York St John University, who worked tirelessly to accommodate my numerous requests for electronic documents and inter-library loans. Thank you for your fantastic support.

I would also like to thank those who have had some input into the writing of the book, either overtly or implicitly. I would like to thank the anonymous reviewer for their comments, which I believe have strengthened the book. I hope, should they read the final iteration, they feel I have achieved this as well. I would also like to say thank you to the students who I have taught on modules covering the Labour Party, discussions with whom helped me think more holistically about the ideas and themes being discussed.

Finally, I wish to express my thanks to my father, who has tirelessly helped to proofread this book and engaged in discussion of some of the themes and ideas contained within it. Talking through the ideas offered a real sense of clarity and helped me to express my ideas on the pages that follow more clearly. Thank you.

I have received a lot of assistance with the book, although I am responsible for its contents and all errors are mine, and mine alone.

1

Introduction: The Labour Party's Economic Policy and Crises

Along with the Conservative Party, the Labour Party has dominated British politics for almost a century. Since its formation in 1906, the Labour Party has produced six Prime Ministers, who between them won ten general elections and held office for 33 years. And since 1923, when the party has not been in government it has formed the official opposition to the Conservative Party.

In the decade following its electoral defeat in 2010, the Labour Party – as well as external commentators – fixated on the shift of the party towards the left, first under Ed Miliband, dubbed 'Red Ed' due to the role of the trade unions in securing his leadership victory ahead of his brother, but most prominently under Jeremy Corbyn – the latter in particular being defined in terms of a return to 'Old Labour' (Ross, Dominiczak and Riley-Smith, 2015). Corbyn's decision to resign after the 2019 general election defeat prompted new talk of ideological battles within the party (Tidey, 2019). Yet such narratives are based on a particular reading of Labour's history: of an ideological party, committed to (vaguely defined) socialism, which by the 1980s had become outdated. According to such a view, Tony Blair's 'creation' of 'New Labour' in 1994 marked a break with what became increasingly homogenised as 'Old Labour'.

The experience of the party in the 2010s, and into the 2020s, reflects Thorpe's (2015, p 1) description of Labour as a party that has spent periods of time in office, but such periods were 'often punctuated by long periods in opposition and even – in the 1930s, 1950s and 1980s – predictions of demise'. As Thorpe notes, and later chapters demonstrate, such periods led to revisionism within the party, battles over the party's ideology and moves to return the party to a position of electability, demonstrating both continuity and change.

However the story of Labour's ideology is told, it is important in understanding British politics and the nature of changes within it.

In government, Labour has been able to instigate wide-ranging changes, such as the creation of the National Health Service (NHS) and devolution. Such policies continue to shape domestic policies and some cases, such as the NHS, have subsequently achieved cross-party consensus.

Yet, despite claiming to be a socialist party throughout this period, Labour has not been consistent in its ideology or policy platforms. Partly this is to be expected – Britain in the third decade of the 21st century is very different from what it was like in the early 20th century when the party was formed. Yet these changes have not been evenly distributed, and have been disproportionately influenced by key events. These include the economic paradigm shifts (Hall, 1993) that occurred as a result of the fall of the Labour government in 1931 and subsequent party split, the economic problems of the 1970s, and the long periods in opposition in the 1950s and 1980s, which shape understandings of the world and challenge(d) the assumptions held by senior figures within the party.

This inconsistency is also due to the term 'socialism' being used loosely to describe a plurality of views. As later chapters emphasise, the leaders of the Labour Party have traditionally been drawn from the right of the contemporary party (Michael Foot and Jeremy Corbyn being two exceptions). The socialism that the right of the Labour Party has traditionally subscribed to is that of ethical (rather than economic) socialism; drawing their intellectual roots from the work of Richard Tawney (see Chapter 2). Such ethical socialism places greater emphasis on notions such as equality of opportunity, rather than equality of outcome. Ethical socialism holds a greater role for agents – who are not seen merely as victims of broader economic structures – to improve their positions and circumstances through education programmes, the maintenance of full employment levels and so on. The role of the state is seen as facilitating such developments and funding programmes to allow agents to realise their full potential. Importantly – certainly for later proponents such as Blair – this could be achieved within the existing capitalist framework (see Chapter 7).

In contrast, other, economic, socialists take as their starting point the need to radically alter (if not break) existing capitalist structures to free workers or the working classes from oppression. Socialism here is seen diametrically opposed to capitalism and requires the state to actively correct the capitalist system by promoting equality of outcome.

Both views have traditionally been represented within the broader Labour Party, but it has also been advantageous to overlook or bury such distinctions. Ideological consistency – or at least appearing to be ideologically consistent – is important for parties in democratic political systems. Divided parties often appear weak and unelectable, and flip-flopping between ideologies diminishes trust with voters (Finlayson, 2013).

Such changes have occurred throughout the party's history, and although occurring at different paces, are more complex than the distinctions of 'Old' and 'New' Labour that have come to define divisions within the Labour Party since the 1990s. The end of the New Labour project is testimony to this, with some arguing that Corbyn especially signalled a return to 'Old' Labour. Equally, following Corbyn's resignation in 2020, the election of Keir Starmer has been presented as Labour shifting back towards the political centre and a return of New Labour. Starmer's premiership has seen the return to Labour's front bench of many who served under Tony Blair and Gordon Brown, such as Yvette Cooper and David Lammy (Stewart and Allegretti, 2021; *The Times*, 2021).

Others have been keen to highlight the continuity that exists between these two factions, at least in a historic sense. Some have employed different terminology to define those factions within the Labour Party that appear more closely aligned with traditional Conservative ideology, such as 'Blue' or 'Purple' Labour (Beech and Page, 2015; see also Chapter 8).

Such divisions and labels further fail to highlight those on the political left who feel underrepresented within the party. Feminist thought provides one example of such a marginalised issue within the party. In the early party, Keir Hardie's commitment to feminist thought (best expressed through his support for the suffragettes) was a minority view, a tradition that has occurred throughout the party's history. Despite feminists joining the Labour Party, Foote (1997, p 295) argues that 'it must be said that feminism remains external to the Labour Party's political thought', not least as the unions, although accepting some changes such as using the language of 'chairperson' instead of 'chairman', remain primarily interested in challenging 'the oppression of working women by individual employers, not their oppression by men'. Foote argues that within the party, feminism has historically been seen as a middle-class movement, which exists 'outside the general wage-relationship', meaning that its aims are often subsidiary to promoting the interests of a party whose aim is to promote working-class interests.

Other historical analysis (Beech and Hickson, 2007) has explored the party's ideology through contributions of key thinkers and in doing so demonstrates how agency has facilitated such ideological shifts. The authors trace the intellectual thought of early thinkers, through to revisionists in the 1950s and 1980s/1990s, highlighting some of the different strands of socialism within the party, and how revisionists such as Anthony Giddens and Gordon Brown drew on the legacy of thinkers such as Tawney to demonstrate continuity in their thought. That those advocating what became known as 'New Labour' felt the need to contextualise their ideology in the writing of Tawney demonstrates that neither 1994 nor 1997 represented a 'year zero' in the Labour Party's history. As Chapter 6 demonstrates, here 'New' was as much an electoral strategy as a desire to distinguish the thought of Giddens and Blair from previous thinkers/leaders.

However, Beech and Hickson's (2007) book has been criticised for being too narrow in focus, relying too much on the social democratic tradition within the Labour Party and ignoring the party's left (Beers, 2008). Key figures such as Sidney Webb, who wrote the much-debated Clause IV of the party's constitution in 1918, Ramsay MacDonald, who was at the forefront of the Labour Party from its creation until 1931, and Barbara Castle, a key figure in Wilson's governments and advocate for women's rights, are omitted from inclusion. More recently, Jeremy Corbyn helped create a mass party with membership figures that enabled supporters to claim it was the largest democratic party in Europe, and in doing so gave his name to 'Corbynomics' (see Chapter 8). In addition to those omitted from the left, it is important to note that not all of those who inspired the party, or key actors within it, subscribed to a socialist ideology; some such as Keynes and Beveridge, both Liberals, did not even support the party. Yet these thinkers came to be associated with the economic ideology of the Labour Party at various times.

This book will highlight some of the distinctions between the ideology of leading Labour thinkers and politicians and the policies pursued by Labour when in power. In combining the effects of structure and agency, this book acknowledges that:

> The development of Labour's thought is not a simple sequence of one set of ideas replacing another, but any tracing of the conceptual connections which make up the web of Labour's thought needs to relate ideas to power, and then to create a model in which ideas are understood as abstractions within history. (Foote, 1997, p 4)

Hall (1993), quoted in (Goes, 2016, p 7), notes that ideas can 'alter the composition of other elements in the political sphere, like a catalyst or binding agent that allows existing ingredients to combine in new ways'. However, at least three external factors affect the power of ideas. The first is their 'power to persuade'; ideas need to offer a coherent and logical solution to a problem. The second requires ideas to be comprehensible; to be explained in an accessible manner. They must 'resonate with people's cause–effect understanding of policy problems and to a certain extent with their worldviews'. Finally, ideas need to come to the (favourable) attention of those who make policy. They must obtain an advantageous position within the decision-making framework of an organisation. Such an endorsement may then lead to a shift in paradigms.

Nor do such ideas emerge in isolation. Ideas and ideologies are means of understanding the world. As the world changes, so too do our ideas and ideologies. External events can support ideological assumptions or challenge them. This book explores some of these events, through the lens of crises, to understand how such events have shaped the Labour Party's ideology.

Such events were, to different degrees, unpredictable and their effects are by no means consistent – events such as the First World War led to the party becoming the main challenger to the Conservative Party, the economic problems of 1931 propelled the party from government and generated deep splits within it, while the party continued to govern for four years after the 1947 sterling crisis, winning the 1950 general election. Yet all of these had profound effects, both positive and negative, on the party's ideology.

Other structures have been more constant, for example the differences between being in government and being in opposition. Tomlinson (2002, p 1) contends that some of the ideological aspirations of the party were watered down once in government, arguing that once in government, Labour 'accommodated itself to markets to a striking degree', noting that even the nationalisation programme of the Attlee government was driven by market forces, which Labour reintroduced to Britain following the Second World War.

There are nuances to the binary of opposition and government – for example, governing with a majority of 179, as Blair was able to do after the landslide 1997 general election, brings different challenges to forming a minority government, as Jim Callaghan had to do after by-election defeats in the autumn of 1976. However, the distinction is important, not only in assessing the development of the party (and thus laying the foundations for future transitions or shifts in economic policy making) but also in understanding the differences between governing and forming the opposition. Political parties also perceive government and opposition very differently, and those with realistic aspirations of forming a government view periods in opposition as failure. Leonard (1975, pp 10–11) notes that 'Labour movements, both in Britain and in other countries, have produced a number of brilliant theoreticians who, when given governmental responsibility, were not capable of putting their ideas into practice'.

Opposition parties have a 'luxury' of ideology not afforded to governments. Debates over ideology are more common or prominent in periods of prolonged opposition (for example, for the Labour Party in the 1950s or 1980s) than they are in government. When faced with large external crises, governments of both the main political persuasions have adopted more pragmatic approaches (for example, Edward Heath's government U-turns and Boris Johnson's economic stimulus in light of the COVID-19 pandemic). Equally, as the experience of the 1929–1931 and 2007–2010 Labour governments demonstrates, when faced with challenges to the existing capitalist model there is a tendency to support existing structures for fear of exacerbating problems such as unemployment (see Chapters 3 and 7). This book will outline some of the choices different Labour leaders faced between trying to advert widespread economic problems and implementing new socialist economic structures and norms. However, it should also be noted that simply changing ideology is not always an easy task. Addressing deeply held approaches can generate opposition from within (for example, the membership opposition to Gaitskell's planned reforms of Clause IV) and there may be strategic reasons for not revealing policies too far in advance of an election.

Rather than viewing the Labour Party as a homogenous entity, this book explores the relationship and battles that exist between different ideologies within the party. These manifest themselves differently throughout the period since 1900, and link to wider debates about the nature of the internal organisation of the party and the relationship(s) that exist between the component parts of the party – for example, Members of Parliament (MPs), party members and the National Executive Council (NEC) of the party.

In order to assess the relationship between the Labour Party and the electorate and the different factions within the party, this book is organised around four themes.

The first explores the relationship between power and ideology, and asks whether the party is ideological, pursing an ultimate goal of creating a socialist society, or driven by electoral success. Others have explored this with reference to what Labour should do. Stewart (1974, p 122), for example, concludes that: 'The public is not all that interested in the semantics of socialism … [Labour] must broaden the basis of its appeal, even at the risk of alienating those groups whose sole interest lies in protest-making. It must continue to act as a coalition.' The relationship between ideology and the pragmatism of government/questions of electability has historically dominated Labour debates. Electoral defeats in the 1950s and 1980s led to the ascendency of revisionist thought within the party and debates over the importance of ideology.

The second theme explores the party's contemporary understanding of socialism. As the 2015 leadership campaigns demonstrated, many Labour politicians have defined themselves as socialists and see socialism as being integral to the party (Payne, 2015). Yet each possesses a different idea of what socialism entails. Herbert Morrison's much-contested definition of socialism as 'what a Labour government does' (Fielding, 1992, p 139) fails largely to resolve this problem and is as allusive as it is problematic. Indeed a more recent understanding of the peripheral role of socialism within the party can be seen in the title of Simon Hannah's (2018) book, *A Party with Socialists In It: A History of the Labour Left*. Some political historians (see for example Tomlinson, 1993) have even questioned the socialist credentials of what are widely understood as some of the greatest achievements of the Labour Party – the creation of the welfare state and the nationalisation programme of the Attlee government.

Attlee (1937, p 15) himself addressed such questions of socialism in his 1937 book *The Labour Party in Perspective*, arguing that 'socialism is not the invention of an individual', but rather a response to 'the evils that capitalism brings'. While Attlee noted that these evils manifest themselves differently in different countries, 'the root cause of the trouble once discerned, the remedy is seen to be the same by thoughtful men and women. The cause is the private ownership of the means of life; the remedy is public ownership.'

Just as others have pointed to varieties of capitalism (see for instance Hancke, 2009), Attlee allows for, and encourages, different understandings of socialism to exist. Socialism developed as a reaction to/critique of capitalism or the capitalist economic system. Given the varieties that exist within such systems it is then to be expected that different means of overcoming economic shortcomings will exist concurrently. Such understandings link to the notions of different strands of socialism outlined earlier.

Attlee was not alone in explicitly outlining his understanding of socialism. Key scholars within the Labour Party have also sought to do so (Beech and Hickson, 2007), as have Labour leaders, including revisionists such as Neil Kinnock (1985a) and Tony Blair (1994a). What is important here is that even those who subscribe to (elements of) capitalism feel the need (but also have the ability) to define their views through a socialist lens.

The third theme relates to the extent to which socialism (however defined, and certainly with the caveats expressed here) can be achieved through parliamentary means. The early Labour Party – and particularly the Marxists within the party – were divided over this question. Labour's socialism was largely constructed and adapted within the British political tradition and the Westminster model. Since the General Strike of 1926, parliamentary socialism, rather than revolutionary socialism – such as that which occurred in Russia following the 1917 revolution – has been favoured by the mainstream of the Labour Party (see Chapter 3). Giddens (1994, p 64), in summarising this intellectual thought within the Labour Party, notes that even following the achievements of the Attlee government, '[m]ost Marxist authors ... were clear that the socialist society of the future would not be much, or at all, like the Soviet Union, but were as reluctant as Marx himself had been to specify the nature of this society in any detail'.

Later leaders also challenged the assumptions and understandings associated with parliamentary socialism. New Labour in office oversaw the weakening of the capacity of the state to bring about economic changes through incorporating private enterprise into the delivery of public services (see Chapter 7) and Corbyn's leadership decoupled understandings of Parliament and democracy with reference to accepting the Brexit referendum result (see Chapter 8).

Labour has historically been a broad church of ideological thought. There have at various times been formal arrangements between the party and the Liberals, the Co-operative Party and the Independent Labour Party. But throughout its history, members of the Labour Party have also left the party to join a plethora of different political groups, from the Communist Party of Great Britain (one member of which – Shapurji Saklatvala – was elected as a Labour MP in 1922) to the Liberal Democrats and the UK Independence Party (UKIP). Even its MPs have defected; senior ministers in the second Labour government, Ramsay MacDonald (Prime Minister) and Philip Snowden (Chancellor), left the party they led to form a national government with Conservative MPs in 1931, while 50 years later the 'gang of four' – including former Cabinet ministers, David Owen and Shirley Williams – broke from the party to establish the Social Democratic Party (SDP) (Butler and Freeman, 1969). More recently, MPs, including former shadow minister and leadership hopeful, Chuka Umunna, have defected to The Independent Group, which was quickly rebranded Change UK, over Labour's stance on the European Union (EU).

The fourth theme to be explored explicitly within the book is that of the trade unions. The relationship between the Labour Party and the trade unions was described by Lewis Minkin (1991) as 'a contentious alliance'. Understanding this relationship is important in understanding the role of the left – those most closely associated with socialist ideology – within the Labour Party. The relationship between socialists and the Labour Party is predicated on the ties the party holds with the trade unions. Such links enable the party to be seen as advancing working-class interests, although as Panitch (2003, p 161) notes, 'more than this is involved. Precisely because the Labour Party is part of the labour movement, this means that the development of class struggle even if not initiated by the party, is bound to affect it considerably within.'

The relationship between the party and trade unions is also questioned by external groups. The closeness between the two and funding settlements are a source of contention for opposition parties. The relationship between the trade unions and Labour's policy formation when in government has led to political opponents questioning the relationship between unelected vested interests and government policies. Within this relationship, however, the trade unions have been able to act independently. While operating closely with the Labour Party to pursue common interests, they have also been able to flex their muscles. And the trade unions have been blamed for a series of events: the Labour Party's fall from power in the 1970s, Labour's absence from power in the 1980s and the election of Miliband in 2010.

Within the party, the trade unions hold a complex role, from being represented on the NEC of the party to providing the party with funding. Minkin (1991, p 509) demonstrates how the trade unions increasingly financed the Labour Party after the Second World War, and argues that in the late 1970s and the 1980s, union funding was central to the Labour

Party to the extent that the party would have been 'devastated without union finance'. Minkin calculates that 95 per cent of the party's general election funding in the 1970s came from the unions. At the same time, the affiliation fees paid by members of trade unions accounted for 89 per cent of all affiliation fees in 1978, and 86 per cent in 1979.

Understanding crises

Another key feature of the book is to explore how crises can, and do, shape policy formations. It seeks to make an important contribution not just to the literature on the Labour Party, but also to wider understandings of crises, and associated concepts such as 'blame' and (crisis) 'resolution'. Gamble (2009, p 38) notes that the term 'crisis' derives from medicine and was first used to describe the 'point in the progress of a disease when a change takes place which is decisive for recovery or death'. Yet Gamble also notes two important qualifications to this definition: first, that a crisis represents not just danger, but also an opportunity – in the medical example, an opportunity for the body to overcome the disease and recover from it; and second, that a crisis should be understood as 'a distinct moment in a process which has a much longer time frame. The process is the disease itself, and the crisis is the turning point in that disease, the moment when the body either starts to shake off the disease or succumbs to it.'

The two caveats identified by Gamble also play out in the political realm. With regard to crises occurring in wider processes, economic crashes and crises exist in wider economic relationships. The Great Slump of 1931 did not emerge in a vacuum, but was a product of a longer disease, borne out by the expansion of credit in the 1920s and the structure of international trade following the Wall Street Crash of 1929. Equally, the financial crisis of 2007/2008 should be seen in the context of the neoliberal reforms of the 1980s (Kirkland, 2017). The opportunity element of crises can also be seen in political crises. Some such as the Second World War have enhanced Labour's credibility and enabled the party to form governments, while others, such as the economic crisis of 1931 and the Winter of Discontent (1978/ 1979) propelled the party from office.

Crises are suboptimal events (O'Connor, 1987). The term 'crisis' denotes that something has gone wrong. Just as we would expect a doctor or medical practitioner to intervene wherever possible to overcome a medical disease, we also expect policy makers to implement (new) policies/solutions that offer a means to correct (or at least explain) a crisis event. One means of deciding which policies to implement is through notions of blame. Here, by blaming an actor/group/institution etcetera, it is possible to propose new measures designed to prevent their same actions occurring (and thus prevent future crises).

Jessop (2018, p 49) notes that crises contain both danger and opportunities for those able to frame particular debates. He outlines five distinct features of crises. First, crises have 'both objective and subjective aspects ... objectively crises occur when a set of social relations cannot be reproduced in the old way. Subjectively, crises tend to disrupt accepted views of the world and create uncertainty on how to "go on" within in.' Second, crises 'do not have predetermined outcomes: how they are resolved, if at all, depends on the actions taken in response to them'. Third, crises may be 'deliberately exaggerated or even manufactured ... based on mis-perception or mis-recognition of real-world events and processes. Sometimes crises may be manufactured or, at least exaggerated, for strategical or tactical purposes.' Fourth, it is the subjective moment that facilitates 'decisive action'; without it, disinterested observers 'will have insufficient resonance ... to spur them into efforts to take decisive action'. Fifth, crises are 'complex, objectively overdetermined moments of subjective indeterminacy, where decisive action can make a major difference to the future'.

Jessop's criteria for crises are important in establishing the relationship between those caught up in a crisis and those responsible for overcoming the crisis. Just as in the medical definition, those who require liberation are likely to be distinct from those who are able/entrusted to enact changes (for example, the patient is, normally, distinct from the doctor who diagnoses the disease they have and establishes a course of treatment). Here Jessop argues that our understanding of crises must (be seen to) reflect a material position that resonates with those caught up in the crisis. While leaders may claim that crises occur, satisfying the subjective understanding of a crisis, if this does not match the perception of those undergoing the crisis then the proposed solutions are unlikely to gain much support.

The crises covered within this book bear this relationship, between subjective and objective understandings, out. In defining crises, different groups within the Labour Party, including Labour's leaders, have had to convince others not only of the existence of the crises but also of the causes of them. Some of these were uncontroversial, for example the problems associated with the lack of union representation in Parliament in the early 20th century; others were more controversial, for example the revisionism offered by Gaitskell in the 1950s or the leftward shift of the party under Corbyn post 2015.

Such narratives are important in orchestrating different responses. For example, although the Labour Party attempted to present the financial crisis of 2007/2008 as a 'global crisis', one that required the state to introduce Keynesian measures to support the wider economy, the opposition Conservative Party – successfully – presented the crisis as one of excessive government spending, leading to a protracted period of austerity (Kirkland, 2017). This redefinition, confirmed following the 2010 general election, changed understandings not only of the crisis but also of the solutions needed to overcome it. Rather than seeing the crisis as one of underinvestment, the Conservatives diagnosed it as being born from excessive spending, meaning that the cure was to reduce public expenditure, in contrast to the previous Labour government, which pursued inflationary policies.

Crises are, according to Hay (1996, p 254), 'moments of decisive intervention', which require additional responses. Hall (1993) further distinguishes crises from 'normal policy making' by arguing that they change conventional wisdom and may instigate 'paradigm shifts'. Hall draws on the experiences of the 1970s and 1980s and argues that the British experience of industrial unrest in this period led to changes in macroeconomic policy making; successive governments focused on inflation, rather than employment, as their key macroeconomic policy objective, in a shift towards monetarism and away from Keynesianism.

Not all crises lead to such fundamental changes, however. One reason for such differences stems from 'social learning'. Hall (1993, p 278) defines social learning as 'a deliberate attempt to adjust the goals or techniques of policy in response to past experience and new information. Learning is indicated when policy changes as the result of such a process.' Here the manner in which such learning occurs has three key features. First, it is defined by the time between previous policy and policy change. According to Sack (quoted in Hall, 1993, p 277), 'the most important influence in this learning is previous policy itself'. The second factor is that 'key agents pushing forward the learning process are the experts in a given field of policy, either working for the state or advising it from privileged positions'. The third determinant is the ability of the state to 'act autonomously from societal pressure' (Hall, 1993, p 278).

Important within these notions is the idea that the collapse or decline of a paradigm is not in itself enough to warrant a crisis. As Blyth (1997) notes, it must be replaced by a competing paradigm. This new paradigm must not only offer an explanation of what went wrong but also create new 'norms' that guide policy. Such transitions can be controversial. Ideas and norms are contested entities and the collapse of a paradigm is often accompanied by a plethora of ideas. Crises, then, do not intrinsically generate new norms. For example, during the economic crisis of 1931, Labour sought to resolve the crisis within the existing paradigm – something that ultimately led to a key split within the party (see Chapter 3).

Crises can be seen as being unequal – they are able to either give groups access to policy makers or policy-making circles or exclude groups from such access, depending on how narratives of blame are constructed/accepted within political discourse. Such differences stem from the ability of actors to engage in such debates. Politicians and those within the media may be able to shape/frame crises in a manner that other agents cannot. Such inequalities

11

may even lead some to generate crises to pursue particular agendas, for example politicians may wish to construct crises to impose martial law and ensure political survival (Fairman, 1942). Furthermore, inequalities may exist outside of the control of those instigating the crisis.

The effects of crises can also be unequal. Depending on the vantage point of the observer(s) and their interests, crises may generate different outcomes. Allocating resources in times of crisis can be politicalised decisions and even being blamed may not necessarily prevent agents or institutions receiving resources. The banking crisis of 2007/2008 led to notions of 'too big to fail' and, despite being blamed for (at least some of) the economic problems, banks received a large amount of capital from government.

This book explores how (understandings of) crises shaped Labour's economic ideology. Understanding crises as inherently unequal is important in this regard. Such inequalities manifest themselves in different ways. Some crises are large, external events, such as the Second World War, which prompted changes not only in Labour's ideology, but also in wider 'social learning', for example relating to the role of the state and inequalities. This crisis extended well beyond simply changing Labour's economic policy, to broader social changes both within the United Kingdom (UK) and internationally. Other crises, such as the trade union crisis of the 1970s, were seen as residing predominantly within British politics. While having implications for other political parties as well (noticeably the rise of the New Right in the Conservative Party led by Margaret Thatcher), the trade union crisis had profound implications for the Labour Party, given it presided over the unions for half of the decade and its historic relationship with the unions. Other crises – such as successive electoral defeats in the 1950s and 1980s – represented internal challenges to Labour, while being seen as the success of the Conservative Party. The causes of such crises were not necessarily economic, but as the following chapters demonstrate, each had an impact on Labour's economic ideology.

Outline of the book

This book proceeds in seven substantive chapters, each exploring one or two crises and outlining how these shaped the Labour Party's economic ideology/ policy. The chapters are centred around the four themes highlighted earlier and follow the same structure. Each one outlines the nature of the crisis/ crises before introducing contemporary figures who contributed to Labour's ideology. It then assesses how the crises transformed Labour's ideology, first by exploring Labour's responses to the crises before unpacking any impact on the party's broad understanding(s) of socialism. The final substantive section of each chapter assesses the implications of the crises for the relationship between the Labour Party and the trade unions.

Chapter 2 explores the Taff Vale crisis and the First World War. It demonstrates the difficulties faced by the early Labour Party in forging consensus on economic policy while responding to the need to differentiate itself from the Liberal Party. Such discussions posed questions over the extent to which socialism could be progressed through parliamentary means.

Chapter 3 explores the Labour Party in the interwar period. Another crisis heavily involving the trade unions – the General Strike of 1926 – placed further strain on the party before the Great Slump of 1931 led to the fall of the second Labour government and the largest-ever split within the party. This chapter explores how the difficulties of the 1929–1931 Labour government prompted greater scrutiny of economic policy and led to a more detailed exploration of economic ideas and ideology within the party.

Chapter 4 highlights some of the ways in which the Second World War changed attitudes towards the ability of the state to meet economic expectations, paving the way for the creation of the welfare state and post-war consensus. It looks at the degree to which the first Labour majority government was able to implement its version of socialism and explores how electoral defeats in 1951, 1955 and 1959 led to a period of revisionist thought within the party.

Chapter 5 explores the difficulties of governing in the 1960s and 1970s. Between 1964 and 1979, the Labour Party held office for all but four years. Yet this was a period during which the tripartite relationships between government, trade unions and businesses collapsed, with many highlighting a rise in union militancy as a, if not *the*, cause. Labour's tenure in office in the 1970s ended following a vote of no confidence in Jim Callaghan's government after a period of industrial unrest known as the Winter of Discontent.

Chapter 6 again highlights a period of revisionist thought in the party, following the electoral nadir of 1983 and further election defeats in 1987 and 1992. It explores how the right of the party and leaders such as Neil Kinnock and Tony Blair redefined the party's commitment to socialism and created 'New Labour'.

Chapter 7 explores the implementation of the 'third way' in office and the end of the Labour government in 2010. It looks at the financial crisis of 2007/2008 and explores the government's response to the events that unfolded. It highlights the shift towards a more Keynesian approach and asks whether this represented the end of the 'third way'.

Chapter 8 looks at the period of opposition from 2010 and the leaderships of Ed Miliband and Jeremy Corbyn. It traces how these leaders sought to distance their party from New Labour and responded to the policies, and discourses, of austerity. It explores each of the three election defeats since 2010 and compares the shift leftwards against that of the early 1980s.

2

Taff Vale and the First World War

Introduction

The origins of the Labour Party are reminiscent of the understanding of crisis outlined in the previous chapter. Different interest groups coming together was symptomatic of the calls to action by marginalised groups who felt misrepresented in Parliament. Throughout the 19th century, the franchise (right to vote) was extended to some working-class men, yet there was not a corresponding change in the party system – which by the end of the century was still dominated by the Conservative and Unionist Party and the Liberal Party. The story of the Labour Party's creation is the coming together of different views – broadly aligned on the political left – to mobilise the issues of the newly franchised workers in formal party politics.

This chapter outlines such relationships, exploring the origins of the Labour Party from early groups that acted as forerunners, such as the Fabian Society and the trade unions, to the sponsoring of parliamentary candidates and MPs in 1900, before outlining how the Taff Vale case of 1901, the subsequent Osborne judgment of 1909 and the First World War helped shape the Labour Party's economic ideology. Along with the next chapter, which explores the interwar period, this helps explain how the Labour Party moved from being an amalgamation of diverse interests to adopting a coherent economic policy.

The early Labour Party

Although often defined in terms of working-class politics, the Labour Party did not create such 'class consciousness'. Rather, the party drew on existing working-class politics. E.P. Thompson (1980, pp 8–11) dates the rise of working-class politics to the 18th century, some 120 years before the Labour Party officially formed. The advent of the Labour Party (or even the Labour Representation Committee – see later in this section) did not represent a 'year zero' for the working class in terms of ideology, or even engagement with the political process, but offered a new means of organisation; the emergence of the working class was 'an active process, which owes as much to agency as to conditioning. The working class did not rise like the sun at an appointed time. It was present at its own making.' Other groups, who retained their independence from the Labour Party, were also important, both implicitly and explicitly, in promoting working-class interests. James Thompson (2011) notes that the Liberal Party had helped ensure working-class representation in Parliament through Liberal–Labour MPs as early as 1874.

Each of these groups had their own ideas and ideologies, and different interests/reasons for participating in such a movement. The Fabian Society appealed to middle-class intellectuals and, according to Sidney Webb, quoted in MacKenzie and MacKenzie (1979, p 346), was 'deliberately kept heterogenous', Marxists saw the party as a means of achieving revolutionary socialism, while the trade union movement had a predominantly working-class membership and ties to the Liberal Party. The challenge for the Labour Party was to present the ideas of these diverse groups in a coherent manner.

As Foote (1997, p 20) notes, 'the political and economic ideas elaborated by Marx were fundamentally opposed to the labourism of the British trade union movement'. It would be too simplistic to conflate the ideology of labourism and the Labour Party. Fielding (1992, p 140) – although writing about the 1940s – notes that the Labour Party, although born from the working classes, never saw itself as exclusively for them. Much debate in later years about the appeal of the Labour Party in opposition would centre on building alliances beyond a working-class base. Socialism, according to the Labour Party, was not just for the workers; 'while workers were to be the main beneficiaries of Labour's socialism, through their liberation from capitalist drudgery, they were not meant to be the only ones. ... Many of these assumptions were infused with elements of both Marxism and Liberalism.'

The Labour Representation Committee (LRC) was established in 1900, following a proposal by the Amalgamated Society of Railway Servants the previous autumn, which called on trade unions 'to devise ways and means for securing the return of an increased number of labour members to Parliament' (Adelman, 2014, p 28). This brought together Marxists, Fabians and trade unionists and the Social Democratic Federation. The LRC would endorse candidates who, once elected, would form 'A distinct Labour Group in Parliament', with distinct elements of a political party, a system of whips and agreed policies. This group would 'embrace a readiness to cooperate with any party which for the time being may be engaged in promoting legislation in the direct interests of labour, and be equally ready to associate themselves with any party in opposing measures having an opposite tendency' (MacKenzie and MacKenzie, 1979, pp 274–275).

While the LRC established a coming together of different interest groups, generating political agreement was harder. At the first meeting it was far from clear that this was the creation of the Labour Party. 'No political programme was agreed on and it was not even decided whether the new body was to work in collaboration with one or other of the existing political parties, as its predecessors had done, or to establish an independent party of its own' (Pelling and Reid, 1996, p 8).

The LRC supported 15 candidates in 1900, although only two were successful: Keir Hardie and Richard Bell. Even this small crop of MPs did not equate to ideological homogeneity. Hardie was a socialist and had fought on an explicitly socialist platform, defeating a Liberal opponent. Bell advocated trade unionism and was elected with the cooperation of the Liberal Party (Martin, 1985, p 17).

Despite such ideological differences, the 1900 manifesto on which the 15 candidates stood, was far more detailed in terms of policies than the manifesto of six years later, a by-product of the internal divisions that existed within the early Labour Party. In 1900, the party established a list of policies or policy objectives, including the 'Abolition of a standing army. ... Graduated income-tax ... payment of members (MPs)' (Labour Party, 1900).

The Labour Party was not the only party to appeal to working-class voters or trade unions. Trade unions had a long history of affiliation to the Liberal Party, and despite the creation of the LRC in 1900 and the Labour Party in 1906, such bonds were not easily broken. Meanwhile the Miners' Federation, which, along with the cotton unions, voted against the Amalgamated Society of Railway Servants' proposal to form the LRC in 1899, did not break its ties with the Liberals until 1909 (Simpson, 1973, p 17; Adelman, 2014, p 29).

The lack of representation was a key theme of Labour's 1906 election campaign. Although the party lacked developed policies, its manifesto highlighted an ideological struggle. It drew from fundamental questions of how any socialist advance could be made – through Parliament or were new institutions needed?

Hardie (1974, p 82) argued that obtaining representation in the House of Commons could help advance the concerns of the working classes in a manner that the trade unions were unable to. He argued that trade unions were unable to combat the 'evil' of unemployment, which ranged from 3 to 8 per cent within skilled trades to more than 14 per cent in unskilled occupations. According to Hardie, the '[m]ost which the trade union can do in [the case of unemployment] is to provide a small out-of-work benefit to tide the unfortunate member over'.

The January 1910 manifesto (Labour Party, 1910) was more explicit in establishing the party's policies. It possessed the headline 'Lords must go', in response to the upper chamber's blockage of the Liberal budget of 1909, which attempted to introduce land taxes and increases in income tax to fund social spending and military rearmament. This argument united two wings of the Labour Party: it accepted that socialist goals could be achieved through a gradual progression and within existing institutions, while at the same time accepting the need for the wide-scale reform of such institutions.

The manifesto was largely reactionary. As Tomlinson (1996, p 3) notes, the Labour Party before the First World War (and, as the next chapter demonstrates, indeed largely up until the 1930s) lacked a coherent ideologically driven economic programme. Rather, the policies it did advocate 'were ad hoc responses to current events'. Tomlinson notes that the first-ever conference 'of MPs and candidates to discuss policy' in 1904 covered numerous policies relating to: trade union legislation; the taxation of the 'unearned increment'; opposition to tariffs; support for universal suffrage; opposition to sectarian education; the expansion of workers' compensation; support for temperance; nationalisation of the railways; and support for referendums.

Tomlinson further notes that there were 'great difference[s] between the pre-1918 Labour Party and its later forms'. The pre-1918 party remained deliberately 'not a socialist but a Labour Party'. Such ideological pluralism, and the lack of expectations about the party forming a parliamentary majority in the short term, meant 'it did not have a "programme", i.e. a comprehensive platform of related policy measures, or the administrative structure to generate and sustain such a programme'. Rather, the policies the party did agree on 'were primarily formulated as tactical responses to particular situations, or as general principles for propaganda purposes'.

The Taff Vale case of 1901, the Osborne judgment of 1909 and the First World War shaped the economic ideology of the early Labour Party, leading to the party's first constitution in 1918. Although Labour's economic policy was incomplete in 1918 (see the next chapter), each of these events are important in understanding how (some of) the tensions between the founding groups were understood and resolved.

Taff Vale, 1900–1901

Nineteenth-century legislation regarding trade unions and their actions was complex. It deliberately established the unions as a legal entity akin to the London Library or the Stock Exchange. This meant that unions were not regarded – in the eyes of the law – as formal corporations (McCord, 1993, p 247) but were considered to be collective entities. Thus, businesses claiming compensation for illegal activity had to take action against individual members, rather than the union concerned at large (unless they were willing to sue all members of the union simultaneously). This meant that despite being awarded large sums in compensation, businesses often found it difficult to collect their compensation. One case, *Bailey v. Pye*, saw a glass merchants (Bailey) successfully claim damages against members of the National Plate Glass Bevellers Trade Union. The firm was awarded a total of £1,217 in

January 1897 but had managed to collect just £5 by September of that year (Clegg, Fox and Thompson, 1977, p 312).

In August 1900, one strike in South Wales changed this understanding. The dispute focused on the Taff Vale rail line, linking the ports of South Wales to the coalfields. Against a backdrop of the Boer War in South Africa nearing its climax, increased demand had led to higher coal prices. Railway workers in South Wales, responsible for transporting coal from 70 Welsh coal mines to docks in Cardiff and Penarth, sought to use the increased demand and prices to 'both improve their position and win recognition for the union'. This line was, according to the counsel for Taff Vale (quoted in Clegg, Fox and Thompson, 1977, p 313), of the 'highest national importance' and of importance for both military and domestic uses.

Upon the decision of the workers to take strike action in August 1900, Beasley hired a number of new recruits, 'free labourers', from the controversial strike-breaking National Free Labour Association. Clashes between these new recruits and those on strike were common as pickets sought to persuade workers to return home. Strikers sought to intimidate those who stayed as strike breakers. Beasley's 'trump card', however, was that the free labourers had all signed a contract on entering service, meaning that those on strike were 'exposed to the charge of incitement to breach contract'. Injunctions against the leaders of the pickets were granted and those on strike were defeated (Harvey and Press, 2000, p 75).

The Taff Vale strike was a failure for the unions. After failing to achieve their original demands, increasingly militant actions combined with the patriotism and nationalism of a popular war the other side of the world (which involved the families of many in South Wales) left the union with little, bar a 'few face saving stipulations' in the return to work agreement, and was symptomatic of the failures of rail workers' strikes in the period (McCord, 1993, p 246).

Defeat was confirmed by the deal to return to work, and the resumption of normal services on 1 September 1900. However, the position of the strikers and strike breakers remained unclear. The union believed it had 'received assurances that all new recruits would be dismissed, all strikers reinstated, and all outstanding court cases against individual workers dropped', but this position was not shared by management (Harvey and Press, 2000, p 76).

This dispute was not in isolation; the previous decade had seen tensions between the manager of the railway line, Beasley, and the unions, at loggerheads over efficiency savings. What turned this short-lived action into a 'landmark' moment in the history of the British trade union movement was the decision of the company to press home its advantage and continue legal action against the union following the strikers' return to work (McCord, 1993; Harvey and Press, 2000). The Taff Vale case was extended from a strike to a legal dispute between the Amalgamated Society of Railway Servants and the Taff Vale Railway Company. During the strike, the railway 'company [had] obtained an injunction against the union for picketing and molestation and another injunction that stopped the union from using union funds to defend the union officers concerned' (Simpson, 1973, pp 45–46). A later judgment argued that as unions had legal rights to own property, they had been afforded the status of corporation; 'in other words the union was liable for the wrongful conduct of its agents and members' (Harvey and Press, 2000, p 77). The company also started action against the workers involved for 'breach of contract' although this was later shelved. The case became significant for unions nationwide. Emmanuel Shinwell, quoted in McCord (1993, p 243), noted that this dispute 'set back the privileges of the trade unions to legally organise strikes by about half a century'.

After a successful appeal against the original decision, the case was escalated to the House of Lords. As the (then) highest court in the land, the House of Lords ruled that the trade union was liable for the actions of its officials and any losses incurred by the company as a result of industrial action. The ruling, made in December 1902, favoured the Taff Vale Railway Company, which 'became the first employer in Britain successfully to sue a union for illegal activities during a strike and for consequent loss of business'. This established a legal precedent, which 'served as a reference point, a symbol of injustice, for the campaign waged by the Parliamentary Committee of the Trades Union Congress to place labour on an equal footing with capital under the law' (Harvey and Press, 2000, p 63).

Following the House of Lords' decision permitting the company to claim damages from the union, the total cost to the Amalgamated Society of Railway Servants amounted to £42,000. Although a significant amount, this represented less than two thirds of its annual income, and by 1904 the society had amassed a fund of more than £300,000 (Clegg, Fox and Thompson, 1977, p 315). However, the effect of the case was to change the wider understanding of the strike. Since earlier court cases were levied against – and limited to – individuals, such decisions had little impact on unions themselves. However, following the Taff Vale judgment, the law extended to include unions as distinct entities, to the extent that 'it seemed that a case could be brought on the grounds of almost anything that might be done in a trade dispute, not only against the members and officers but against the union itself', with little safeguard for the union's funds (Clegg, Fox and Thompson, 1977, pp 315–316).

Following the House of Lords' judgment, a Royal Commission was appointed in 1903 to review industrial relations, although it would not report until 1906, after the Liberal Party's general election victory. The report recommended upholding the House of Lords' ruling. Its recommendation of 'protecting union benefit funds and the right to picket peacefully' was too 'tame for [the] vociferous cohort of newly elected Labour Members of Parliament and their Liberal allies', who instead brought forward the Trade Disputes Act (which became law in December 1906), which 'nullified the Taff Vale judgment, clarifying the positions of unions under the law while safeguarding their funds and protecting them from legal action' (Harvey and Press, 2000, p 63).

A further judgment in 1909, the Osborne judgment, also threatened the relationship between the Labour Party and the trade unions. This judgment, brought about by a Liberal trade unionist, prohibited the practice of trade unions collecting funds for political purposes (that is, to fund the Labour Party). It noted that 'there is nothing in the Trade Union Acts from which it can reasonably be inferred that trade unions as defined by Parliament were meant to have the power of collecting and administering funds for political purposes' (Moher, 2009).

This was the second time in the decade that the House of Lords had found the actions of the trade unions, and in particular the Amalgamated Society of Railway Servants' actions, to be illegal. The ruling was made in the lower courts, but challenged by the Labour Party and the Railway Servants, with the backing of the Trades Union Congress (TUC). The House of Lords ruled that as the definition of a trade union, expressed in legislation from 1875, 'did not include the support of a political party, such support was *ultra vires*' ('beyond the powers') (Pelling, 1982, p 890).

As Pelling summarises, this case had not gained salience or traction necessarily for its outcome – the decision was overturned through an Act of Parliament in 1913, which permitted unions to finance political action so long as such payments came from a discrete political fund and that each member of the union had the option of opting out of making contributions to such a fund – but rather the symbolism of the state acting against the interests of the trade unions.

The repercussions for the House of Lords were 'not insignificant'. The unions' second defeat at the hands of the upper chamber, in less than a decade, demonstrated the different interests presented in the House of Lords and the unions. The Osborne judgment 'strengthened the willingness of trade unionists to support the Liberal government in its constitutional struggle against the Lords' (Pelling, 1982, pp 889–890).

The First World War

Most studies exploring the Labour Party in the First World War note that it led to the party adopting a more coherent foreign policy. For example, Pelling and Reid (1996, p 32) argue that the First World War meant the questions of foreign policy became 'of paramount importance'. Yet the war had significant implications for the party in other areas.

The war changed the relationship between employer and employee and put the government at the heart of new collective bargaining processes. In 1915, the government introduced compulsory arbitration to resolve disputes. Along with the government's control 'of certain industries [this] encouraged the development of industry-wide pay settlements'. Such settlements were used in the railways (from 1915), coal (1916) and engineering (1917), before spreading to munitions and other transport services by 1918 (Lovell, 1986, p 50).

The war also required government borrowing not seen on such a scale before. During the war, Britain accumulated debts equivalent to 136 per cent of its Gross National Product (GNP) (National Archives, nd). The funding of the war was based on the McKenna rule, named after the Liberal Chancellor of the Exchequer, Reginald McKenna (1915–1916). This rule had as its basis 'a desire to treat labour and capital fairly and equitably, not pass WWI [World War I] costs onto future generations, and commit to a debt retirement path and higher taxes'. Although the war debts were only fully repaid in 2015, this rule shaped British economic policy from 1915 to the onset of the Second World War (Nason and Vahey, 2007, p 290; BBC News, 2014).

The manner of debt repayments would influence British economic policy for decades. Arthur Cecil Pigou, a lecturer in economics at Cambridge University, argued that there existed three methods of raising enough money to pay off the debt (rejecting the notion of defaulting as something that '[n]o serious person would consider for a moment'): first, raising a short-term levy; second, increasing taxation to pay the interest plus a minimal amount of capital each year; or third, a combination of the two (Pigou, 1918, p 136). Pigou noted that there were no problem-free solutions, but advocated a mix of the two – partly to avoid the intergenerational problems of leaving too much debt, but also to overcome expectations of how such levies may be used in the future. Pigou (1918, p 139) was especially concerned that other social projects that politicians deemed necessary could invoke large-scale government spending – particularly if the Labour Party were to form a government.

In its 1918 manifesto, the Labour Party advocated funding the debt through 'a conscription on wealth', which would introduce a levy on capital. The manifesto promised that 'Labour will place the burden on the broadest backs by a special tax on capital. Those who have made fortunes out of the war must pay for the war; and Labour will insist on heavily graduated direct taxation with a raising of the exemption limit' (Labour Party, 1918). Although Labour was keen to demonstrate the temporary nature of this tax, other measures facilitated by the expansion of the state during the First World War appealed to the party. The document *Labour Party and the New Social Order*, written by Sidney Webb (1918a), advocated retaining the wartime excess profits tax and updating death duties.

Even the coalition government acknowledged that the economic impact of the war could not simply mean a return to business as usual. Writing in the Conservative Party's election manifesto of 1918, David Lloyd George and Andrew Bonar Law argued that: 'Until the country has returned to normal industrial conditions it would be premature to prescribe a fiscal policy intended for permanence. We must endeavour to reduce the war debt in such a manner as may inflict the least injury to industry and credit' (Conservative Party, 1918).

However, the debt did not get paid off in the manner that Pigou or even the Labour Party advocated. Instead, high levels of debt became the new norm. Britain, having left the gold standard in 1914, did not return to it until 1925, easing the burden of accumulating government debt. Additionally, the government benefited from 'capital and foreign exchange controls [which] meant British lenders could not freely buy bonds issued by governments abroad, meaning there were fewer alternatives to UK Government debt for investors' (Thompson, Hawkins, Dar and Taylor, 2012, p 106).

Outside of the question of debt, there is limited evidence to suggest that the wartime experience led to significant socioeconomic change. Tanner (1990, p 351) argues that the First World War did not produce the paradigm shift it is often assumed to have. This was because 'social and economic conditions did not create a homogenous working class, or a uniform class experience. ... Neither did participation in the war effort transform the British working class.'

Although not producing the socialist revolution that occurred in the Soviet Union, in terms of electoral politics the war greatly aided the position of the Labour Party. Upon the resignation of Herbert Asquith, in December 1916, Lloyd George invited three Labour MPs to join his coalition government: Arthur Henderson was appointed minister without portfolio, and included in the War Cabinet; and John Hodge and George Barnes were responsible for labour and pensions respectively. Lloyd George's government further represented 'a rapid expansion of the machinery of government and of government control over the economy' (Harrison, 1971, p 236).

Debates over foreign policy had left the Labour Party close to being divided or even splitting in 1914. However, incorporation into government enabled the party to be united around its patriotism, by focusing on domestic issues (ironically, one of the effects of the coalition government was to generate a split in the Liberal Party). Outside of government, and prior to 1916, Labour had effectively managed to emphasise domestic rather than foreign issues. One manner in which this was achieved was through the creation of the War Emergency Workers' National Committee, the first meeting of which was after the declaration of war. This further helped incorporate a greater number of trade unionists into the broader party, without ceding substantive powers from the centre (Harrison, 1971).

Compared with the pre-war party, Labour was now more united and more coherent. In 1914 it was the fourth party in Parliament and by 1922 it was able to position itself as the main opposition party to the Conservatives, and even form a government in 1923. Throughout this period, Labour was able to distance itself ideologically from the Liberal Party, which was plagued by divisions over the wartime coalition government and questions of Irish Home Rule (Thorpe, 2015, p 36; see also later in this chapter).

Labour's ideology

Although the policies of the Labour Party were often limited to responding to events during its formative years, this did not mean that there was no discussion about broader ideology. Ramsay MacDonald was important in the early shaping of the Labour Party. Although not regarded as a 'key thinker' by Beech and Hickson (2007), MacDonald's potential to shape the party's ideology is evident in the positions he held: Party Secretary (1900–1912), Chairman of the Parliamentary Party (1911–1914), Chairman and Leader (1922–1931) and Labour Prime Minister (1923–1924 and 1929–1931). Barker (1976, p 51) describes MacDonald as the 'party's principal propagandist and mythologist'.

Barker (1976, pp 52–53) dissects MacDonald's socialism from his writings between 1905 and 1918. He argues that it contained four important points. First that socialism was a historical process; 'the new world was not to replace the old so much as to grow out of it'. This was important as 'the vision of ultimate socialism gave [the Labour Party its] purpose, while the insistence of continuity allowed for piecemeal reform and did not scare away the liberals, trade union pragmatists, and non-socialist social reformers among the party's supporters both in Parliament and in the country'. Second, MacDonald acknowledged that socialism would lead to a markedly differently economic and political character for society, providing a 'moral basis for particular reforms which could thus be justified as part of a larger, and slower, scheme of social reconstruction and development'. Third, MacDonald's proposals were 'flexible, even imprecise', allowing him 'room for manoeuvre' in Parliament and the wider Labour Party; MacDonald (quoted by Barker, 1976, p 52) told the 1907 national conference of the Independent Labour Party that the 'mere principles of socialism do not carry us very far, because they are capable of application in so many different ways, and their meaning in relation to existing things is so very general'. The final theme of MacDonald's socialism, identified by Barker, is that he 'emphasised the assimilative rather than the divisive purpose of socialism': transforming the existing order was preferable to simply destroying it, and doing so would enable the inclusion of the working classes.

However, MacDonald's belief in the capacities of existing institutions, and his reluctance even for political reforms such as proportional representation and an elected second chamber, let alone revolution, led Cannan (1910, p 64) to note 'that he would rank as a very good Conservative, if that word was used in its original significance'. Rather than such radicalism, MacDonald's philosophy was designed to appeal broadly to three distinct groups, each with different ideological perspectives. These were: those engaged in parliamentary politics, who could be won over through 'progressive arguments', such as Liberal supporters; the electorate, which the 1918 Representation of the People Act had greatly expanded, and diversified; and the rank-and-file membership, who were committed socialists. Barker (1976, pp 53–54) argues that MacDonald's vision of socialism attempted to unite these three groups through 'the socialist myth'.

MacDonald's – and other figures' – desire to offer as broad an appeal as possible explains why Labour throughout this period lacked a sense of economic ideology, instead favouring a broad strategy and a pragmatic understanding of socialism (see also the next chapter). The initial formation of the Labour Party saw a number of different perspectives amalgamated to form the party. The early Labour Party was one of a defensive nature – defensive against the attacks on the trade unions, as exemplified in the response to the Taff Vale case and Osborne judgment – and one that had to forge a distinct political space from existing political parties (for example the Liberals).

Throughout its early decades, Labour adopted ethical socialism, promoted by Richard Tawney, an economist who was led to socialism through his Christian roots. Tawney saw socialism as an ethical critique of Victorian liberalism – he did not seek to offer an outright rejection of capitalism, for he understood that capitalism, while destroying older customs and norms, also created 'new kinds of cohesion' (Rogan, 2017, p 17). In outlining his ethical socialism, Tawney (1921, pp 22–24, 26) distinguished between functions and rights (including the right to accumulate profit). He argued that the former should take precedence over the latter, which was 'to imply that property and economic activity exist to promote the ends of society, whereas hitherto society has been regarded in the world of business to support them'. Tawney criticised existing 'acquisitive societies' as their 'whole tendency and interest and preoccupations is to promote the acquisition of wealth' (Tawney, 1921, p 29).

Linked to these notions of ethical or Christian socialism, Tawney was a firm believer in adult education. Having seen the possibilities that education could open up for individuals, he was keen to offer this to the highest number of people. Here Tawney differed from Marxists/socialists – the role of the state was to provide services that would encourage agents to improve their opportunities, not merely correct for material inequalities. The existing structures of capitalism were not, according to Tawney, inherently negative or restrictive, but could be overcome through means such as education.

Such an emphasis on adult education went unfulfilled until the Attlee government of 1945–1951 and the acceptance of the Beveridge Report of 1942 (Beveridge, 1942).

According to Tawney, the state was not the sole organisation of importance in a socialist society. Tawney (1921, pp 30–31) critiqued the prevailing industrialism and capitalist model as it promoted individualism, offering 'an invitation to men to use the powers … without enquiring whether there is any principle by which their exercise should be limited … it assures men that there are no ends other than their ends, no law other than their desires, no limit other than that which they think advisable'. Such individualism promoted the acquisition of riches at the expense of moral principles, allowing humankind to avoid distinctions between forms of economic activity and 'different sources of wealth, between enterprise and avarice, energy and unscrupulous greed, property which is legitimate and property which is theft, the just employment of the fruits of labour and the idle parasitism of birth of fortune'. This lack of ethical considerations within economic activity stemmed from the prevailing wisdom within the economic system, which held 'a contempt for all interests which do not contribute obviously to economic activity' (Tawney, 1921, p 31). Rather than accept a moral vacuum within industry, Tawney (1921, pp 7, 46) argued that industry should be 'subordinate to the community in such a way as to render the best service technically possible', and that industries should be 'conducted by self-governing guilds developed out of the trade unions' (Wright, 1987, p 58).

Tawney's legacy within the Labour Party is debatable, although he offered the party a 'coherent socialist philosophy', which rested on an ethical, rather than economic, understanding of socialism. Foote (1997, p 72) notes that Tawney's position within the party changed over time, from that of a gradualist in the 1920s to a critic of gradualism in the 1930s and an advocate of revisionism in the 1950s, allowing his work to be interpreted so widely that both Shirley Williams and Michael Foot 'could claim his as their intellectual ancestor'. Diamond (2004, p 2) presents Tawney as a revisionist, and Gaitskell called Tawney 'the Democratic socialist par excellence'. Beech and Hickson (2007) note he has been cited as influencing a wide range of Labour scholars, up to and including proponents of New Labour.

Tawney was not the only person within the early Labour Party to defend socialist positions on the grounds of morality. Others too argued that morality rather than economics should guide socialist thought; Philip Snowden (1974, p 12) argued in 1906 that 'on the ground of morality, justice and necessity, the taxation of the rich for social reform purposes is justifiable'. Just as MacDonald emphasised the inclusive nature of socialism, the party's commitment to ethical, rather than revolutionary, socialism was designed to accommodate (if not appeal to) the broadest section of the electorate as possible.

Labour's responses to the crises

Throughout this period, the Labour Party sought to amalgamate different perceptions of socialism, including unionism. Undoubtedly, many unions and societies joined the Labour Party for ideological reasons, although these were not necessarily homogenous, and key Labour figures such as MacDonald were keen to point out the fluid nature of socialist thought. Labour's growth and success was in part due to its appeal beyond a single cause, although this would lead to Marxist groups later leaving the party as it developed a more coherent (moderate) understanding of socialism and the links between socialism and economic planning in the following decades (see the next chapter).

Nairn (1964) concludes that the early Labour Party 'did not come into being in response to any theory about what a socialist party should be; it arose empirically, in quite a piece-meal fashion'. The first two decades of the 20th century were testimony to that and highlighted the divisions that were present in the early Labour Party. They also highlighted the limited range of views advocated by the different groups within the party, for example the unions adopted a defensive position in the wake of the Taff Vale and Osborne judgments. Here the party in its formative years spent more energy defending its position and the position of associated groups, such as the trade unions, than exploring questions of ideology. Such positional weaknesses (for example, a reliance on other political parties and a low membership base) encouraged MacDonald (and others) to emphasise the fluidity of socialism, to try to maximise the party's appeal and solidify its position.

The First World War increased the role of the state in economic planning, particularly in key industries such as coal and the railways (although the scope of state involvement was not as broad as it was during the Second World War). Yet this was seen by the Labour Party through a pragmatic lens. The expansion of the state was seen as a necessity of the war and supporting the efforts was more a symbol of patriotism than accepting or overcoming the deficiencies of the capitalist economy system. The main effect of the war was to promote, within the party, an ethical, rather than economic, rationale for socialism.

Nor is it to say that the Labour Party – or at least its leaders – did not see the party as being ideologically driven. The Labour Party's 1918 constitution demonstrated the balance between the ideology of socialism and the need to build the Labour Party.

The 1918 constitution established a clear, ideological understanding of the Labour Party. It offered a 'new formula', changing the party from a pre-war party that had sought to 'organise and maintain in Parliament and the country a political Labour Party' to one that offered a new, more ideological foundation, especially in its much-quoted Clause IV, which promised 'to secure for the producers by hand or by brain the full fruits of their industry, and the most equitable distribution thereof that may be possible, upon the common ownership of the means of production and the best obtainable system of popular administration and control of each industry and service' (Butler and Freeman, 1969, p 109).

This constitution was part of Labour's transition into a 'mass party', further facilitated by the extension of the franchise in 1918, which extended the vote to non-property-owning men and some women. Barker (1976, p 54) quotes Sidney Webb's address to the second conference of 1918 where he noted that the party's programme as outlined in *Labour and the New Social Order* was 'not an appeal to the converted but the basis of an appeal to the 20 million electors – 10 or 12 million of them being new electors'. It was not until 1918 that the Labour Party created 'a wide ranging programme, an elaborate extra-parliamentary party structure and [offered], for the first time in its history, an opportunity for individuals to join as members' (Seyd and Whiteley, 1992, p 13). This allowed those who did not come to the party through the trade unions, or express a socialist ideology, to join (Webb, 1918b), although it did dilute the importance of both of these groups within the party (see the next chapter).

Labour's understanding of socialism

Without any period of office (other than the wartime coalition, which for Labour's leaders had a particular, self-contained purpose), manifestos offer the best guides as to what the party may have done if it had been presented with the opportunity of government. Labour Party manifestos before the First World War did not mention the terms 'socialist' or 'socialism'. The first use of either was not until 1924 (although the 1900 manifesto mentioned the 'socialisation of the means of production, distribution and exchange'; Labour Party, 1900).

Labour's commitment to socialism stemmed more from the ethical socialism of Tawney (although he was not the first to advocate such policies) than from the economic understanding of Marx. The socialism adopted by Labour was 'not solely about the common ownership of the means of production ... [but] about the abolition of immoralities – such as poverty, and inequities – such as opportunity based on, or denied, because of wealth, not individual worth'. Those who advocated such forms of socialism were '"rational", often self-educated men and women, who despised ignorance and wished to transform working class life'. For ethical socialists, the role of the state was not to eradicate the inequalities of the capitalist system but to offer agents an equal chance of realising their potential, through schemes such as adult education. MacDonald also emphasised this ethical socialism and rejected notions of 'economic struggle as a mobilising agent' for three reasons.

First, because 'the working class were both producers and consumers; they did not have a single economic interest'. Second, because MacDonald 'had less faith than the moral revolutionaries in the possibility of achieving broad working class support for the construction of a new social order'. And finally, because 'conflict, animosity, and class prejudice could not suddenly be transformed into the social spirit which was the true basis of socialism' (Tanner, 1990, pp 32–34).

Attlee (1937, p 33) saw the formation of the Labour Party as a coming together of socialist propaganda and the recognition of the limitations of the existing union structures, principally that 'methods of strikes and mutual assistance must be supplemented by parliamentary action'. While some recognised the limits of trade unionism, there existed tensions between Labour's appeal to the views or ideologies held by the trade unionists and the broader working classes, which were by no means homogenous, and the need for Labour to achieve significant representation in Parliament.

Labour's parliamentary ambitions risked splitting the anti-Conservative vote, making it harder for progressives to achieve representation in Parliament. Awareness of this led to agreements between the Liberals and Labour as to which seats each party would contest. While such agreements enabled Labour to gain representation in Parliament, it also signified its reliance on the Liberals, and in doing so forced Labour to adopt a more moderate or pragmatic form of socialism. Labour acknowledged that it was unable to gain the support of the entire working classes, and MacDonald identified that it did not have a homogenous ideology, let alone subscribe to revolutionary (or economic) socialism – a point others returned to later in the 20th century (for example, Parkin, 1967) – but sought to appeal to as wide a range of the working classes as possible. There was, prior to the First World War, no reason to suspect that Labour was imminently poised to overtake the Liberals as the main challenger to the Conservative Party in British politics.

The experiences of the late 19th and early 20th centuries (for example the Taff Vale judgment) demonstrated, for the working classes, the need to obtain representation within Parliament. Although questions remained regarding the extent to which socialism could be achieved within the existing institutional framework, for the unions in particular, parliamentary representation was needed to maintain their relative position. Parliamentary representation then was linked to protecting existing structures as much as it was about creating new ones. Representatives were needed to balance out the vested class interests of the Conservative Party. The reversal of the Taff Vale judgment in 1906 demonstrated this point; this did not enhance the powers of the trade unions but returned the unions to their pre-1900 legal standing. 'It was similar with the reversal of the Osborne judgment and the promulgation of the 1913 Trade Union Act; not a total victory but one enabling the unions to sustain a political role' (Minkin, 1991, p 11).

Ramsay MacDonald (quoted by Marquand, 1977, p 75), writing in the left-wing evening newspaper, *The Echo*, made a similar link between such judgments and the need for parliamentary representation: '[T]rade unionism is being assailed, not by what the law says of it, but by what judges think the law ought to say of it … that being so it becomes necessary for the unions to place men in the House of Commons, to challenge the decisions which I have no doubt will follow this.' The Taff Vale judgment of 1902 convinced MacDonald of the need to secure money through a levy on trade unions, having previously considered the idea premature. Following the LRC's decision in principle to pursue this at its conference in 1902, MacDonald, again writing in *The Echo* (and quoted by Marquand, 1977, p 75), noted that '[n]ow we are to have a Trade Union levy paid into a common fund, and Labour candidate[s] – not necessarily Trade Unionists – run from that fund'. Important here is the 'not necessarily trade unionists' caveat. Although the fund was to be comprised of union levies, the selection of candidates would be at the discretion of the Labour Party, again allowing for a plurality of ideologies within the party.

Labour's growth over the period, especially during the First World War, aided the belief that Parliament could be a vehicle used by socialists to achieve radical change. The 1910 general elections exposed the weakness of the Labour Party. These elections were fought on the theme of House of Lords reform, following the House of Lords' refusal to pass the Liberal budget of 1909. Labour's position in Parliament was not sustained on the basis of competing against the Conservative and Liberal parties in three-way constituencies but rather through forging local electoral truces with the Liberal Party. Such dependency weakened Labour's position and limited the extent to which the party could form its own positions/campaign tactics. This was clear in 1910: although the Labour Party fielded 78 candidates in January 1910, this was reduced to 56 in December of that year following 'Liberal threats of retaliation' (see for example *The Times*, 1909; McKibbin, 1970, p 219) where Liberal chief whip, Mr Pease, warned Labour against trying to compete in Liberal seats and that doing so would lead to 'retaliatory attacks on their own candidates'.

The Labour Party won 57 seats in the 1918 election, up 15 on December 1910, making it the fourth largest party, after the coalition partners and Sinn Fein and ahead of the Liberals led by Asquith, a feat made more impressive given the continuation of the Conservative and Liberal coalition, which reduced the number of candidates standing in many constituencies. Such results again emphasised Labour as the main (national) opposition party. The First World War further gave hope that the state could be a vehicle of change within British society. The war had seen an extension in the role of the state, particularly in economic planning, something that the Labour Party was keen to utilise and continue. The 1918 manifesto advocated the nationalisation of land as 'a vital necessity', along with proposals to build 1 million new houses (for a population estimated at being fewer than 40 million) at the expense of the state (Labour Party, 1918; Office for National Statistics, 2015).

Despite these gains in parliamentary seats, the 1918 election 'left the Labour Party badly short of leaders'. Key figures such as Ramsay MacDonald, Arthur Henderson, Philip Snowden and George Lansbury were all defeated by coalition candidates. Although most were soon returned in by-elections, the post-election Parliamentary Labour Party (PLP) 'was overwhelmingly a trade union party, and half of the Trade Union representation was drawn from a single union [the Miners' Federation]', weakening the development of a coherent political ideology (Cole, 1948, p 84).

Attlee (1937, pp 44–45) noted that the war enabled the creation of a socialist party; he stated that the Great War represented a turning point, first through highlighting the differences that existed within the party, principally between national patriotism and Christian pacifism. In overcoming these – or at least not being torn apart by such divisions – the war had two effects. First, it led to organisational changes within the party and an agreement that the party needed to appeal to broader sections of the electorate than it had pre-1914 (not least due to the expanding, and more diverse, electorate). Second, it provoked ideological changes: 'the party now accepted socialism as its aim. No longer is the mere return of Labour members sufficient. In 1918 the objects of the party were set out.'

Others on the left point to 1918, and the implementation of the party's constitution, as a turning point; G.D.H. Cole, an economist, member of the Fabian society, influential Labour thinkker and later advocate of guild socialism, (1948, p 56) noted that this 'unequivocally committed the Labour Party to Socialist objectives', while Ralph Miliband (1961, p 61) saw it as Labour's rejection of (its own version of) liberalism. This was symbolic both in the ideological positioning of the party, and in asserting Labour's independence from the Liberal Party (Beer, 1965, p 140). However, such understandings were challenged by commitments to expand the party (see earlier) through individual memberships, suggesting that the party saw socialism as one of multiple ideologies, rather than its only ideology. Labour's 1918 manifesto did not mention the term 'socialism', but instead argued that its programme was one 'of national and international justice, founded on permanent democratic principles' (Labour Party, 1918).

The Labour Party and the trade unions

Prior to 1906, the working classes, due to the restrictive nature of the franchise, represented a minority in the vast majority of constituencies, with notable exceptions in mining areas of the north-east of England and South Wales. The franchise at the turn of the 20th century was still very much dominated by property-owning men. While approximately every other male trade unionist was able to cast a ballot in England, about half a million voters were able to cast two ballots (Clegg et al, 1977, pp 269–271).

The Taff Vale case, and subsequent House of Lords decision, were seen as an attack on the practices of trade unions. They encouraged unions to seek additional avenues for reversing or overturning the decision. As Minkin (1974, p 8) notes, it 'had the effect of stimulating increased trade union affiliation to the [Labour] party'. In 1901, 41 unions were affiliated to the Labour Party (or LRC) and membership totalled 455,450. By 1904, the number of unions affiliating had quadrupled and the number of affiliated members had more than doubled (Simpson, 1973, p 46). The 'judgement, which put the finances of every union at risk, made them see that they needed spokesmen in Parliament to work for legislation to reverse it' (MacKenzie and MacKenzie, 1979, p 310). While the growth in union affiliation was a success for the Labour Party, its appeal beyond unions was severely limited; Porritt (1910, p 309) explains that Labour's increase from 323,195 votes in 1906 to 499,011 in the January 1910 general election 'was due to ... the Miners' Federation', which had put forward 12 of the 40 Labour MPs who were elected.

To contextualise these figures, the entire trade union movement accounted for fewer than 2 million workers in 1901 and, between 1901 and 1914, union density stood at only 15–25 per cent, with children and adolescents prohibited from joining unions, and only a small proportion of female workers joining. Such limitations would, after the First World War, encourage Labour to place greater emphasis on individual membership (McKibbin, 1984, pp 298–299). Although, as Thompson (2011, p 28) demonstrates, this period also represented vast increases in union membership, albeit from the low base highlighted by McKibbin, 'union membership grew markedly from about 750,000 in 1888 to 2.6 million in 1910, reaching 4 million in 1914 before peaking in 1920 at over 8 million'. Despite overall growth, differences existed between different industries and unions; in 1910, the mining union accounted for a quarter of all trade union members.

Exploring why the trade unions came to see the Labour Party, rather than the Liberal Party, as their parliamentary representation is critical to understanding the development of the early Labour Party. Once Labour had accepted the need to obtain representation in Parliament and pursue a parliamentary route to socialism (even if this was not seen as an exclusive route prior to the First World War), there were clear overlaps in the electoral coalitions both it and the Liberals were seeking to form, particularly with respect to the working-class or trade union votes. The Liberal Party had a strong claim to be seen as progressive – not only had it demonstrated an ability to win elections and form governments, but in doing so it had enacted legislation introducing old-age pensions and sick pay. Such policies appealed to those groups who were to become Labour's core voters in the interwar period and after.

McKibbin (1970, p 216) also notes that prior to 1914, the Liberal Party was the main challenger to the Labour Party, renewed by 'old debates' relating to free trade, the question of Irish Home Rule and House of Lords reform. However, Labour's success was reliant on the Liberals, leaving the party with 'no real tradition of independent electoral activity. For the most part Labour had achieved its parliamentary strength not by struggle, but by arrangement – an arrangement embodied in the MacDonald-Gladstone Agreement.' McKibbin (1970, p 217) acknowledges that much of the agreement was needed to ensure an effective Labour challenge, but notes that it created two unintended consequences: '[I]t ensured, excluding a couple of areas, that there was no known reservoir of true Labour voters and it got MacDonald into the habit of assuming that arranged victories were as satisfactory as any other form of victory.'

Lovell (1986, pp 30–31) notes that the Taff Vale case was not the first instance of trade unions' activity being impeded by the media, politicians or employers. However, historians agree that Taff Vale was important in changing relationships between formal politics and the trade unions. '[A]lthough the Labour Representation Committee had been set up in 1900; it was not until after Taff Vale that the Committee won widespread support among the unions.' Taff Vale, and later the Osborne judgment, demonstrated the pragmatic relationships between the trade unions and the Labour Party. Union support was by no means unanimous at the founding of the Labour Party but grew throughout the post-war period in response to changes in the law and Liberal unwillingness to reverse the Osborne judgment in full (Klarman, 1989).

Yet it would be wrong to assume that the Taff Vale experience homogenised the views of trade unionists. Many still pursued narrow, sectional interests, seeking to maximise their members, with little concern for other groups (Clegg, Fox and Thompson, 1977, p 488). While Taff Vale demonstrated the importance of links between political representation and a defence of trade union activities, there remained a large number of union members who did not vote for the Labour Party and rejected notions of socialism, instead finding political homes in either the Liberal or Conservative parties. The party's performance in the December 1910 general election is testimony to this: Labour only stood 56 candidates and won just 42 seats, with a national vote share of 6.4 per cent – a decline of 0.6 per cent from January (Blewett, 1972, p 390).

While Sydney Webb identified 'exceptional political opportunities' within the coal and cotton industries, due to them being concentrated in specific regions, Clegg, Fox and Thompson (1977, p 271) note that the geographical distribution of the working classes limited their propensity to enact change. Working-class political representation was used most effectively, before 1906, in Northumberland and Durham. These two regions, although accounting for only 20 per cent of the coal industry's labour force, accounted for 60 per cent (three out of five) of MPs sponsored by the miners in 1889, who added a further seat in 1904. This was the first addition to the nationwide miners' tally since 1889.

Labour, however, used the crises to forge stronger ties with the unions. The party's response to the Osborne judgment and the Trade Union Act of 1913 was to establish 'voluntary contribution schemes to the party funds'. Such schemes were 'not only financially unsuccessful, but MacDonald's dispiriting tussles with trade union leaders must have doubly convinced him that there was still much hostility to the Labour party in the unions' (McKibbin, 1970, p 220).

Although both of these initiatives ended in failure, they help to explain why those such as Webb were keen to demonstrate Labour's appeal beyond the unions. The unions, certainly in the period before the First World War, lacked the funds and/or appetite to transform Labour into a serious challenger to the Conservative or Liberal parties.

The First World War also impacted on the unions in their own right. Union membership increased by 50 per cent between 1914 and 1918, and the number of unions affiliated to the Labour Party doubled (Barker, 1976, p 47). Barker argues that the incorporation of the Labour Party into government was based on 'the government's estimation of the importance of gaining the support of organized industrial labour for the war efforts, and the ability of parliament Labour to further that end'. The Labour Party could ensure that the government was more effective in making agreements with the unions.

The First World War aided the Labour Party through exposing weaknesses in its main political opponent – the Liberals – and in doing so helped establish the Labour Party as the dominant party of the left. Although both parties were divided on offering support to the war, the Labour Party emerged from the war more unified than its main competitor for left-wing votes. The Liberals throughout the war were divided between 'coalition Liberals' who supported Lloyd George (who replaced Asquith as Prime Minister in 1916) and the coalition with the Conservative Party, and those led by Asquith. Divisions had emerged during the war over conscription and the direction of travel towards total war pursued by Lloyd George following the onset of the coalition government. In contrast, the Labour Party had demonstrated relative unity throughout the war, offering incentives for unions to join the party, even though Labour was simultaneously seeking to broaden its support. Unions were converted to Labour's socialism by a widespread belief in coordinated economic planning. As Clegg (1985, p 232) notes: 'Under wartime controls, living standards had been maintained at a reasonable level while about half the nation's productive capacity had been devoted to the manufacture of armaments and other materials of war, and millions of men had been away in the armed forces.'

Given the effectiveness of government control over the economy in wartime, the propensity for government control once peace was declared looked promising. Such optimism was reflected in the Labour Party's 1918 constitution, and in particular the famous commitments to nationalisation contained within Clause IV (see earlier).

Labour's decision to leave the coalition and fight the December election further emphasised the extent to which Lloyd George was willing to work with the Conservative Party. The 1918 election saw Labour emerge as the principal opposition to the Conservatives in Britain, as the majority of the Liberal Party remained in coalition with the Conservatives. Coalition candidates stood in 541 of the 602 constituencies in England, Scotland and Wales. The coupons outlined the coalition's preferred candidate; 364 went to Conservatives and 159 to Liberals, with the remaining 18 offered to the National Democratic Party, 'a "patriotic" working-class party of transient existence hostile to the Labour Party'. Of the 541 candidates 478 were successful (333 Conservatives, 136 Liberals and 9 National Democratic Party) (Wilson, 1964, p 38; Morgan, 2011). The issuing of coupons confirmed the coalition Liberals as the junior partners in the coalition and left Labour as the main opposition to the government.

Conclusion

Given that the Labour Party was born out of a coming together of different, marginalised groups, broadly aligned on the left of British politics, its transition to the forefront of British politics fewer than two decades later was in many respects remarkable. Maintaining this expansion was in part due to Labour's ability to describe socialism in the broadest possible terms, drawing on the ethical rather than revolutionary aspects to appeal to as many working-class voters and sympathisers as it could.

Many of the crises explored later on in this book will outline negative consequences for the Labour Party, but the Taff Vale judgment and the First World War, outlined in this chapter, can be seen to have strengthened its position within British politics. Labour's key task in this period was to attract trade unionists who had previously been supporters of, or at least sympathetic to, the Liberal Party. The Taff Vale judgment demonstrated the need – from the perspective of the unions – for political representation but in the first decade of the 20th century there was no guarantee that Labour would be the main vehicle for this. The First World War and Labour's ability to remain both united and patriotic (as demonstrated through its involvement in the coalition government) helped the unions come to see the party, rather than the Liberal Party, as their political home.

The crises further helped wed the party to the institutions of the British political tradition. Such alignment in turn promoted an ethical, rather than revolutionary, understanding of socialism as the party's key ideology. The need for working-class political class representation as well as the inclusion of Labour in the wartime coalition committed the party to Parliament. Alongside this, the party appealed to trade unions who themselves promoted labourism, rather than revolution.

Some problems were yet to be resolved. The party's broad appeal also meant that it included some who held revolutionary views (which led to expulsions from the party in the next two decades). The relationship between the trade unions and the Labour Party would be debated at various points over the next 80 years, as would aspects of the 1918 constitution, and prove contentious for both the party and political opponents (see Minkin, 1991). Equally, Labour's commitment to existing institutions such as the Treasury would, according to those on the left, constrain the party's response to the crisis of 1931.

3

Governing in Hard Times: The Second Labour Government and Need for a Coherent Economic Policy

Introduction

The 1920s and 1930s were a period of great instability for the Labour Party. Although the interwar period offered Labour the chance to form both its first and second governments, consolidating its electoral position vis-à-vis the Liberals as the main opposition to the Conservative Party, both of these were minority governments. The party's socialist advance in many ways lost momentum due to two crises: first, the General Strike of 1926 – orchestrated by the trade unions – which challenged the relationship between the party and the unions described in the previous chapter and highlighted the differences between revolutionary socialism and parliamentary socialism; and, second, the Great Slump of 1931, which led to the downfall of the second Labour government in 1931.

This chapter asseses the Labour Party's responses to these crises. It outlines the internal party splits that caused the party to distinguish itself from the national government, and lose the 1931 and 1935 general elections, only returning to government under the wartime coalition government of 1940–1945. It explores what Diamond (2004, p 2) labels as the first period of revisionism in Labour's history, principally through the works of Evan Durbin and Ernest Bevin, who offered the Labour Party a more coherent economic ideology.

The General Strike of 1926

Although the General Strike lasted for nine days in May 1926, its origins lay in the post-First World War economy. The end of the First World War saw a decline in coal outputs, and domestic coal production was under threat from cheaper foreign imports. In 1924, the government had intervened in the coal industry to offer subsidies but gave one month's notice at the end of June 1925 that this was to end. This meant that miners faced pay reductions in order to compete with production overseas. In addition to these longer-term trends, British competitiveness had weakened following the decision to rejoin the gold standard in February 1925 (Mason, 1969, p 1).

The ending of the coal subsidy was postponed following the government's appointment of a Royal Commission to assess the future of the mining industry, something that was initially seen as a victory for the unions. This deferred the proposed cuts to the industry until the commission reported – but, importantly, also gave the government time to prepare for any industrial action that arose. The report, published in March 1926, recommended reorganisation (not nationalisation) of the industry alongside wage reductions at the end of the subsidy.

The report was unacceptable to the miners, leading to conferences between the government and trade unions. Mine owners posted lockout notices, set to expire on 30 April, informing the miners that if they did not agree with the new conditions, they would be locked out of their places of work. This deadline passed without agreement and on 1 May, unions supported a TUC proposal for a general strike (which commenced on 4 May) in support of the miners.

The miners have a special symbolism with the British trade union movement, partly as they were 'the best organized and most conscious members of the British trade union movement' (Mason, 1969, p 2), but have at times had a fractious relationship with other unions. An agreement between the miners, railwaymen and transport workers forged prior to the First World War broke down in 1921 due to the lack of support for a miners' strike. However, in 1926, the trade union movement united in their support for the miners, calling out a total of one and a half million workers in a variety of industries, such as dockers, railwaymen, printers, builders and those responsible for electricity generation (Catterall, 2017).

The General Strike was called off after nine days following questions about the legality of strikes outside the mining industry under the Trades Dispute Act 1906 (for a discussion of these arguments see Goodhart, 1927). The miners remained on strike until the autumn but also returned to work defeated, having won no concession.

Although the Labour Party was not in government at the time, the strike still posed considerable questions for the party. Defeat in the strike may not have tested the revolutionary aims of the trade unions (see Lovell, 1986, pp 56–57) but it did close 'an era of industrial militancy' and emphasised, for the Labour Party, a lack of broad support for revolutionary means and the need to coordinate reform and work within the parliamentary tradition. According to Minkin (1991, p 20), the strike 'severely weakened the trade unions and undermined for many years the appeal of large-scale militant industrial action'.

Following the strike, the Conservative government passed the Trade Union Act in 1927, reinstating provisions of the Osbourne judgment and banning sympathetic strikes. Among restrictions on the actions of trade unions it replaced the system of contracting out with one of contracting in. This meant that members of trade unions were no longer automatically registered as Labour Party members; rather, they now had to explicitly state a preference to be. This placed a renewed emphasis on the party obtaining individual members and for the first time in the party's history it overtly attempted to recruit men. Previous attempts had focused on newly enfranchised women as it was assumed that men would belong to a trade union and therefore already be affiliated (Seyd and Whiteley, 1992, pp 13–14).

Others saw the strike as centralising the place of the Labour Party within the British political left. Following the strike, Cole, who previously had viewed the trade unions as the primary vehicle for realising benefits to the working classes, distanced himself from notions of revolution advocating instead a statist approach to instigating socialism. Cole had assumed that if the unions grew stronger so too would the Labour Party and the unions would be increasingly influential in determining Labour policy. In the period after the First World War Cole became more active within the Labour Party and came to see it, rather than the unions, as the most likely instigators of socialism (Foote, 1997, 115–119). Cole (1929), in his book, *The Next Ten Years in British Social and Economic History*, revised his understanding of workers in two ways to reflect this lack of revolutionary tendencies. First, he now accepted that the workplace was not necessarily the central interest in the worker's life and that a great deal of work, which was unavoidably dull, would always remain 'primarily an obligation' no matter how the workplace was organised. Second, Cole argued that the worker was not so much of a political animal, as he once thought, and was not interested in spending his non-working hours setting up a great number of committees. Cole did not abandon the idea of workers' control altogether, but rather promoted guild socialism. In doing so, Cole refined this to a more limited idea of work councils. Rather than seeing the workplace as the key institution of social reform, this role now lay with an interventionist centralised state.

This stemmed from an alternative understanding of the state. For Cole the state stood above class struggles and could be persuaded to support the unions' cause. There was no need, according to Cole, to undertake a revolution or overthrow the state, which he warned was bigger than any single employer. Democratic unions could achieve socialism but only 'in partnership with, and not opposition to, the state' (Foote, 1997, p 119).

Cole argued that only the state was able to solve the problem of unemployment. He argued for a 'national labour corps', which would be 'a national organisation of workers available for any use of national service'. Although forward thinking, the experience of the New Deal in the United States (US) demonstrated that this would have problems. Cole was aware of many of these. One telling response was Cole's remedy to the opposition of the trade unions. Cole acknowledged that the trade unions may see his proposal as being a militarisation of labour and an attack on the labour movement. However, Cole 'argued that a Labour government must be prepared to override the objections of the unions and that the risk of a conservative reaction was one that it had to be prepared to take' (Riddell, 1999, p 43).

The Great Slump of 1931

The 1929 general election permitted another minority Labour government. Labour gained 287 seats, a net increase of 136 from the 1924 general election, but just 27 seats more than the Conservatives and 21 seats short of an overall majority. Yet it still offered Labour and its supporters optimism; this was the first time Labour had won the most seats in a general election and was thus able to form a second government in five years, the election further firmly establishing its credentials as the dominant party of the British political left. The Liberals won just 59 seats, a meagre increase of 19. Labour gained 15 seats from the Liberals in the election, with just two going the other way.

Thorpe (1991, p 9) notes that the 1929 general election was unique in the optimism that was exhibited within the Labour Party and the broader political left. Both the PLP and affiliated trade unions were delighted. Thorpe quotes one union general secretary, W.A. Robinson, who while emphasising the need for loyalty 'added that he had "never at any time moved about in such an atmosphere of enthusiasm". The party activists reflected this mood; York divisional Labour Party (DLP) "congratulate[d] the Working Class on at last becoming the Ruling Class".'

The Labour government of 1929 was not markedly different from that of 1924 in terms of personnel, but was ideologically to the right of its predecessor (Cole, 1948, p 228). Snowden (1934, p 767) notes that the Cabinet was 'composed overwhelmingly of the right section of the movement' and also altered the dynamics of the party's relationship with the unions. Of the 54 'major and minor appointments', trade unionists were given less than half (21). Yet, importantly, unlike in 1924, the government did not seek the support of any other parties – the Cabinet was comprised solely of Labour members.

Although easy to present/view such progress in linear terms, the pursuit of ideological ends was (and would continue to be) tempered by a number of factors, as MacDonald (quoted by Snowden, 1934, p 772) made clear to the new House of Commons:

> I want to say something else. It is not because I happen to be at the head of a Minority that I say this. ... I wonder how far it is possible, without in any way abandoning any of our party positions, without in any way surrendering any item of our Party principles to consider ourselves more as a Council of State and less as arrayed regiments facing each other in battle?

Any optimism, however, was short lived. After a short-sitting Parliament entered into a three-month-long summer recess. Parliament was recalled following the Wall Street Crash of 29 October 1929 (Snowden, 1934, p 843; Cole, 1948, p 230). This prompted the US to ask for repayments of First World War loans and reduced its investment in Britain and much of Western Europe, events which, alongside the decline in traditional manufacturing and high unemployment, further weakened Britain's balance of payments position and government deficit.

The government, keen to balance the budget, appointed the May Committee, led by the liberal Sir George May, in February 1931. This committee reported at the end of July that year and proposed a combination of cuts (comprised of cuts to unemployment benefit and public sector pay cuts) and increases in taxation at a ratio of 4:1. By far the largest cuts were to unemployment benefit (£66.5 million).

Some argued that the forming of such a committee was not entirely at the behest of the Labour government, due to its minority nature. Webb (1931) blamed the parliamentary arithmetic for the forming of the committee. He noted that despite the Liberal Party's previous requests for public expenditure to alleviate unemployment, they opportunely brought about the crisis of 1931 by choosing 'suddenly to demand of the government the immediate appointment of a non-political Royal Commission of businessmen, which, in order to lighten the burden that the heavy taxation was declared to be pressing on industry' and advocate 'drastic reductions in public expenditure'. The Liberal proposals were adopted by the opposition Conservative Party, which was 'eager to join in a defeat of the Government on any issue promised unanimous support'.

Cole (1948, p 252) noted that although the committee's report was designed to help the Chancellor, Philip Snowden, achieve his objective of balancing the budget, while weakening opposition within the party, it 'create[d] abroad a belief in the insolvency of Great Britain and in the insecurity of the British currency. ... Foreign-owned sterling now began to be withdrawn at an increasing pace, and exchanged into gold or dollars.' As Ball (1988, p 174) outlines, the May report then led to wider problems. By

August 1931 two distinct problems combined: a banking crisis that left the City of London exposed and a budget deficit of £120 million in 1931–1932. 'These factors combined to produce a serious run on the gold reserves, and sterling's position could only be saved by propping up the parity through loans from financiers in the markets of Paris and New York.' Experts at the Bank of England advised the government that such loans would not be offered unless overseas confidence was restored by instigating policies to balance the budget. Such policies would 'require a substantial reduction of expenditure, in particular in the area of the unemployment benefit, which under the impact of the slump was a heavy charge on the Treasury. In other words, the crisis had become as much political as financial.'

Unemployment was a particular problem for the Labour Party. A party designed to be the representation of the working class and the trade union movement saw unemployment as one of the – if not *the* – key indicators of how well society was functioning. The Great Slump posed a question about the extent to which the Labour Party could cut unemployment support. As Seaman (1993, p 243) notes, deflationary pressures meant that the relative position of unemployed people was improving in comparison with those in employment to the extent that 'a man on unemployment benefit at the depths of the depression in 1933 was no worse off than an unskilled labourer in work in 1913'. In addition to this, 'the lack of work at skilled rates in the most depressed areas, the only jobs which the unemployed might take in the thirties, were often so intermittent and so badly paid that they really were better off on the dole'.

The problem for the Labour Party was that government spending is naturally progressive. Those in receipt of government spending are typically poorer than those who receive no such benefit. Here, through emphasising the crisis as stemming from the balance of payments, the costs of (and implicitly also the blame for) Britain's problems were being shifted to those in receipt of government spending (traditionally the poorest within society). Brookes (1985, p 49) cites an example of one article in the *Daily Express* from July 1931, entitled 'Cheap Fares for "Dole" Excursions', reporting subsidised rail fares for unemployed people in Horwich, Lancashire. The article, although presented as objective, offered no 'mention of whether [the subsidised fares] would be taken up by the unemployed'. There was nothing assessing the costs of train fares relative to the level of unemployment benefit, but rather the article sought to reinforce notions of 'common sense'; although the seriousness of unemployment was well documented, the public also believed 'that there is always a "shiftless" element of the population who will not work. The "man in the street" knows that a good proportion of "his" hard-earned wages will be taken from "him" by the state.' These views were juxtaposed with the subsidised holidays offered to unemployed people.

In addition to concerns over Parliament, further arguments that institutions were seen to be acting against the Labour government drew on the Bank of England's and the media's commitments to the gold standard. Britain had rejoined the gold standard in 1925, leaving little room to manoeuvre when the sterling crisis emerged. Webb (1931, pp 6, 9) noted that in August 1931, 'no question was raised as to the possibility of going off the gold standard, a step then apparently regarded as unthinkable'. Rather the Bank of England outlined the government needed to borrow 'no less than 50 million pounds' from New York or Paris. Yet 'within four weeks of the formation of the National Government … on September 21, London was off the Gold Standard! Far from this "terrible calamity" providing instantly ruinous to British credit or British trade, as Mr MacDonald had so recently threatened, the press welcomed it.'

This resulted in a major split in the Labour Party. The leader (and Prime Minister, Ramsay MacDonald), along with other senior members of the party, left to form a national government with the Conservatives. This, alongside electoral defeat in 1931, significantly reduced the number of Labour MPs. For those who remained, the actions of Ramsay MacDonald, and others who left the party to form the national government, were defined as deserting the working class. Some proposed a more militant approach and alignment with the Communists, provoking fierce debates and leading to the temporary expulsion of 'several left-wing leaders' from the party (Foote, 1997, p 145). In 1932, the Independent Labour Party (ILP) also split with the Labour Party and other left-wing groups, such as the Socialist League, were founded shortly after (Pimlott, 1971).

Labour's ideology

The late 1920s saw a change in Cole's attitude in particular. Riddell (1995, pp 934, 937) notes that his 'conversion from pluralism to statist socialism from the 1920s was deeply symbolic of the ideological predominance of the latter in Labour's thought thereafter'. The General Strike left Cole, according to Webb, 'disillusioned about workers' control'. In 1928, Cole rejoined the Fabian Society and such was the change of emphasis that in 1929 he was fearful, according to Riddell, that 'the TUC would attempt to dictate policy to a future Labour government and argued that a move away from union dependence could only be beneficial to the party'.

Against this backdrop of internal divisions and poor electoral performance, the Labour Party used the 1930s to reassess its policies and in particular establish a more coherent economic ideology, in the wake of the Great Depression and mass unemployment. For those who remained in the party, this period committed Labour to the principles of parliamentary socialism, working within the existing structures rather than seeking to create new institutions as the more extreme elements of the party had previously advocated. This debate can be divided between those who looked towards liberal thinkers such as Keynes (Evan Durbin and Ernest Bevin) and socialist critics (G.D.H. Cole and Harold Laski) (Howell, 1980, p 60).

Evan Durbin argued for a mixed economy, drawing on the work of John Maynard Keynes. Durbin synthesised many of Keynes's arguments with critiques of J.A. Hobson. Unlike earlier contributors to Labour's ideology, Durbin was a trained economist who did not intrinsically accept that economics was 'committed to laissez-faire, or ... rationalising immoral, acquisitive behaviour', but saw it as offering 'a powerful set of analytical tools that could be used to serve a variety of ideological ends' (Jackson, 2007, p 126).

It was only through intellectuals such as Durbin that the Labour Party was introduced to Keynesian ideas. Keynes himself was very much distant from this process. Only by engaging with Keynesianism at a distance was the Labour Party able to reconcile aspects of his ideas, developing what Pilmott (1985, p 224) describes as policies that were at least 'semi-Keynesianism', with traditional understandings of/debates around control and planning (Barberis, 2006).

Durbin was a representative of the moderate wing of the Labour Party. He rejected 'the traditional radicalism of the Labour left' while simultaneously arguing that the market was 'not able to increase social wealth' (Foote, 1997, p 161). Durbin's key publications include *Purchasing Power and Trade Depression: A Critique of Under-Consumption Theories* (1933) and *The Politics of Democratic Socialism* (1940).

In *Purchasing Power and Trade Depression*, Durbin explored and critiqued Hobson's ideas of under-consumption. He argued that an excess of saving as a result of low consumption was not necessarily disastrous. Rather, such accumulation could simply lead to an expansion of investment, as had occurred in the industrialism of the 19th century. Durbin (1933, pp 151–152) stated that the Great Depression was generated by a large fall in prices. But unlike other economists, Durbin was keen to distinguish between falling prices as a result of falling costs and other reasons for a fall in prices, arguing that 'there comes a point at which the choice is between pure inflation and the critical step of credit restriction'. Crisis was inevitable 'from the moment at which prices fail to fall as rapidly as costs'. This meant that theories of under-consumption were 'radically wrong in tracing the origin of cyclical depression to a shortage of money'. Rather, Durbin argued that governments have two policy options available: increasing the rate of voluntary savings, which could only be achieved, at least in the short term, through a regressive measure (that is, giving more money to those who have a greater predisposition to save) or reducing 'the size of the capital good industries ... [moving] young labour and new capital ... into the less unprofitable production of consumption goods' (Durbin, 1933, pp 155, 167, 170–171).

Durbin advocated the second option and was in favour of democratic socialism, arguing that the central task of the state was the control of industry and the distribution of income, meaning the transfer of economic power from private interests into the hands of the state, allowing the redistribution of income from the rich to the poor. Although Durbin (1933, p 171) acknowledged that this transition would be slow and painful, he argued that it was the only means to avoid further depressions.

In contrast to the revolutionary socialist, who wished to create new structures, the democratic element of democratic socialism saw Parliament act as a key safeguard. This was the only method through which lasting socialist revolution could be achieved. If parties in Britain believed that their opponents were out to destroy them, they would never cede power in elections. Equally, if Labour implemented 'extreme measures', it risked, once removed from office, Conservative repercussions. Durbin (quoted in Foote, 1997, p 191) argued that 'to betray democracy is to betray socialism'.

Bevan (2008, p 169) argued that democratic socialism viewed society in a relationship with nature and with an awareness of the limitations imposed by physical conditions. Democratic socialism views the 'the individual in his context with society and is therefore compassionate and tolerant. Because it knows that all political action must be a choice between a number of alternatives it eschews all absolute proscriptions and final decisions.'

Democracy, for Bevan (2008, p 5), is important as it 'brings the welfare of ordinary men and women on to the agenda of political discussion and demands its consideration'. Equally, Parliament, in a British context, was central to instigating change. Bevan argues that the key problem in MacDonald's response to 1931 was his willingness to let capitalism resolve its own crisis. Bevan (2008, p 31) argues that in the case of 1931, 'parliamentary action was still to be the handmaiden of private economy activity. ... This is wholly opposed to socialism, for to the socialist, parliamentary power is to be used progressively until the main streams of economic activity are brought under public direction.'

Durbin saw four types of measures as being necessary to transform Britain's capitalist society:

- an extension of social services;
- socialisation measures: the nationalisation of industry and the acquisition of economic power by the state for central planning;
- prosperity measures: legislative and administrative acts to maintain and increase the volume of industrial activity – Durbin argued that socialist economists had overlooked the importance of maintaining production, especially during the transition from capitalism to socialism, which could take a very long time; and
- egalitarian measures aimed at changing the inequality between classes, towards a fairer distribution of income and wealth.

Labour's economic policy should be, according to Durbin (quoted in Foote, 1997, p 162, emphasis in original), 'based upon the necessity of making a large quantity of *private* industry expand its demand for labour at the existing level of wages, and upon the demand of the trade unions for the maintenance of money wage rates'.

Alongside Durbin, Bevin argued in the 1930s for state intervention in the world of high finance so that increased investment through the creation of credit would lead Britain away from the vicious circle of low investment and high unemployment. A minimum programme of reform within capitalism required Labour to 'socialise the Bank of England, as other countries have socialised their central banks in order to be free to pursue an expansionist monetary policy on the basis of a managed currency' (Bevin, quoted in Foote, 1997, p 165).

Scholars such Durbin and Bevin facilitated Labour's gradual adoption of Keynesian economics (Diamond, 2004, p 61). Importantly, Keynes was never a Labour supporter nor a party member; his reasons for not joining are quoted in Foote (1997, p 137). Keynes viewed Labour as 'a class party and the class is not my class. If I am going to pursue sectional interests at all, I shall pursue my own.' Despite this, Keynes's ideas were introduced to the party by those with a more egalitarian persuasion (Jackson, 2007, p 119). Bevin saw a planned economy situated very much within a national context. Here the protection of British workers would take precedence. This offered the left 'a bridge' to Keynesianism and overcame, in part, objections to Keynes's conceptualisation (or lack of) of class power (Foote, 1997, pp 165–166).

Alternative ideas were formulated by those on the left of the party who had become increasingly frustrated with the economic policy of the Labour governments, such as Harold Laski and G.D.H. Cole. These authors were drawn to ideas of guild socialism, ideas that had emerged in the immediate pre-First World War period and remained within socialist discourse afterwards (Stears, 1998).

As early as the end of 1929, Cole, although appreciating the difficulties the government faced, 'feared the government's minority position was being used as a fig-leaf to hide its shortcomings and as an excuse for a policy which will fail because it lacks courage and does not go far enough' (Riddell, 1999, p 190).

From 1929, Cole realised that Labour's understanding of economics was woefully inadequate. 'He believed that if Labour was going to achieve a peaceful transition to socialism it was essential it should have a coherent strategy for dealing with a capitalist system which, following the logic of socialist analysis, would be subject to continual crisis' (Riddell, 1995, p 950). Cole established the New Fabian Research Bureau (NFRB) as he was concerned with the generation gap within the Labour Party and questioned the party's appeal to younger voters. Important figures, such as

Clement Attlee, Stafford Cripps, George Lansbury, Hugh Gaitskell and Evan Durbin, attended NRFB meetings. By the summer of 1931, the NFRB had established three wide-ranging inquiries to study all aspects of economics, international affairs and the political system, respectively.

Cole was important in understanding Labour's response to the crisis faced by the second Labour government. According to Riddle (1995, p 934). 'Not only did Cole make a significant contribution to the reshaping of the party's ideology in the 1930s; in addition, his conversion from pluralism to statist socialism from the late 1920s was deeply symbolic of the ideological predominance of the latter in Labour's thought thereafter.'

The experiences of the interwar governments further shaped Harold Laski's views. He increasingly 'came to see that people whose interests were entrenched in the capitalist system would vigorously contest the rights that were essential to the development of a socialist–pluralist democracy' (Lamb, 2004, p 45).

Laski and Cole both argued that the state was one of a number of organisations within society, and if socialism was to flourish it would require a grounding in a plurality of organisations. Guild socialism promoted democratic participation at levels below that of the state, such as within unions, insisting that true democracy was self-government of the individual in all spheres of social life: political and industrial. Cole suggested that specific guilds would operate in regions of the country and would themselves be made up of workers within districts where factories are situated, and within the factories different sections or 'shops' would democratically elect their supervisors, foremen and managers.

Cole (2011, p 196) distinguished between socialisation and nation-alisation: 'Nationalisation in the true sense of the word, as it is used in common by capitalist and by labour advocates, means national management; socialisation, whether in the mouth of a social democrat or of a hireling of the Anti-Socialist notion, means national ownership with a system of controlling industry.' Nationalisation for Cole did not refer to one single centralised body, but rather nationwide coverage of decentralised guilds. Indeed, Cole, in the 1920s, argued that a bureaucratic form of nationalisation would represent a worse outcome than if the Labour Party dropped its commitments to nationalisation altogether (Beech and Hickson, 2007, p 46).

One area where Cole's (1929) book, *The Next Ten Years in British Social and Economic History*, was forward looking was in its assessment of banking and finance. Cole argued for the socialisation of banking and finance, noting that this was more important than the nationalisation of industry as banks control credit for the ends of big business. Cole (1929) argued that a Labour government should immediately nationalise both the Bank of England and the joint stock banks. Together with the nationalisation of insurance and the development of a board of national investment to administer public loans, a Labour government would hold the power necessary to aid suffering industries and more importantly develop new ones.

Here Cole moved away from prioritising the nationalisation of industry. Instead, he argued that control, and not ownership, was the key socialist transformation. He argued that the mining industry should remain privately owned initially, although the state would supervise the compulsory amalgamation of the mines into more economic units. A similar proposal was developed with regards to the railways whereby a gradual socialisation after a state of transition would be required. Through advocating such measures, Cole attempted to avoid the problems of the state taking over industries that were suffering economic problems.

Many of the ideas and thoughts developed in the 1930s would not come to fruition until the late 1940s (see Chapter 4). Labour lost both the 1931 and 1935 general elections, and it was not until the Second World War that the party returned to government, first in a coalition led by Winston Churchill and after 1945 under a majority government led by Clement Attlee. Yet this did not mean that the party did not adapt and respond to the crises of the early 1930s.

Some elements of the 1929–1931 government and crisis hindered the party. Losing the 1931 general election along with the splits that led to the loss of its leader and other senior figures ensured that the party would spend the rest of the decade in opposition. This naturally hindered the party's ability to forge ahead with a socialist agenda, but the crisis pushed Labour to develop a more holistic understanding of economic policy. Splits within the left of the party further offered the party a (relatively) more ideologically homogenous membership, making it easier to agree board policy goals.

The splits of 1931 generated immediate responses from the Labour Party. The reorganisation of the party in the face of losing senior personnel occurred within a matter of weeks. The first significant consequence was an increase in the importance of the trade unions. The trade union movement was again formalised within the decision-making processes of the party. The National Joint Council was revived in December 1931 to 'consider all questions affecting the labour movement as a whole' and 'to secure a common policy and joint action'. The TUC was given seven seats on the council, giving it a majority, with three afforded to each of the NEC and PLP (Brooke, 1992, p 13).

The crisis of 1931 prompted the Labour Party to change the way in which policy was determined, and encouraged it to think more about economic ideology and policy in particular. Four new standing committees were established, of which two dealt directly with economic questions (Booth, 1996, p 8). The 1930s were also characterised as a decade of economic soul searching, exemplified here by the differences between Durbin and Cole. Arguably it was not until the party returned to government that it became clear that the work of Keynes took precedent over Marx's, but as Elizabeth Durbin (daughter of Evan) notes (Durbin, 1985, pp 261–262), this did not mean that the party had not advanced its understanding of economic issues. Indeed, she argues that by the end of the decade 'the Labour party had travelled light-years' in its understanding and knowledge of economic policy. Durbin notes that the 1930s represented 'a long process of research and debate'. Through this, Labour adopted a 'programme of institutional reform ... which would ensure central control over the forces determining money supply, exchange rates and investment'. Great attention now focused on economic ideology and questions. Emanating from such discussions were specific proposals regarding unemployment, regional investment and a detailed programme of nationalisations, and 'detailed and systematic plans to cope with negative banking, business or speculative reactions ... had been worked out by the party's powerful finance and trade committee. Neither the financial crisis of 1931 nor the failure to deal with depression unemployment was likely to be repeated out of ignorance.'

This period saw the Labour Party advocate the nationalisation of a range of industries (Singleton, 1995, p 16). At the start of the interwar period, Labour manifestos were guided by the experience of the wartime economy. The 1918 manifesto proposed the nationalisation of coal, the railways, electricity, shipping, armaments and land. By 1924, only the coal mines and railways survived from that list, although these were supplemented with canals. Following the spilt of 1931, the list was again extended, encompassing coal, transport, iron and steel, land and also banks, to overcome some of the problems faced by the Labour government. The last manifesto before the Second World War proposed to nationalise all of the industries that the 1931 manifesto proposed (substituting electricity for power) and added cotton and armaments. The expansion of armaments again demonstrates that these proposals were driven more by the contemporary landscape than by ideological commitments.

Despite expanding the industries to be nationalised throughout the 1930s, the rationale for nationalisation was not universally accepted. For scholars such as Tawney, nationalisation represented an ethical approach to organising economic relationships (see the previous chapter); for others such as Cole and guild socialists, nationalisation was a means of overcoming some of the weaknesses of the trade unions. Others noted that workers had more immediate concerns than the ownership of industry. Morrison (1933, pp 224–225) argued that 'the majority of workmen are ... more interested in the organisation, conditions, and life of their own workshop than in those finer balances of financial, and commercial policy which are discussed in the Board room'.

Labour's (1934) document, *For Socialism and Peace*, promised 'to establish a policy of full and rapid socialist economic planning, under central direction, to establish public ownership of and control of the primary industries and services as a foundation step'. The document promised to repeal the Trade Disputes and Trade Unions Act 1927, the establishment of a 40-hour working week and the promotion of higher wages (Labour Party, 1934). The document further rejected compromises, noting:

> There is no half-way house between a society based on private ownership as a means of production, with the profit of the few as the measure of success, and a society where public ownership of those means enables the resources of the nation to be deliberately planned for attaining the maximum of general well-being. (Labour Party, 1934, p 6)

Labour's manifesto in 1935, its last before the Second World War, was far more developed than its election manifesto in 1918. Although it focused primarily on the international context, the manifesto drew on some of the themes outlined in *For Socialism and Peace*, such as the repeal of the Trade Disputes and Trade Unions Act 1927, and promised 'the public ownership of land' and the abolition of means testing for unemployed people; it also promised to 'vigorously develop the health service' and to raise the school leaving age (which would be implemented following the Beveridge Report of 1942; Labour Party, 1935; Beveridge, 1942). The party had come a long way in outlining and establishing explicit economy policies, although it was not until after the party's landslide election victory in 1945 that some of the policies outlined in the 1930s were incorporated into Labour's programme.

Labour's responses to the crises

The General Strike of 1926 highlighted some divisions in Labour's ideology. Ramsay MacDonald refused to support the strike, instead advocating for Parliament to resolve the issues through legislation. Labour politicians rejected such a strike as a means of securing revolution and instead sought solutions to the question of unemployment within capitalism. This emphasis on Parliament was itself divisive and generated splits between those who believed that the Labour Party, after the experiences of 1924, should not take power again without a parliamentary majority and the party leadership – particularly after the 1929 general election who viewed the ability to form a second minority governments in the 1920s as evidence of 'the inevitability of gradualism – the slow evolution of capitalism into socialism' (Foote, 1997, pp 123–124).

The 1926 and 1931 crises highlighted the weakness of Labour's ideology, what Foote (1997, p 124) refers to as 'its bankruptcy of economic solutions'. Each crisis was important in encouraging the party to think about external relations and further develop its ideology, but the crises themselves prompted few immediate ideological responses. The crisis faced by the second Labour government in particular forced the party to develop a stronger, more coherent, economic ideology, but this did not begin until after the split of 1931. The mounting pressures of unemployment weakened the trade union movement and the more pragmatic elements of the Labour Party (including members such as MacDonald and Snowden who left the party to form a national government) saw or defined the crisis in terms of governance rather than ideological debates between capitalism and socialism.

The 1929–1931 government gave 'foremost place' to the 'question of unemployment' (Snowden, 1934, p 770). However, far from Snowden's (1934, p 770) assertions of an 'ambitious' programme, Cole (1948, p 229) noted that the programme introduced in the King's Speech was essentially a '[m]oderate [one], with no hint in it of any sort of "socialism now"'. Cole noted that Snowden's own ideology – a belief in the gold standard and in free trade – would come to dominate the party. Cole (1948, p 236) argued that 'Snowden held a very strong position in the party as its one recognized financial expert ... neither MacDonald nor most of the other members of the cabinet had any understanding of finance, or even thought they had'. When faced with increasing unemployment, Labour appeared to accept the workings of the capitalist system – debating levels of unemployment insurance rather than undertaking revolutionary policies aimed at instigating socialism.

Although the party had, in ideological terms, deliberately sought to appeal to the maximum number of voters/sympathisers (see the previous chapter), the lack of an economic ideology and understanding was telling in moments of crisis. Michael Foot (1977, p 70) would later note that the failings of 1931 were not just personal to Ramsay MacDonald – who was labelled as a traitor to the party and movement for his actions – but could also be levied at the entire Cabinet and wider parliamentary party. MacDonald was 'surrounded by moderates but they had no notion even [of] what to be moderate about'. Foot notes that such moderates, in the absence of other policies, 'were all content to become immoderate deflationists. Certainly, the moderates of every shade offered no solution for the national crisis. It can be much more plausibly argued that the crying need of the hour was an extremist revolt against Treasury domination.'

If the 1926 General Strike showed that socialism could not be achieved in a revolution, then 1931 showed that the path to socialism had not yet been paved or even forged. The party split of 1931 underpinned wider problems within the Labour Party – that its leadership (but also a significant proportion of its members) could not agree on how socialism could/would be introduced into Britain, even when faced with a crisis of capitalism. MacDonald's position reflected this lack of imagination. Labour in government was 'incapable of implementing any economic policy other than the palliatives of Treasury and Bank of England orthodoxy. When the international bankers demanded "economies" as a condition of a loan, [the government] found it necessary to accept the conventional, capitalist, wisdom' (Eatwell and Wright, 1978, p 38).

The 1931 split had left a smaller parliamentary party, but arguably a more cohesive one. Many of those who left the party to join the national government were ideologically from the right wing of the party. Yet this did not necessarily ensure that the party would adopt a more cohesive understanding of socialism or economic policy. Throughout the interwar period, Labour Party thinkers sought to unpack concepts such as 'nationalism' and 'socialism'. As Howell (quoted by Jackson, 2007, p 93) argued, the 1930s were 'a contest between Marx and Keynes'.

The result of these ideological debates was the emergence of corporate socialism and corporatism. These tendencies offered an economic understanding to Labour's ethical socialism and untied the Labour Party by demonstrating that 'politics could not be restricted to the parliamentary sphere, but must incorporate the great economic corporations of labour and capital into the hitherto sacrosanct realm of the state' (Foote, 1997, p 182).

While Labour did not pursue ideological responses to the crises of 1926 and 1931, these events did help to shape the party's ideology. Although 1945 is often seen as a turning point, and it would plainly be wrong to deny that the Second World War had a significant impact on Labour Party thinking on economic and social policy (see the next chapter), its impact in many cases was to crystallise existing tendencies rather than bring about an abrupt change of line. The emphasis on nationalisation as a necessary condition for efficiency, on planning as vital to the maintenance of full employment, on social welfare to be provided by radical reform and the building of national systems of provision were all clearly established before 1939. In many ways, the war provided a political opportunity to assert what was already believed in by the party (Tomlinson, 1996, p 21).

Labour's understanding of socialism

Much like the earlier Labour Party, Labour in the 1920s, according to Dowse (1974, p xxii), advocated socialism only in general terms to appeal to as broad a section of the electorate as possible, covering those who advocated for radical change, and as a means of explaining contemporary dissatisfaction, such hollow narratives were 'to conceal the need for a system of policy priorities, [and] prevented any systematic thought about administering an advanced capitalist society'.

Hugh Dalton (1945, p 319), a moderate of the Labour Party in the 1930s, and later Chancellor in the 1945–1950 government, argued that 'socialists seek, by the abolition of poverty and the establishment of social equality, to build a prosperous and classless society'. For Dalton (1945, p 27), the degree of socialism in any given society was inevitably linked to questions of nationalisation: 'we may measure the degree in which any particular community is Socialist by the relative extent of the "socialised sector", and of the "private sector", in its economic life. Within the socialised sector public ownership and control, in some form, are present, and private profit-making is absent.'

This broad and fluid definition of socialism enabled the party to adapt its policies once in government. As Dalton (1945, pp 20–21) further argued, the radicalism of the Labour Party in opposition did not seep through into government and noted that ministers as early as 1929 were 'in full retreat from their election pledges'. The situation was made worse by the Great Slump and banking crisis of 1931, which demonstrated the dominance the Treasury held over the government.

In *Labour and the Nation*, the Labour Party (1928, p 36) noted that at the 'forefront of its programme [existed] a prudent and economic administration of the nation's income'. Accepting that this was a common theme across all parties, the Labour Party 'differs from its opponents ... as to the methods by which that result is most likely to be achieved'. The pamphlet went on to defend public spending against the opposition's charges of being 'burdensome' and advocated for increasing 'revenue by direct taxation'. Yet just three years later, when faced with the economic problems of 1931, the leadership of the party, in a continued effort to balance the books, proposed a combination of spending cuts and increases in taxation at a ratio of 4:1.

If the party remained unsure or divided on an understanding of socialism, the interwar period did, however, convince its leadership that Parliament was the avenue for its inception. Defeat in the General Strike of 1926 demonstrated the lack of alternatives to achieving change through parliamentary channels. Nye Bevan (2008, p 25), in *In Place of Fear*, outlines this point, noting that the General Strike 'seemed to have exhausted the possibilities of mass industrial action. ... The trade union leaders were theoretically unprepared for the implications involved. They had forged a revolutionary weapon without having a revolutionary intention.'

Such ideas were not novel, or indeed new, within the labour movement. Cole had come to these conclusions before the General Strike. Trade unions, according to Cole, could not defeat a modern state. Rather, in order 'to change capitalism into socialism a Labour government had to control capital rather than industry' (Beech and Hickson, 2007, p 47).

The failures of the first Labour government led to a debate about the conditions under which a Labour government should assume office – principally, should it assume office without a parliamentary majority? Although a majority favoured not imposing limitations on the party leadership after the first labour government fell in 1924, as they acknowledged that 'no such majority seemed to be in sight and the prospect of an indefinite spell of Tory rule was no means pleasant' (Cole, 1948, p 177), similar questions were asked following the collapse of the 1929–1931 government too.

Although the Labour Party was removed from office in 1931, the reasons for this and solutions to overcoming similar crises in the future were seen to lay within the party. The experience of government had highlighted some important limitations regarding the pace and scope of change but had not fostered a sense of the need to abandon the parliamentary process. Rather, the solutions were to be found from within; there was a requirement to pursue a more holistic understanding of economic ideology.

Tomlinson (1996, p 290) notes that Labour's defence of democracy rested on a 'fundamental faith in Parliament as the sovereign body', although with significant reforms. Labour in the interwar period was committed to the abolition of the House of Lords, reform of the voting process and wider changes in parliamentary practices. Through such 'limited reforms', Labour argued that Parliament could be 'made the instrument of the people's will'.

The question was not whether socialism could be achieved through parliamentary means alone, but rather which organisations alongside Parliament would need to be incorporated into the socialist drive. Corporate socialism and the commitment to economic planning demonstrated that socialism could not simply be imposed on Britain.

The failings of the Labour government demonstrated Labour's inexperience in government, but also a continued ideological vacuum. There was no coordination or 'coordinating brain'. Despite these flaws, Bevin rejected what he saw as the intrusion of 'new factions' proposing ideas for attaining socialism. Such factions according to Bevin (quoted by Seaman, 1993, p 175) derived 'knowledge of the working class … from the theoretical treatises in the University library'. Rather Bevin argued 'to understand the workers one must live with them and work with them'.

Eatwell and Wright (1978, p 40) note that the experience of 1931 encouraged widespread ideological debate(s) within the Labour Party but changed very little ideologically. One of the most frequently advocated positions was that the party should never again form a minority government. In part this is understandable given the problems Labour faced in 1924 as well as the split of 1931, but as the authors note, 'this lesson made sense [only] in so far as a socialist party could hardly hope to implement socialist measures when dependent on non-socialist support'.

The experience of 1931 highlighted key failures in the existing political and economic system. MacDonald was presented as being vain and sought to desert the party in favour of his aristocratic friends (Eatwell and Wright, 1978, p 40). Alongside this view, of class determining MacDonald's actions, many on the left attributed 'particular historical significance' to Labour's inability to agree on cuts to unemployment benefits. It demonstrated the entrenched institutional opposition to the gradualist understanding of socialist transformation. The government's failure to move beyond contemporary economic orthodoxy demonstrated 'the true distribution of power concealed by the formally democratic procedures of the British state. The parliamentary road to socialism was ineffective, such critics suggested, because British democracy was essentially managed for the economic benefit of the ruling class' (Jackson, 2007, p 94).

Many within or close to the Labour Party saw the governing institutions (for example, Parliament and the Treasury) as frustrating the socialist cause. Yet this did not generate within the party the same revolutionary or anti-establishment feelings as occurred in other European political systems during the 1930s. The experience of 1926 had demonstrated that such tactics would not work in Britain. Dalton (1945) started his analysis by noting the differences between the British and European politics systems. Labour was still committed to the institutions of the British state, such as the role played by opposition parties (Webb, 1931). Rather than adopt more radical approaches, the party reaffirmed such commitments throughout the 1930s as it became more concerned with questions of 'entryism' or concerns about those holding Labour Party membership while subscribing to extreme views of communism. The party prosecuted such entryism 'from 1934, and thereafter with mounting vigour' (Campbell and McIlroy, 2018, p 543).

Of course, opting to pursue a parliamentary route was no guarantee of its success. Harold Laski (1933, p 233), Labour Party chairman from 1945 to 1946, following the crisis of 1931, set out 'the revolutionary claim' noting that 'capitalism is presented with the choice of co-operating in the effort at socialist experiment, or fighting it; and I have given reasons for believing that it may well prefer the alternative of fighting'.

The 1920s dispelled the idea, for Labour at least, that revolutionary socialism could take hold in Britain as it had in other countries. Despite facing a crisis that propelled Labour from office in 1931 in spectacular fashion, the party still saw parliamentary means as the best method of achieving socialism, which itself was still broadly defined in the interwar period.

The Labour Party and the trade unions

The increased number of strikes between 1910 and 1926 was a challenge for the Labour Party, briefly tempered by the First World War. While what Holton (1985) identifies as the first phase of syndicalism (1900–1910) saw a small hard core of extremism emerge and was largely overlooked by the Labour Party keen to distinguish itself from the Liberal Party, the second phase lasted until the General Strike of 1926 and provided 'the greatest challenge to labourism since Marx' (Foote, 1997, p 84).

Syndicalism argued that representation in Parliament was insufficient on its own to achieve emancipation. Here the Labour Party represented an elitism that existed outside of the control of the working classes; enfranchisement without strong economic organisations to protect workers was a hollow promise (Foote, 1997, pp 88–89). Such arguments posed a direct challenge to the Labour Party and understandings of state socialism, which saw the institutions of the state as central to creating a socialist society. Syndicalists' proposal that 'unions should have a direct role to perform in governing an industrial economy was, of course, intimately connected to their proposition that neither the state nor capitalist corporations should have any role whatsoever in such government. As such it was inimical to everything that the Labour Party stood for' (Foote, 1997, p 94).

Throughout the 1920s, the Labour Party had sought to increase its ties with individual members – partly for financial reasons, but also to reflect legislative changes following the passing of the Trade Disputes and Trade Unions Act 1927 (see later in this chapter). Cole (1948, p 174) noted following the 1924 election that the party had fought three elections in three years, placing great strain on its finances, leaving many seats under-resourced. New solutions to this problem included increasing individual memberships, offering a further revenue stream for the party but also weakening the relative powers of the unions within the party, for it was not 'felt to be desirable that the Labour Party should become any more than it was already a trade union party'.

The General Strike of 1926, however, was a 'turning point' in the interwar years. Mason (1969, p 1) argues that: 'The defeat which the trade unions suffered at the hands of the Government successfully discredited the idea of wide-spread industrial action as a method of obtaining the demands of labour. It did much to ensure the relatively quiescent acceptance by Labour of the persistent unemployment.' The failure of the strike forced the trade unions to view the Labour Party as a means of achieving their objectives, which in turn strengthened the position of the Labour Party vis-à-vis the trade unions.

Lovell and others (see for example Clegg, 1985) dispute the argument that 1926 provided a turning point in the manner that Mason identifies. Lovell (1986, p 56) argues that the failure of the strike highlighted problems of organisation within the trade unions. Although notions of a general strike were referred to between 1919 and 1926, little thought was devoted to the logistics of such an undertaking. Rather, these scholars present 1926 as a product of longer-term trends, which demonstrated how mutually important the relationship between the party and unions was/could be. The 1930s saw the trade unions renew their commitments to the Labour Party, but the decade also helped prepare the ground 'for the functional pluralism and the tripartite planning in which the unions and the party would to some extent go their own ways' (Minkin, 1991, p 21).

The General Strike, however, did lead to the passage of the Trade Disputes and Trade Unions Act 1927, which again highlights the precarious nature of funding strikes and the economic relationship between the trade unions and the Labour Party. Although the bill did not revoke the Trade Disputes Act 1906, it created a new class of 'illegal strikes', which meant that 'when a strike was held to be illegal an injunction could be issued preventing the use of any trade unions funds in its support'. Other measures that pertained directly to the relationship between the unions and the Labour Party included the banning of civil servants from joining 'trade unions which were associated with either the Trades Union Council or the Labour Party'. The Trade Disputes and Trade Unions Act 1927 also reversed the Trade Union Act 1913 and restored the process of 'contracting in' to the unions' political fund (which was the unions' financial contribution to the Labour Party). The result was dramatic: Labour's affiliated membership fell from 3,388,000 to 2,077,000 in two years, set against a more modest fall in trade union membership of just over 400,000 (Cole, 1948, pp 192–195). Such a measure led the party to face financial hardship and encouraged it to strengthen the situation by building up individual memberships, a policy that in turn would weaken the unions' power with the party and encourage or facilitate the party to move to the right.

Although the General Strike had resulted in failure for the trade unions, the guild socialism of Cole incorporated some aspects of syndicalism into the Labour Party's ideology. This argued that institutions other than the state were important in realising socialism and helped pave the way for the tripartite relationship of the post-war settlement (see the next chapter).

The collapse of the Labour government in 1931 further demonstrated the asymmetric relationship between the party and trade unions that developed during this period. The government, despite advocating for cuts to unemployment insurance and accepting higher levels of unemployment, was largely immune from trade union protests and only capitulated due to its adherence to existing norms and understandings, which were themselves favourable to capital rather than labour with a small 'l'.

Conclusion

Although Elizabeth Durbin's argument that the Labour Party had travelled light-years in terms of economic policy was much debated and contested (see earlier in this chapter and in particular Booth, 1996), the interwar period saw significant changes within the party. The party that had gained just 57 seats in the 1918 general election had formed a government twice in the 1920s and, by the end of the 1930s, despite a significant split, was still considered to be the main challenger to the Conservative Party.

While both governments (1924 and 1929–1931) can be seen as, at least ending in, failure(s), their experiences encouraged the Labour Party to think more broadly and strategically about the relationship between democratic government and socialism. Equally, neither of the government collapses encouraged the party to adopt a more radical stance (as it would do after 1979); the 1926 General Strike, and later purges of communist sympathisers within the party, further put to bed the idea that socialism in Britain could be achieved through any other means than Parliament.

Further failure can be seen in the weaknesses of the trade union movement in 1926. Although few within the movement saw this as a revolutionary endeavour, the defeat of both the General Strike and the miners showed the limitations of syndicalism and, along with the Liberal collapse after the First World War, left the Labour Party as the predominant, if not only, progressive force within British politics. Yet while this strengthened Labour's position on the left of centre within British politics, it weakened it vis-à-vis the Conservatives and forced the party to place more emphasis on individual party memberships, which in turn encouraged the party to move away from more radical understandings of socialism.

As the party's response to the crisis of 1931 demonstrated, when faced with a crisis of capitalism, Labour sought to adhere to economic orthodoxy, in particular through defending the pound's position within the gold standard. In part this was acceptable and necessary because the party's understanding of the transition to socialism was still based on an ethical understanding of socialism. For the Labour Party of the 1930s, the route to socialism was through a strong economy; not through the inherent contradictions of capitalism that Marx highlighted. In the meantime, as the responses to the economic problems of 1931 demonstrated, Labour attempted to prioritise improving the day-to-day conditions of the working classes within the confines of the existing system.

Such experiences of failure in government also prompted the Labour Party to develop its economic ideology. The split in 1931, and in particular Snowden's defection, highlighted the Party's poor grasp of economic ideology. But by means of compensation it also meant that the party was more ideologically concentrated and this paved the way for new influences, such as Keynes, to be discussed.

Opposition is never a good vehicle for instigating change, and many of the changes put forward in the 1930s, such as the extension of the nationalisation programme, could not be realised until Labour returned to office after the Second World War (see the next chapter). Although the split of 1931 left the party in opposition for the remainder of the decade, it may have had some benefits: the quick defections prevented some of the prolonged discussions/arguments that occurred in the 1980s or even after the 2010 general election defeat.

This is not to say that such divisions did not occur, but that the party was able to take a firm stance on particular issues (for example in expelling Stafford Cripps in 1939 over proposing an alliance with the Liberals). Here Labour's response was couched in ideology; arguing that Cripps was willing to sacrifice socialism to achieve a 'popular front' (Cole, 1948, p 358). The party was also able to develop a more robust economic programme, with the nationalisation of key industries (albeit broadly defined) at its heart. In addition to this, the Second World War provided a means for the party to unite and (from 1940) to share in governing responsibilities, further supressing internal divisions.

4

The Second World War, Reconstruction and Revisionism

Introduction

The eve of the Second World War found the Labour Party still recovering electorally from the split of 1931. The party had won just 154 seats in the 1935 general election, only a quarter of all MPs. However, just as the First World War gave Labour the experience of governing and accelerated its claim to being Britain's second party, the Second World War 'speeded the party's opportunity of competing with the Conservatives on equal, or even superior terms' (Thorpe, 2015, p 103).

The 1945 general election, conducted while fighting in the Far East was still ongoing, saw a drastic change in the party's fortunes. Labour won the election with a majority of 145, allowing it to form its first-ever majority government. This was a government unconstrained by other parties as the governments of 1924 and 1929–1931 had proved to be (see the previous chapter), and – at least in theory – it was able to impose its ideology on Britain.

This chapter explores how the party approached issues of reconstruction and how questions over the balance of payments, leading to the 1947 sterling crisis, affected its macroeconomic planning. It looks at how the plans for nationalisation, developed in the 1930s, came to fruition in the 1940s and early 1950s, before exploring the ideological challenges posed by revisionists following Labour's election defeat in 1951 and 13 years in opposition.

The Second World War and the immediate post-war period

As in 1914, once war was declared in September 1939, the vast majority of 'the Labour Party and the Trade Unions ... assumed unhesitatingly ... the responsibility for sustaining the war effort, despite their lack of confidence in the government by which the war machine was to be directed'.

The Independent Labour Party and communists took a different approach (Cole, 1948, p 373).

Labour initially fulfilled the part of 'cooperative critic' of the Conservative government. Following the declaration of war, this allowed the party to emphasise social changes and a greater role for the state while maintaining a patriotic commitment to the fight. Cole (1948, p 377) noted that, in opposition, Labour 'raised many issues connected with' the economics of the war, covering service pay and allowances, the hardships attendant on the call-up for the armed forces and the effective maintenance and supplementation of social services to meet the needs of war. The party later turned its attention to unemployment and argued that this could be better utilised within the war effort. It called for the 'more effective mobilisation of the nation's economic resources, and especially for the setting up of proper machinery for economic co-ordination under an Economic General Staff'.

Labour's position changed in 1940 as the party accepted an invitation to join a coalition government, following Chamberlain's replacement as Prime Minister by Churchill. Addison (1977, pp 17–18) described the formation of the coalition government as '*the* crucial change', arguing that this change replicated/enhanced shifts in public opinion; 'it should also go down as the year when the foundations of political power shifted decisively leftwards for a decade. ... the struggle for survival dictated that the right should recruit the left'. Through this process, not only were Labour ministers incorporated in government but also the TUC 'virtually [became] a department of government in Whitehall'. Social democratic ideas were entertained by key institutions such as the BBC, the army and information services and greater priority was offered to understanding and improving the morale and welfare of the working classes. Taken together, these changes led to a new phrase: 'the people's war'.

The Labour Party was important in presenting a united front against the threat of German aggression and ensuring the compliance of millions of workers. Yet Labour's incentives were not completely selfless. In deciding to join the wartime Cabinet, Labour also looked beyond the war, seeing engagement as an opportunity to help shape the political landscape of the post-war period. As Atlee (quoted in Toye, 2013, p 88) put it in November 1939, '[p]eople want to know for what kind of country they are fighting ... many of us remember the hopes that we entertained at the end of the last war and what happened after the peace'. Others, such as Nye Bevan, saw the war as forming social revolution to defeat not only fascism abroad but also conservatism at home; these were 'two enemies to be fought as part of the same process' (Toye, 2013, p 88).

Labour's position in the wartime coalition Cabinet was relatively strong, considering the number of MPs the party had. Attlee, Morrison and Bevin held 'posts of prime importance'; Attlee became Deputy Prime Minister and he and Arthur Greenwood (who was appointed as a minister without portfolio) were incorporated into Churchill's small War Cabinet. The other posts had distinct economic roles: Ernest Bevin became Minister of Labour and National Service and Herbert Morrison Minister of Supply; 'upon them was bound to fall the main brunt of the organisation of man-power and of industry'. In addition to these 'four front rank ministers, A.V. Alexander went to the Admiralty, Hugh Dalton was Minister of Economic Warfare, and Sir William Jowitt was Solicitor-General' (Cole, 1948, p 383).

Attlee (2019, p 167) certainly saw the war as enabling elements of Labour's new programme. The Second World War required greater shared experiences and sacrifices than the First World War. The governance involved in the former conflict was also more robust, 'profiteering had been repressed, rationing had been better managed, high rates of interest had not been allowed and very heavy taxation had been imposed'.

The Labour Party at the outbreak of the Second World War was more united than in 1914. The experiences of the 1930s helped form a more ideologically coherent party; however, this did not translate to every policy area. Labour in the 1940s was far more united on issues of economic policy than it was on foreign policy. In terms of economic policy, groups such as The Finance Group played a key role in giving backbenchers a 'creative role' in policy making. The Finance Group included Evan Durbin, Hugh Gaitskell, Jim Callaghan and Douglas Jay, among others. Attlee for his part 'took less interest in the nuts and bolts of some aspects of policy, especially economic policy. Attlee was no economist although he usually knew whom to ask.' This was much in keeping with MacDonald, who had relied on Snowden for economic guidance. But, just as in the crisis of 1931, it meant that Attlee when faced with 'crises such as the huge outflow of funds after the convertibility of sterling in July 1947 and even more the devaluation of the pound in September 1949 ... seemed totally at a loss'. Decisions in such crises were referred to Gaitskell and Jay (Morgan, 2004, p 41).

Despite seeing a large expansion in the role of the state, the war also challenged some of the understandings held by the Labour leadership, in particular over nationalisation. Nationalisation was the key pillar of Labour's economic policy in the 1930s – although as the previous chapter demonstrated, different rationales for this were advocated, and although rhetorically the war offered legitimacy for such a programme, it also challenged assumptions regarding its scope. 'Nationalization was simply the highest form of physical planning, not an end in itself. The rhetorical arguments for nationalization had been vindicated by the war, but they had been given little depth' (Brooke, 1992, p 245).

Labour's 1945 manifesto was clear about the aims of the new government. The party's ultimate goal was 'the establishment of a Socialist Commonwealth of Great Britain' (Labour Party, 1945). The Attlee government was undoubtedly much better placed than previous Labour governments, primarily due to the large parliamentary majority it was afforded but also in terms of the wartime controls that it inherited, to pursue socialist ends. Wartime controls had changed politicians' and the public's understanding of the economy and potential or capacity of the state in economic planning. Attlee's government was arguably the first Labour government to present a coherent economic ideology – what Coates (2013) refers to as 'the first way'.

Attlee's government oversaw the transfer of large industries into public hands, including the Bank of England (1946), British European Airways (1946), National Coal Board (1947), British Electricity Authority (1948), British Transport Commission (1948), Gas Council (1949) and Iron and Steel Corporation (1951). The nationalisation of these industries helped increase public sector employment from 3.35 million in 1946 to 5.67 million in 1949 and accounted for 80 per cent of all transfers of private industry to the public sphere over the 20th century (Millward, 1997, p 210; Office for National Statistics, 2019a). With the exception of iron and steel (and parts of the road haulage industry), this means of organisation was preserved until the 1980s.

The sterling crisis of 1947

By the end of the Second World War, Britain was the 'world's leading debtor country ... [owing] more than £3,000 million to her war time creditors ... [alongside this] she faced a prospective balance of payments deficit of £1,250 million between 1945 and 1950' (Newton, 1984, p 392).

The balance of payments proved difficult for the Labour government. At the end of 1945, the government restricted a range of imports that required payment in US dollars. In order to rectify the balance of payments – or at least to not exacerbate the problem – the key task of macroeconomic policy was to 'restrain demand sufficiently to keep it roughly in balance with productivity' (Allen, 2014, p 3). A continued deficit in 1946 led to further restrictions and saw the introduction of bread rationing – something that 'had not been thought necessary even in the darkest days of war'. Such restrictions, although in many ways an extension of the wartime regulations, and identified by Atlee as being relatively successful, were at odds with the expectations of the public. Although there was an appreciation that developments would take time, there was an expectation that restrictions on some luxuries would be eased. Wages had increased three times faster than inflation during the war, increasing the spending power of many (Robertson, 1987, pp 4–5).

Along with the fact that Britain had relied heavily on imports as part of the war effort, under the lend-lease scheme, the war had devastated its export market. Cole (1948, p 461) argued that the only way to avert a serious balance of payments crisis would be to find new markets in the Western hemisphere, principally Argentina, Canada and the US, although he also recognised that 'it was not likely that these countries would be willing to take anything like an equivalent quantity of British goods, even if the goods could be made available for them'.

By 1947, Britain was facing 'a major balance of payments crisis' (Miliband, 2009, p 304). This crisis is often seen as a turning point for the socialist aims of the Attlee governments. Post 1947, the government 'eagerly embraced a cross-party consensus constructed along the lines dictated by Beveridge and Keynes', scholars who did not align themselves to the overly socialist aims of the Labour government (Francis, 1996, p 40). This 'consensus', however, extended to little more than 'broad agreement among political elites about the basic direction of policy-making'. Other authors have described this not as a consensus but as a settlement, arguing that the term 'consensus' is used by those 'who look back nostalgically to a pre-Thatcherite past where ... things were done differently' (Ellision, 1996, p 17).

As a result of the balance of payments deficit, Britain sought a loan from the US, the world's largest creditor. There was an assumption that, as former allies, the US would offer Britain a good deal, and Britain attempted to negotiate an interest-free credit, or grant, of US$5 billion. Ultimately, the offer was just US$3,750 million, to be repaid over a 50-year period at an interest rate of 2 per cent, on the condition that sterling was made convertible by 15 July 1947 (Newton, 1984, pp 392–393).

From 1947 onwards the Labour Party began to lose its reputation for competence. Crises such as the fuel crisis and the devaluation of sterling in 1949 led to Conservative leads in opinion polling and gains in the local elections of 1947 and 1949. This prompted senior figures within the party to call for a pause in the nationalisation programme and other programmes with large government expenditure (see later in this chapter). Such a pause meant that 'by the late 1940s, and very obviously in 1950–51, Labour seemed to have run out of steam; it displayed few new policy ideas, its leaders were physically exhausted, and factional splits were emerging' (Crowcroft and Theakston, 2013, p 62).

This lack of steam was replicated in opposition. Although Labour won more votes than the Conservatives in the 1951 general election, there was no quick return to office that some had assumed/predicted. Labour lost further general elections in 1955, after which Attlee resigned as leader, and in 1959. More ominously for Labour, each general election saw its vote share decline and the Conservative Party's majority increase.

By the end of the decade, Labour's route to electoral success was by no means guaranteed. Perceptions of economic success were widespread, even if these masked a relative decline, something the Conservative Prime Minister, Harold Macmillan, summarised in a speech to Conservative Party members in Bedford in 1957 when he noted that 'most of our people have never had it so good', a phrase that is often misquoted as 'you've never had it so good' (Crafts, 1995, p 246).

Successive election defeats forced the Labour Party to look inwards and explore its own ideology. Such debates were not confined to economic understandings – issues over nuclear weapons and the campaign for nuclear disarmament highlighted large divisions within the broad Labour Party – but did lead to a wave of revisionist thought led by the right of the party.

Labour's ideology

The Second World War changed the relationship between Keynes and the Labour Party, affecting Labour's ideology. Throughout the interwar period, Keynes was critical of British socialism and the Labour Party, which he saw as being too concerned with sectional interests. Rather, he called on the Liberal Party to assert its progressive credentials (Foote, 1997; see also Chapter 7). As Labour endeavoured to gain a systematic understanding of economic policy in the 1930s, moderates such as Dalton and Durbin engaged with Keynes's ideas relating to employment (see the previous chapter; see also Dalton, 1945). Labour's response to the Beveridge Report of 1942 (Beveridge, 1942) and the question of full employment, as developed from the *Employment Policy* White Paper of 1944 (HM Government, 1944), demonstrated the liberal influences within the party, even if these were, as Foote (1997, p 186) notes, 'echoes of the process of policy development which Labour had already evolved'.

Controlling inflation was a key goal within the wartime economy, and the Treasury drew heavily on Keynes's work to achieve this. The success of the Keynes plan – increasing taxation and making saving compulsory through deferred pay to reduce consumption – which was incorporated into the 1941 budget, influenced the post-war Labour government. Keynes's theories proved able to effectively 'influence demand', policies Labour had 'little to offer against'. This lack of alternatives meant that economic planning was developed, both during and after the war, within a Keynesian framework or paradigm (Brooke, 1992, pp 245–246).

Minkin (1991, p 70) notes that the 1945–1951 Labour government was in many ways unique when compared with its successors. Although 'the legislative programme of the Attlee Government was not in the end to be as sweeping or as fundamental in its redistribution of wealth and power as some of the left had hoped', it achieved 'virtually' all of its domestic policy manifesto commitments, 'a feat which future Labour governments were to find beyond them'. Minkin argues that the crisis of 1947 did not affect the version of socialism Labour put forward in 1945, but instead suggests that this vision was itself conservative with a small 'c'. In contrast, Francis (1997, p 7) argues that while Labour's 1945 manifesto 'claimed that the [L]abour [P] arty is a socialist party and proud of it … it would have been more accurate to have said that the Labour [P]arty was not so much a socialist party as a party which contained socialists', highlighting that the different strands of ideological thought that had combined to create the party at the turn of the century were clearly distinguishable. The party by the 1940s 'essentially remained the federal alliance between socialists and organised labour'.

Much analysis of the Labour Party in government between 1945 and 1951 follows a similar pattern. It argues that the government made some progressive strides and reconceptualised the role of the state as an enabler with its nationalisation programme and expansion of the welfare state. Although pensions and sickness pay had been introduced by the Liberal government of 1906–1910, it was not until the creation of the NHS that the term 'welfare state' gained traction. Yet as Coates (2013, p 40) notes, '[t]his is not to claim, of course, that the record of the Attlee government was all unalloyed radicalism. It was not.' Much of the economic understanding was based on planning and Keynesian assumptions of aggregate demand rather than commitments to economic socialism. There was little if any emphasis on replacing existing capitalist structures. 'Ministers belatedly experimented with incomes policies as a way of squaring price stability and full employment, and they certainly stopped short of taking full ownership of successful private firms.'

Labour's programme in government epitomised the ethical, rather than economic, socialism identified in earlier chapters. It was designed 'on the basis of a capitalist economy', rather than to radically overturn it. As Saville (1967, p 44) notes, 'by 1948 the nationalisation proposals of *Let Us Face the Future* – except for Iron and Steel – had been placed on the Statute Book and the Government had brought into operation its universal insurance system and the National Health Service'. Ralph Miliband (2003, p 31) saw this as Labour's 'moment of truth; what now had to be decided was whether it would go forward with a nationalization programme which, by eating really deep into capitalist enterprise, would be immeasurably more significant than the previous one, or whether it would stop at bankrupt industries and public utilities'.

After this, the government appeared to 'run out of steam' (Francis, 1997). Others see the second Attlee administration (1950–1951) as being 'on the defensive' or representing a 'retreat from Jerusalem' (Pelling, 1984, p 235; Morgan, 1985). From 1948, senior figures within the Labour Party advocated a period of consolidation. Those on the right of the party – Morrison, Durbin and Jay – argued for a more piecemeal expansion of the state (Foote, 1997, p 187). Broad understandings of the relationship between capitalism and socialism were overlooked in favour of ethical approaches. Jay in particular focused on 'equality and security, rather than class power' (Foote, 1997, p 195).

After general election defeats in 1951 and 1955, Gaitskell became Labour leader and sought to modernise the party, the need for which was demonstrated by defeat in 1955 and the Conservative landslide of 1959, which gave the Conservatives a majority of more than 100 seats. As leader, Gaitskell became the leading 'social democratic politician of his generation' (Diamond, 2004, p 95) and sought to establish his understanding of nationalisation in *Socialism and Nationalism* (Gaitskell, 1956). He outlined three socialist ideals: equality of opportunity, full employment and industrial democracy and cooperation. On equality of opportunity, Gaitskell (quoted in Diamond, 2004, pp 97–110) suggested that income differentials could be justified on 'generally accepted criteria of merit – such as the nature of the work – more being paid for dirty, harder, more skilled, better performed, more responsible jobs'. This was born out of an ethical understanding, with the overall goal not to reduce natural inequalities that emerge due to age, intelligence, health or work ethic, but to offer 'equal opportunity for the pursuit of happiness'. Gaitskell clarified that full employment cannot be 'taken to mean that everybody is guaranteed the same job for life. ... But it has been interpreted as at least implying that there are more jobs available than persons seeking for them.'

Gaitskell, Anthony Crosland and Roy Jenkins, along with others, extended the debate of the 1940s between the 'consolidators' and 'fundamentalists' by offering a revisionist approach. Although revisionism only gained traction within the party under Gaitskell's leadership, those advocating such positions had been developing their ideas since the 1930s (Jones, 1996, pp 20–22). Underpinning the success of this revisionism was the idea that capitalism and the electorate had shifted. Following defeat in 1959, it was argued that 'the Labour Party's traditional sources of support in the environment, in traditional values and party loyalties had been weakening' (Abrams, Rose and Hinden, 1960, p 97).

Central to the revisionist ideas was a belief that governments did not need to own industry in order to control it. Nationalisation was seen to be electorally unpopular and that it should be viewed only as a last resort. For Crosland, 'planning should be used to regulate macroeconomic activity and supplement fiscal policy. Public ownership should be used where existing government policy tools proved insufficient to meet social objectives' (Beech and Hickson, 2007, p 160). Public ownership did not resolve the day-to-day issues of workers, which he saw as being local issues, caused by 'managerial shortcomings'. Crosland (2006, p 288) argued that:

[N]ationalisation is no panacea for bad relations. It has, it is true, removed particular grievances in particular cases, notably in the coal industry. But nobody could claim that morale in the public sector was uniformly high, or even better than on average in good private firms and in two industries, coal and the railways, it is quite exceptionally low.

Rather than adopting this one-size-fits-all approach, Crosland contended that the expansion of public ownership should be confined to two forms, first related to land ownership and second through individual firms, rather than entire industries.

Throughout his premiership, Gaitskell was clear that such a programme was to be achieved through parliamentary democracy, which was ascribed equal importance to socialist ideals. This entailed that further nationalisations would be introduced gradually. Such gradualism was incorporated into Labour's 1957 publication, *Industry and Society: Labour's Policy on Future Public Ownership*, which stated (quoted by Favretoo, 2000, p 58):

> In the past, public ownership has meant the taking over and reorganising of an entire industry under a single authority. This was the form best suited to the basic industries in which a complete change of structure was called for. But there may be other cases where, if the needs of the nation are to be met, the public ownership of a single company or group of companies will be more appropriate.

Industry and Society was a controversial publication. It drew on Crosland's ideas of changes within British capitalism, which he argued necessitated a new form or understanding of socialism. Two developments were identified as generating changes within capitalism. First, an increase in government's economic power and activity alongside the 'greater strength of organised labour' had reduced 'the economic power of the capitalist'. Second, this had 'coincided with the achievement of rapid and sustained economic growth'. Taken together, these two developments had not only transformed classical capitalism but also thereby 'rendered obsolete' the established 'intellectual framework within which most pre-war socialist discussion was conducted' (Jones, 1996, p 23).

Challenging the policy of nationalisation went to the very heart of Labour's socialist commitments, as expressed in the 1918 constitution. By decoupling nationalisation from socialism, Crosland and others focused on the outcomes of equality, rather than the means by which this was to be achieved. This also led to the decoupling of socialism from the notion of community (Jackson, 2007). Revisionists argued that socialism could be achieved without a nationalisation programme. Doing so redefined socialism, which for revisionists was defined by 'values and ideals such as personal liberty, social welfare and, above all, social equality. This approach implied a view of socialism that was, in Gaitskell's words "a collection of ideals towards what we hope to advance" rather than as a distinct form of economic organisation' (Jones, 1997, p 2).

Nationalisation, rather than being a component part of socialism, was seen through a pragmatic and instrumentalist lens, a technique rather than a goal in and of itself. Such decoupling led Gaitskell to propose changing the Labour Party's constitution, in particular to rewrite Clause IV – Labour's commitment to nationalisation. The ethical socialism of revisionists did not hold nationalisation as essential to achieving socialism. '[P]ublic ownership was considered by Labour revisionists to be merely one useful means among several others for realising socialist values and ideals. It was not to be regarded as the most distinctive feature of a future socialist society' (Jones, 1997, p 2).

Such attempts to revise Clause IV put Gaitskell at odds with the trade unions. The attempt to rewrite it has been described as 'one of the most explosive episodes in Labour's long search for its true identity' (Haseler, 1969, p 157). This was the first attempt to amend the party's 1918 constitution and such proposals shifted the debate away from which industries should be nationalised to fundamentally questioning the link between nationalisation, socialism and Labour Party ideology.

Nor was it the case that revisionism in the 1950s had a free hand to shape the Labour Party's views. Gaitskell's attempts to reform Clause IV were defeated and it was even agreed that the clause should be 'included on party membership cards' (Gano, 2015). Throughout the next two decades, revisionism would be in retreat, in part due to Labour's electoral success (see the next chapter), but even the period of opposition did not offer revisionists an opportunity to rewrite Labour's history. Jobson (2013, p 139) demonstrates that Gaitskell's attempt and ultimate defeat in the rewriting of Clause IV was 'not simply a battle over ideology or policy: it represented a struggle over the party's nostalgic attachment to the past'.

Labour's responses to the crises

Labour's decision to join the Wartime Cabinet was agreed only after 'thorough consultations between the Parliamentary leadership, the party executive and the General Council of the TUC'. Each group was acutely aware of the dangers of sacrificing Labour's independence, but the potential rewards were attractive. As Bevin told the TUC special conference called to discuss these matters, 'if ... our class rise with all their energy and save the people, the country will always turn with confidence to the people who saved them' (Minkin, 1991, p 55).

Labour's commitment to nationalisation during the war rested on notions of 'practical socialism'. This involved 'national ownership, or at least control, of the railways and mines' (Toye, 2013, p 89). Labour argued that the planning of the economy was of strategic importance. In 1940, Herbert Morrison led calls for a minister of war economy, moving a parliamentary motion '[t]hat, recognising the vital necessity of planning to the best advantage the resources of the nation for the successful prosecution of the war and for meeting the requirements of the civilian population ... there should be in the War Cabinet a Minister specially charged with this function' and in doing so critiqued existing plans of 'co-ordination' claiming 'co-ordination has its uses, but it is no substitute for government, for decision, drive or direction' (Morrison, 1940).

Shinwell (1944, pp 44–45) also offered pragmatic, rather than ideological, understandings for nationalisation, advocating state planning on the grounds of efficiency and national security. Shinwell argued that the market system had almost caused Britain to be 'starved out' during the war as agricultural production prior to 1939 fell to just two thirds of home demand. Shinwell also called for the nationalisation of 'all natural resources' and maintained that 'instead of profits being the first charge on industrial undertakings, they must take their place in the queue behind such priorities as the consumer's interest and the standards of living of the workers'. Further to this, the nationalisation of the banking system was seen as necessary for democracy; 'in the past we have suffered too much from the dictation of the Bank of England and the satellite joint stock banks. It is of little use having a democratic government at Westminster while reactionary finance is free to sabotage all attempts at comprehensive reconstruction.'

While Labour may have been committed to some form of socialism, this was clearly not the same as its flagship economic programme of nationalisation. Speaking at the party's 1945 annual conference, Morrison (quoted by Miliband, 2009, p 279) offered a defensive, pragmatic case for nationalisation rather than seeing this as an ideological venture, stating that the case for nationalisation must be made 'industry by industry on the merits of each case. ... it is no good saying that we are going to socialize electricity, fuel and power because it is in accordance with Labour Party principles to do so'. Morrison argued that the minds of British voters were not as abstract as ideological arguments often assume, rather that in order to achieve popular support, 'you must spend substantial time in arguing the case for the socialization of these industries on the merits of their specific cases'. Even rail nationalisation – something that had been popular historically – was defended not on ideological grounds but on 'the track record of inadequate investment by private transport companies, the fact that the industries contained "strong elements of natural monopoly and externalities" and the "widespread support for the realization of scale economies"' (Jupe, 2011, p 325).

Millward (1997, p 209) further argues that the nationalisations of the post-war period were not ideologically driven, nor did they represent a pinnacle of socialism. In critiquing the limits of the policies, he asks why 'should the socialist vision be restricted to transport and fuel? Why should the "means of production" not include the machinery and other capital assets in manufacturing, construction, commerce, and agriculture, let alone the original indestructible capital in land?' Such pragmatic understandings were apparent in the manner in which the government assumed control of industries. The Labour Party did not confiscate industries, or view nationalisation as a tax on private industry, but rather acquired industries by paying, often generous sums, to bring them into public ownership, Edgerton (2002, p 164) estimates that the 'major nationalisations' of the late 1940s cost the UK government £2.6 million in compensation.

Others such as Woodrow Wyatt (1977, pp 22–23), a Labour MP who would become a strong critic of the Labour Party in the 1970s, argued that many of the nationalised industries were not radical departures from the actions of previous governments; the Sankey commission in 1919 recommended the nationalisation of coal, the Conservative government in 1926 had created the Electricity Board and 'many free enterprise countries nationalize their civil aviation, or subsidise it to such an extent that it might as well be nationalised'.

Even the creation of the NHS, which Foot (1973, p 106) would later refer to as 'the Labour government's most intrinsically socialist proposition', demonstrated elements of pragmatism. Funding the NHS was a key issue for the Attlee administration, one that would eventually lead to party splits (over prescription charges) and the downfall of the administration in 1951. Bevan (2008, pp 91–92), when creating the NHS, accepted the need for pay beds to entice specialists to work in the nationalised health service (or at least not to migrate to private care) but argued that 'the number of pay beds should be reduced until, in time they are abolished' as they promoted a commercial practice that undermined the principle of free universal health care. However, to overcome financial constraints, Bevan altered these arguments and suggested that revenue could increasingly be obtained from the number of 'amenity beds', which commanded a small fee in exchange for patient privacy.

The fall of Attlee's government in 1951 was far less dramatic than the fall of MacDonald's in 1931 or Callaghan's in 1979. Labour actually won more votes than the Conservatives in the 1951 general election. Some in the party saw the results as a success – Hugh Dalton described the result as 'wonderful', and argued that the Conservative Party, with a mere 17-seat majority, 'would quickly encounter economic and political problems and [that Labour] would be back in office sooner rather than later' (Crowcroft and Theakston, 2013, p 61). However, further electoral defeat in the 1955 general election led to Attlee's resignation as leader and a period of revisionism.

Labour's understanding of socialism

Labour's commitment to socialism continued to be demonstrated rhetorically throughout party publications (such as the manifesto) and leading figures. Its socialist commitments as expressed in the 1950 manifesto were outlined in the third paragraph, which read:

Socialism is not bread alone. Economic security and freedom from the enslaving material bonds of capitalism are not the final goals. They are means to the greater end – the evolution of a people more kindly, intelligent, free, co-operative, enterprising and rich in culture. They are means to the greater end of the full and free development of every individual person. We in the Labour Party – men and women from all occupations and from every sphere of life – have set out to create a community that relies for its driving power on the release of all the finer constructive impulses of man. We believe that all citizens have obligations to fulfil as well as rights to enjoy. (Labour Party, 1950)

Such claims came at the expense of a detailed understanding of socialism. As Fielding (1992, p 139) notes, 'Herbert Morrison's alleged maxim that "Socialism is what the Labour Government does" has caused some to bemoan the party's "mindlessness"'. Although, as Fielding notes, there is a serious question mark over the authenticity of Morrison's remarks, the ease at which socialism became synonymous with the Labour Party in the post-war period, by both those with favourable and those with unfavourable dispositions to the party, led to a lack of engagement in debates surrounding the drivers of Labour's ideology.

Although Labour's nationalisation programme is often seen – along with the creation of the NHS – as the pinnacle of socialism in Britain, revisionists have suggested that such socialism did not extend to other policy areas. They argue that Labour's industrial policy has been guided by factors other than socialist ideology. Francis (1997, p 91) argues that although revisionists were 'reluctant to renounce public ownership, they were aware of its limitations as an instrument of economic planning, but they felt it still had an important role to play in Labour's egalitarian objectives'. Ralph Miliband (1969, p 109) argues that the modernisation of capitalist enterprise, not a socialist revolution, was the goal of Labour's programme. Such views are strengthened by Crosland's (1975a) analysis, which argued that capitalism was not a static entity, but one that had changed in the immediate post-war period.

Prior to the Second World War, the future Conservative Prime Minister, Harold Macmillan, described 'Labour's programme for the nationalisation of the Bank of England, coalmining, power, land and transport as mild compared with his own plan' (Millward and Singleton, 1995, p 311). Attlee (2019) himself noted that only the proposal to nationalise iron and steel invoked much opposition, although the opposition did come from significant actors. The decision to nationalise the iron and steel industry stemmed from a conference resolution passed in 1944, against the wishes of the NEC. Addison (1977, p 273) notes that even some within Labour's cabinet were not convinced that nationalisation was the right approach. 'Morrison, encouraged by Attlee, [tried] to evade the commitment by devising a system of control which fell short of public ownership' before the industry was nationalised in February 1951.

Given the relative lack of opposition, the government's nationalisation proposals appeared thin. As *The Economist* (quoted by Miliband, 1969, p 108) highlighted, 'an avowedly socialist government, with a clear parliamentary majority ... might well have been expected to go several steps further'.

Labour historians, looking back at the Attlee governments of 1945–1951, have broadly agreed that the Labour government – even before the 1947 crisis – was guided more by pragmatism than socialism. Strachey, quoted by Beech and Hickson (2007, p 108), argued that the government 'appreciably modified the nature of British capitalism'. Crosland (2006, p 46), who in 1956 answered 'no' to his question 'Is this still capitalism?', did not conclude that any revolution was completed and continued in *The Future of Socialism* to establish how socialism could be achieved.

Other scholars or thinkers place different emphasis on such consolidation. Those on the left saw the period as a betrayal and argued that its changes should be seen only as the first stage of a broader transition to socialism. Miliband (1969, p 110) notes those on the political right, either of the party or broader spectrum, accepted that pausing was the correct approach, defending it in order to maintain political stability.

Crosland (2006, p 31) admitted that even following the electoral defeat in 1951 he – and others within the party – did not fear that the socialist project was under threat, as the changes stemmed not solely from legislation but also from 'fundamental changes in the social framework'. This meant that such changes were immune from governments of different persuasions. Even if a new government could reverse the successes of socialism, 'a wholesale counter revolution would still be rather unlikely. It is not, for one thing, in the nature of the British Conservative Party ... indeed it lacks the essential attribute of a counter revolutionary party – a faith, dogma, even a theory.'

Two issues are significant in this analysis – first the limited role of Parliament in orchestrating socialism. Crosland highlighted changes that occurred beyond the legislative programme of the Labour Party. He pointed to wider social interactions. It is unclear whether Crosland saw the chain of causality as stemming from public opinion on the legislative programme or vice versa (or indeed if he would have rejected such a crude binary option). Yet once these social changes had occurred there is little to suggest – despite the electorate voting for a Conservative government – that they could be reversed (especially by subsequent legislation).

Crosland differed from earlier socialists who downplayed the role of Parliament in favour of more direct actions including a more traditional revolution. The second issue relates to this and concerns the speed at which socialism can be or needs to be introduced. Crosland saw socialism as piecemeal, something that does not have to happen overnight – and indeed a transition that can be interrupted by successive parliamentary defeats.

Crosland, along with Attlee, offered a pragmatic view of socialism. They both presented socialism as a goal as separate from utopian understandings and argued that socialism can and indeed needs to be pragmatic in responding to developments in society (Attlee pointed to further human development; Crosland talked about changes in capitalism).

Attlee's Labour Party did not – as Marxists may have hoped – reimagine the relationship between Labour and capital. Here the ease at which the Conservatives, following their return to office in 1951, adopted the key tenants of the post-war settlement, has been used to demonstrate the limited nature of the Attlee government's reforms (Minkin, 1991; Francis, 1997).

Attlee (1937, p 138) was keen to reject the links between utopianism and socialism. He saw socialism not as something that could be arrived at or 'completed'. The establishment of a socialist system was not comparable to the creation of other political systems; a 'future historian will not be able to point to a particular date as that on which the [s]ocialist state was established in the same way as the United States of America dates from the declaration of Independence, because socialists envisage human progress as continuous'.

Attlee (2019, p 165) instead preferred to link notions of socialism with critiques of capitalist economy, arguing that 'we had not been elected to patch up the old system but to make something new. Our policy was not a reformed capitalism but progress towards a democratic socialism.' However, following the 1951 election defeat, critics of the government suggested that the government had not plotted a path to socialism. Through rejecting viewing an end goal, Attlee's version of socialism had 'ultimately failed according to Crossman, since it lacked a distinctly socialist theory – it had instead, in keeping with the British political tradition – been largely empiricist, pragmatic, cautious; it lacked ... a "map" to guide it to socialism' (Beech and Hickson, 2007, p 122).

The government largely adopted existing understandings of the economy and orthodox measures of economic performance remained prevalent. This appeared at odds with conceptualisations of socialism as creating a new economic system. There was no reimagining of economic concepts such as inflation and unemployment, as occurred in the 1980s, and existing assumptions, inherited from the capitalist structures, formed the basis of the government's approach. In October 1946, Herbert Morrison (quoted by Tomlinson, 1993, p 2) declared that he 'would put [the] problem of increased productivity first among the current problems to which planning must help to find an answer'.

If tensions existed over the party's understanding of socialism and its relationship to issues of community and nationalisation, the same could not be said for the party's understanding of the importance of Parliament.

Any socialism was by the 1940s rooted in parliamentary, rather than revolutionary, socialism. The party's 'managerial transformation', which had led to the party expelling those (especially communists) who were seen to be unsympathetic to its views (Shaw, 1988, pp 26–29), along with the experience of fighting extreme governments in the war, had centralised theories of social democracy within the party and committed it to existing means of governance. As Arthur Greenwood (1945) noted in the House of Commons:

> We are not unreasonable people. We are constitutionally-minded. In fact in some respects we are quite conservative, for example about the conduct of affairs in this House. We represent a different attitude. I claim that we are really a national party. I look around among my colleagues and I see landlords, capitalists, and lawyers. We are a cross-section of the national life, and this is something that has never happened before.

The Labour Party, especially after 1947, was primarily concerned with 'stabilisation rather than modernisation' and demonstrated a pragmatic, rather than ideological, approach to nationalisation. The industries that were nationalised, such as coal, the railways, electricity, gas and even iron and steel were key industries within the context of not only the Second World War – and the strategic importance to the war effort – but also the post-war economic recovery. Far from Attlee's assertions of creating something new, other 'ailing' industries, such as cotton and shipbuilding, were not nationalised but maintained existing structures (Millward, 1997, p 210; see also Tomlinson, 1993, p 1).

The effect of revisionism can be seen in the 1959 manifesto (Labour Party, 1959), which in contrast to earlier manifestos only outlined Labour's commitment to socialism in the final section, four paragraphs from the end. Here the party defended its programme not in terms of a broad understanding of socialism but in terms of the 'socialist belief in the equal value of every human being'.

Labour's 1959 manifesto acutely demonstrated a pragmatic rationale for nationalisation. Despite stating that it 'will be necessary to extend the area of public ownership', only two industries were specifically mentioned: the steel industry and commercial long-distance road haulage. Both of these had been privatised under the Conservative governments of the 1950s. The criteria for incorporating other industries into public ownership were broadly akin to those of the Attlee administration; 'where an industry is shown, after thorough enquiry, to be failing the nation we reserve the right to take all or any part of it into public ownership if this is necessary' (Labour Party, 1959).

Jones and Keating (1985, p 83) argue that tensions existed between the role of the state and economic planning. Although the authors credit Attlee for an 'ambitious' programme of nationalisation, they note that this was mostly confined to 'declining basic industries', which were afforded independence from government and not 'used as the instruments of purposive planning'. For Jones and Keating, such tensions between socialism and nationalisation were born out of a wider inconsistency with regards to Labour's view of the nation state.

The institutions of the British state, unlike countries such as France and the US, emerged over time and were not radically shaped by revolutions. This lack of either a revolutionary or a democratic foundation for the British state 'frustrated the development of a general set of principles by which the Labour Party could assess the institutions and practices of the state. The party's approach to the interconnected issues of the state and political power has consequently tended to be piecemeal and guided by pragmatic considerations.' Such issues further frustrated Labour's nationalisation plans although 'the party [was] firmly identified with central economic planning and to a form of state collectivism epitomized by the nationalized industries ... there [existed] an element of confusion in whether nationalization should primarily reflect the needs of central planning or transform the economic and political balance of British society' (Jones and Keating, 1985, pp 193–194).

Such stabilisation was also explored by Wootton (1945, pp 130–134), who highlighted that parliamentary sovereignty and the right of the electorate to remove unpopular governments can lead to weaknesses in the planning processes. Wootton argued that the house-building programme was subjected to fluctuations and changes in the 1920s and instead made the case for the establishment of boards or corporations, rather than ministers, to oversee the industries concerned – drawing on examples of the BBC and London Transport. In comparing the Central Electricity Board to the experience of house building in the immediate period following the First World War, Wootton argued that while new changes in governments may be designed to reverse existing policies or arrangements, 'there is in practice far greater reluctance to wind up an independent going concern, which is charged with a specific task, even though this may have been established by a government of a different political complexion'.

The Labour Party and the trade unions

The end of the Second World War led to a decentralisation of industrial relations, encompassing both the trade unions and employers' associations. While this was comparable to the end of the First World War and other developed nations , 'the centrifugal tendencies at work in Britain were more powerful than most, if not all other industrialised countries'. Employers in the engineering industry, for example, recognised more than 30 unions, with up to three or more individual unions operating in the same plant (Clegg, 1994, p 300).

The TUC also grew in strength in the Second World War, just as it had done during the first. Membership in 1938 stood at 4,460,167, growing to 6,642,317 by 1944, led by expansions in important wartime industries such as engineering and agriculture. In exchange for their cooperation during the war – principally through an official agreement not to take part in industrial action (although some short-term localised strikes did occur), Bevin, as Minister for Labour, pushed through 'a broad range of measures to alleviate working conditions' and encouraged employers to recognise trade unions (Minkin, 1991, p 57).

The composition of the PLP in 1945 was very different from the pre-war PLP. In 1945, the percentage of 'trade union sponsored MPs had declined from 51 to 31 per cent' (Minkin, 1991, p 71). Of those MPs, the number of ex-teachers in the post-war PLP was 'greater than the number of ex-miners and those with university education was almost a third'. Labour's victory in 1945 and subsequent nationalisations further led to personnel changes within the unions, which in turn led to a weakening of their political influence. The highest profile among these was Ernest Bevin, who took up the position of Foreign Secretary in Attlee's Cabinet and was replaced by Arthur Deakin as General Secretary of the Transport and General Workers' Union. This change served as a double blow to the unions; it meant that Bevin was no longer on secondment to the government from the unions – as he had been during the war – but also meant that he would leave his post as Minister for Labour and was replaced by George Isaacs (Clegg, 1994, p 320).

Nationalisations, such as those in coal or electricity, also incorporated trade unionists to the boards of national industries. Such personnel changes, according to Clegg (1994, p 319), meant that in 'the immediate post-war years ... the top leadership of British trade unions fell below the standard of its predecessors who had led the unions before the war and, with the exception of Bevin, through the war years'.

Ties between the party and the unions, however, were enhanced by the fulfilment of Labour's long-term commitment to repeal the Trade Disputes and Trade Unions Act 1927, which was achieved in 1946. This reversed the practice of contracting in and allowed unions to revert to the pre-1927 practice of contracting out, whereby those not wishing to join the party had to explicitly say so. Labour's affiliated trade union membership increased from 2,635,346 in 1946 to 4,386,074 in a year (Clegg, 1994, p 321). The unions' commitment to free collective bargaining put them at odds with some of the party's leadership – especially the overt references to socialism contained within the party's 1945 manifesto.

Throughout the Labour government, the unions, although being incorporated into government planning under the tripartite consensus structure, retained independence, and on certain issues operated at arm's-length. Millward (1997, p 209) demonstrated that with the exception of coal there is little evidence to suggest that trade unions had a persuasive influence on Labour's nationalisation plans. Equally, the unions may have prevented the party from more radical reforms in certain areas. Nijhuis (2009, p 371) argues that union opposition to pension reform prevented the Labour government from introducing a redistributive superannuation pension scheme, meaning that the British pension lagged behind its competitors in terms of generosity.

There further existed a tension between the role of the state in economic planning and the freedoms enjoyed by the trade unions. In 1935, Durbin warned that, for a successful programme of nationalisation to be realised, 'the unions had to be convinced that protecting the rights of collective bargaining was a legacy of the past, unnecessary and even dangerous to a socialist economy' (Brooke, 1991, p 692).

Although there was an agreement between the unions and the Labour Party that wartime economic planning should remain, this did not cover the processes of free collective bargaining. Incorporating such ideas was advocated only by a left-wing minority in both the government and the unions themselves. However, 'the large unions were adamantly opposed to any such interference in what was considered to be not only their legitimate industrial functions but also their right to freedom' (Minkin, 1991, p 72).

This period saw the unions adopt a defensive strategy within the Labour movement and successfully sideline attempts to engage with a new political role. The unions between 1948 and 1959 offered years of stability, with the leadership being passed from one generation from the right of the unions to another. The unions had a large input into the post-war settlement. It was a union initiative that led to the Beveridge Report (Beveridge, 1942), the unions helped shaped the nationalisation programme (and its limitations), they preserved free collective bargaining and they persuaded the government to repeal the Trade Disputes and Trade Union Act 1927. They also combined with the Labour Party, sharing a common enemy in the communists. In this sense, the unions helped moderate the left of the party; by the late 1940s it became apparent to those on the right of the party, as well as those on the left of the party, that there 'might be a problem in reconciling traditional trade union behaviour with socialist objectives', for example the relationship between free collective bargaining and government macroeconomic planning or control of industry (Minkin, 1991, pp 77–81).

This defensive strategy was also important in organising opposition to Gaitskell's attempts to remove Clause IV. Changing Clause IV would have weakened the links between the Labour Party and the trade unions. Union opposition, however, managed to water down such proposals, first by encouraging Gaitskell to propose a compromise, keeping Clause IV but with an updated statement establishing Labour's fundamental principles. Under this plan, the constitution and Gaitskell's statement would represent the 'Old and New Testaments'. Second, by the middle of 1960, the unions had helped harden opposition to any form of change to the constitution. Such opposition made it clear to Gaitskell that he would be defeated should he bring the proposals to conference in 1960. This forced the 'demotion of Gaitskell's "New Testament" to a lower status' confirming Clause IV's unamended position within the constitution. Such divisions between the leadership and the trade unions were costly with respect to other policy areas, such as nuclear disarmament, but the unions' success in opposing changes to Clause IV demonstrated that they still wielded significant power within the Labour Party (Jones, 1996, pp 36–44).

Conclusion

Between 1940 and 1963, the Labour Party was both aided and inhibited by crises. As the previous chapter demonstrated, the Great Slump of 1931 forced the party to think more deeply about its economic ideology and in particular how socialism could be achieved within the current British state. The Second World War had a two-fold effect on the party. First, it offered Labour another chance to join the government through Churchill's cross-party coalition. It is highly unlikely that Labour would have been afforded such an opportunity if there had been a general election in 1939 or 1940, which would have occurred without the onset of war. The coalition, and victory in the war, allowed voters to associate the party with responsible or 'good' government. Second, the impending victory in the war helped to shift the focus in the 1945 general election to domestic issues, wrong-footing the Conservative campaign. Labour membership had also grown during the war and trade union voices had been incorporated into governance structures.

Labour's success in the 1945 election, and subsequent government, owed much to the collective wartime experience. This encouraged the party to promote state planning and pursue the nationalisation programmes developed in the 1930s. The war offered a practical defence for such nationalisations. It also encouraged the Labour Party to adopt liberal influences via Keynes and Beveridge – although moderates within the party were advocating such measures in the 1930s.

The direct effects of the sterling crisis of 1947 were clouded by the fact that, unlike other crises, this did not propel the government from office, and by historic scepticism of Labour's initial ambitions to promote nationalisation and advance socialism. However, by the end of the decade (and before the fall of the Attlee administration), it is clear that the once-sacred links between nationalisation and socialism were being questioned. Consolidation, rather than socialism, took centre stage within Labour's programme, prompting divisions between those who saw this as a means of testing the water for further nationalisations and those who advocated greater state control.

Such debates became more pronounced following general election defeats in 1951 and 1955 as the right of the party, including Attlee's successor, Gaitskell, embarked on a period of revisionism. Successive elections defeats in 1955 and 1959 eroded any initial optimism that may have occurred after 1951. Just as defeats in the 1930s encouraged the party to think about its economic ideology, the 1950s saw the emergence of a new revisionist tendency.

This new approach sought to map changes in the existing capitalist structure and argue more readily for a mixed approach between the ideologies of socialism and those of capitalism, drawing on advocates of consolidation. This helped shift the leadership of the party to the right, under Gaitskell, epitomised by the leader's decision to seek to change Clause IV.

Labour's 1959 manifesto summed up the revisionist position by stating that the party had 'no other plans for further nationalisations' other than the road haulage and steel industries, which had been privatised since 1951 (Labour Party, 1959). Such revisionism established the path that proponents of New Labour would later follow, to a more successful conclusion, attempting to break the commitment to state planning, and fundamentally alter the relationship between the party and trade unions through changing Clause IV.

5

Testing the Labour–Unions
Relationship

Introduction

Over the 15 years between 1964 and 1979, Labour was in office for all but four. Yet this was by no means a period of stability, and by the end of the 1970s the key tenets of the post-war consensus – the tripartite relationship and a commitment to full employment – that had shaped British economic policy for more than three decades were no longer the policy goals of government. Although the 1979 election of Margaret Thatcher as Prime Minister is often described as a watershed moment (Coates, 2005, p 42), much of the monetarist shift in economic policy was instigated by Callaghan.

The period 1964–1979 became synonymous with crises and questions over governability. These narratives were aided by poor economic performance. Since the end of the Second World War, British growth had been lower than growth in its continental neighbours. While there were structural reasons for this (for example, the higher opportunities/greater need for reconstruction in countries such as West Germany and France), the relative decline was marked by a corresponding decline in Britain's international position. In 1950, Britain accounted for more than a quarter of world manufactured exports, but by 1973 this had fallen to below a tenth and had not increased by the end of the decade (Crafts, 1998, p 4).

The late 1960s and the 1970s saw large-scale changes to the British economic model. Some of these were due to the deliberate policies of government; for example, entry into the European Economic Community (EEC) in 1973. Others were the result of crises, themselves a result of external groups, for example an increase in the number of working days lost due to industrial action, culminating in the 'Winter of Discontent' in 1979. And some were due to wider structural economic problems, for example the devaluation of sterling in 1967. This chapter outlines how the Labour Party responded to these challenges.

Throughout this period, both revisionists and traditionalists sought to develop new means of understanding how government could control the economy, moving away from the Keynesian paradigm. Others, outside the party, such as Anthony King (1975) and Samuel Brittan (1977), began to question the extent to which the government was able to effectively control the economy.

The devaluation of sterling in 1967

Labour's 1964 manifesto highlighted a promise to stop the prevailing 'stop–go' economic policies of the Conservative government, whereby policies of fiscal expansion were followed by economic tightening, arguing that their time in office represented 'thirteen wasted years'. The manifesto argued that 'only a major change in economic and fiscal policy can break the defeatist stop–go cycle and prevent another bout of stagnant production, rising unemployment and declining national strength' (Labour Party, 1964). By offering a new, technocratic approach to macroeconomic management, Harold Wilson and Labour sought a new approach to the combined problems of inflation and low growth, otherwise known as 'stagflation'.

Williams (1975) notes that far from being free to implement such approaches, the Wilson government of 1964–1966 had little space to breath and was beset by a balance of payments crisis immediately after taking office. One estimate of the deficit stood at £800 million (Caincross and Eichengreen, 2003, p 166). The government's economic agenda was set out in the National Plan, launched in 1965, and led by the new Department of Economic Affairs, which itself was designed as a rival to the Treasury. The plan established a target of increasing output by 25 per cent by the end of the decade – a target that George Brown, Secretary of State for Economic Affairs, effectively abandoned a year later due, Brown explained in a letter to Wilson, to external factors (Department of Economic Affairs, 1965; Brown, 1966). Without the plan the Department of Economic Affairs had lost its raison d'être and was eventually wound up in 1969 (Blick, 2006, p 343).

Blaazer (1999, pp 122–123) notes that the expansion in economic activity in the 1950s and 1960s stemmed from increases in imports. This increase in demand further increased demand for foreign currencies, in particular US dollars. This led to downward pressure on the value of the pound, increasing the prospects of devaluation. These problems were exacerbated due to different speeds in paying: while British importers paid promptly, to minimise potential costs, foreign buyers 'dawdled' amid increasing 'speculation, with some operators willing to borrow sterling through short-term loans with interest rates of up to five hundred per cent per annum, in order to sell it at the current rate in the hope of soon buying it back at a much lower rate'.

The government decided not to devalue sterling upon assuming office in 1964, partly due to the legacy of the previous devaluation in 1949. The Labour Party could not afford to be known as the party of devaluation. Others, such as Callaghan, presented moral arguments, arguing that devaluation was 'unjust to those for whom Britain acted as international banker', although this was not the first time such a policy had been mentioned. Callaghan was joined in opposition to devaluation by Chancellor George Brown. Wilson for his part thought he could 'accomplish a "re-structuring" of the British economy' to relieve pressure on the balance of payments without relying on market forces but instead by 'organisation and administration' (Caincross and Eichengreen, 2003, pp 156, 167).

Election victory in 1966 did not offer respite from the contemporary economic problems. Although Labour's majority had increased to 97, dispelling talk of an alliance or coalition with the Liberals (Fielding, 2003, pp 45–46), Wilson and his government were faced with mounting economic pressures and a majority, which now offered potential rebels the option of stepping out of line, without bringing down the government.

The decision not to devalue sterling came at a political cost: the 'only alternative way to overcome balance of payments crises was to slow economic growth, thus curbing prosperity and increasing unemployment' (Blaazer, 1999, p 123), which Neef and Holland (1967, p 19) noted was not an even process: unemployment declined in 1964 and 1965 but increased 'sharply in the last 4 months of [1966] as a result of measures adopted in late July to improve the balance of payments'.

Unemployment continued to increase, rising to 2 per cent by mid-1967 with no signs of the balance of payments problems abating. The seasonally adjusted deficit stood at £280 million in the second quarter of 1967 and economic activity was stagnating, 'labo(u)r costs and export prices for manufactures were still rising faster in the United Kingdom than in most other industrialised countries [and] foreign exchange reserves were low' (Artus, 1975, pp 625–626).

In November 1967, the government devalued the pound by just over 14 per cent, from US$2.80 to US$2.40. This placed great strain on the public finances and affected the party's wider domestic agenda, leading to cuts to 'the road and housing programmes, increased weekly national insurance contributions, the deferment of the raising of the school-leaving age, and the introduction of higher dental charges and NHS prescriptions'. Government expenditure was reduced by £716 million over the next two years (Crossman, 1977, p 15) and Wilson had to publicly address the nation to reassure the public, in his famous 'pound in your pocket' television address. Wilson (quoted by Steele, 2008, p 68) argued that although the pound's value abroad had declined by about 14 per cent, '[i]t does not mean, of course, that the pound here in Britain, in your pocket or purse or in your bank, has been devalued. What it does mean is that we shall now be able to sell more goods abroad on a competitive basis.'

Postponing devaluation until 1967 is often portrayed as a crisis brought about by the culmination of economic problems that the Wilson government inherited, namely the balance of payments deficit. In such understandings, Labour 'failed to devalue early enough. As a result they abandoned their objectives of full employment and growth' (Graham and Beckerman, 1972, p 11), although such arguments, Graham and Beckerman note, are too simplistic and fail to explore questions such as: 'Why did the Labour government not devalue earlier? Why did the balance of payments assume such an important role and become an objective instead of just a constraint on the extent to which more basic objectives were pursued?'

Graham and Beckerman (1972, pp 14–16) argue that there were compelling arguments against devaluation, and anti-devaluation sentiment was shared not only within the Labour government but also in the City of London and the opposition Conservative Party. The Labour government saw the problem as one of inflation, the balance of payments problem being a symptom, rather than a cause, of this problem (although this argument was not without its simplifications). One adviser to Wilson argued that devaluation could only be avoided if a workable incomes policy could be developed with the cooperation of the trade unions (although they also noted that any devaluation would increase – rather than decrease – the need for such an incomes policy).

Wilson, for his part, saw the solution to Britain's economic problems as managing the relationship between costs and productivity. In short, the government sought to link increases in wages to increases in productivity. Doing so helped generate a new system of decentralised industrial relations. The main objective of industrial policy was 'to raise productivity and efficiency so that real national output can increase, and to keep increases in wages, salaries and other forms of incomes in line with this increase' (Minkin, 1991, p 112).

The government was willing to take an active role in the creation of this new system of industrial relations. A commission was established with the remit of considering 'relations between management and employees and the role of the trade unions and employers' associations in promoting the interests of their members and in accelerating the social and economic advance of the nation' (Turner, 1969, p 1).

In 1968, the Royal Commission on Trade Unions and Employers' Associations (also known as the Donovan Commission) made its recommendations, noting that the contemporary system of industrial relations was markedly different from the last Royal Commission report, some 62 years previous. It recommended adopting a decentralised bargaining framework with company- or plant-based arrangements replacing national ones. It further sought to codify the processes of industrial relations, by requiring all agreements involving firms with more than 5,000 employees to be registered with the Department of Employment and Productivity and recommended creating a permanent Industrial Relations Commission (Banks, 1969, pp 340–342).

There was growing concern about the nature of unofficial strikes. The government's White Paper, *In Place of Strife*, estimated that 'about 95 per cent' of all strikes in 1969 were unofficial (Castle, 1969). The commission only reached a final agreement on the issue 'immediately prior to the preparation of its final report' (Banks, 1969, p 344). This rejected incorporating collective agreements into a legally binding contract, something that disappointed the unions. The commission was 'essentially pragmatic as it argues that legally binding contracts on their own are both impractical and irrelevant as a solution to Britain's unofficial strike problem'. It saw the law as an inappropriate 'instrument for an effective reform of industrial relations, if it seeks to change union–management behaviour simply through a process of direct coercion' (Banks, 1969, p 344).

However, the proposed system of industrial relations was ultimately a failure. It did not receive the same consensus as its predecessor had. Opting for such localised agreements weakened the national trade unions and the overall policy was 'undermined by wage restraint policies that made reform hostage to economic crisis management, and by resistance on the part of a group of employers for whom the institutionalisation of trade unions' power inside the firm was vastly more threatening' (Howell, 2007a, p 88). Turner (1969, pp 7–8) further emphasised weaknesses within the commission's theorising of contemporary industrial relations, questioning in particular the distinction between factories and workshops – which help inform proposals for collective bargaining – as units of employment, and noted that 'the commission's analysis is thus largely irrelevant to the conditions and situation of most British employees: while its proposal for reform involves a large ambiguity'.

Castle originally published *In Place of Strife* to stimulate debate, ahead of legislation to be brought forward later in 1969; the proposals on the one hand 'included new rights to trade union recognition; the right of individuals to join a trade union; and protection against unfair dismissal'. However, discretionary powers were also given to the Secretary of State 'to order a strike ballot prior to official strikes, and to order a "conciliation pause", an immediate return to work lasting for up to 28 days, in the case of unconstitutional or unofficial strike' (Tyler, 2006, pp 461–462).

Rather than pausing for a prolonged consultation, the government brought forward a bill in June 1969 containing many of the provisions within *In Place of Strife*, but only a 'limited number of the new trade union rights'.

The TUC responded to this by publishing its own set of proposals entitled *Programme for Action*, published the same month, and endorsed by the TUC general council on 5 June (Tyler, 2006, p 462).

Opposition from both within the party and the wider trade union movement led to Castle presenting a watered-down version of the commission's report. This only became law following the Industrial Relations Act 1971 under Edward Heath, as the Labour government was defeated in the 1970 general election before the bill could be given a second reading in Parliament. The bill proved very controversial and 'came closer to dividing the labour movement than any event since Ramsay MacDonald formed his national government in 1931' (Tyler, 2006, p 461).

Labour, the IMF crisis and the Winter of Discontent

Although Labour lost the 1970 general election, the party was returned to power four years later. This avoided some of the problems of prolonged periods in opposition in the 1930s and 1950s. Harold Wilson remained leader and returned to Number 10 in February 1974, amid a miners' strike, despite winning fewer votes than the Conservative Party, led by Edward Heath.

Traditionally, Wilson's second spell in Number 10 has been viewed markedly different from his first in the 1960s (Morgan, 1997). Wilson's ideology and vision were replaced with growing concerns about government leaks and models, and insecurities, which Hennessy (2000) argues resulted in Wilson, to use a football analogy, shifting from an attacking 'centre forward' to a defensive-minded 'centre half'.

However, both governments were beset by crises – and indeed the legacy of the 1964–1970 government affected both the governments of Wilson and Callaghan in the 1970s. For example, Hannah (2018, p 125) argues that the government's responses to crises in the 1960s provided a disappointment to many voters, particularly the working classes: '[T]he economy suffered numerous problems which saw promised government spending curtailed. Ministers managed to limit wage rises but union leaders bitterly complained that Wilson was too preoccupied with middle class concerns.' One direct U-turn was the abolition of prescription charges in 1965, only to be replaced by higher rates in 1968.

Working-class concerns were, however, brought to the forefront in the social contract, which offered legislation on rent controls and the cost of living in exchange for wage moderation. The social contract was initially designed to be a voluntary agreement between the government and the trade unions. At least in theory this recognised that taming inflationary pressures rested on more than simply curbing wages.

The idea of a social contract was established in *Labour's Programme* (Labour Party, 1974). During the February 1974 general election, Wilson (quoted in Butler and Kavanagh, 1974, p 98) set out the need for a:

> 'social contract' between government, industry and the trade unions, with each party willing to make sacrifices to reach agreement on a strategy to curb rising prices. He added 'we have agreed such a new contract with the TUC [although this agreement was later revealed to be incomplete by an interview with Hugh Scanlon]'.

As Minkin (1991, p 121) notes, 'the highly publicised "social contract" arose out of the necessity of an understanding with the unions'. Yet it was not universally accepted; 'some on the right continued to be skeptical of the value of association with the adverse image of trade unions'.

The contract was seen as largely successful until the autumn of 1978; inflation (measured according to the Consumer Price Index) halved between 1974 and 1978 (and decreased by two thirds from a high of 22.6 per cent in 1975 to 7.6 per cent in 1978) (Office for National Statistics, 2019b), although some have pointed to imbalances in maintaining such promises (see for instance Rogers, 2009, who claimed that while the unions upheld their end of the bargain, the government was less committed to doing so). Inflation explicitly became the government's (now under Callaghan) key priority following further downward pressure on the pound over the summer of 1976.

The 1970s saw inflationary pressures increase for many developed countries, including Britain. Many of Britain's economic competitors such as France, Germany and Italy saw inflation rise due to a combination of increases in import prices and expansionary policies to boost economic growth following the collapse of Bretton Woods and oil price shocks earlier in the decade. Such countries explicitly made inflation their key priority in 1974/1975. By contrast Wilson, initially, prioritised employment as part of the government's commitments to the social contract, something that 'proved completely ineffective in the critical period up to the middle of 1975 while the harsher measures elsewhere were somewhat more successful' (Burk and Cairncross, 1992, p 220).

By 1975/1976, inflation once again generated problems in Britain's balance of payments, just as it did in 1947 and 1967. The balance of payments in 1974 stood at £4.1 billion; although that declined over the next two years as the broader economic situation improved the pound continued to decline (Burk and Cairncross, 1992; Ward, 2020, p 8). In order to shore up the UK finances in September 1976, the government requested a loan of US$3.9 billion from the International Monetary Fund (IMF) – the largest loan requested that point in history, and a total so large that additional funding had to be sought from the US and Germany. Such was the severity of events that Chancellor Denis Healey made a 'dramatic turnaround at Heathrow', staying in London to negotiate the loan and later flying to the Labour Party conference in Blackpool – to announce the details of the loan – rather than going to Hong Kong for a scheduled meeting of Commonwealth finance ministers (Castle, 1993, p 499).

As part of this loan, the government undertook a period of austerity, with budget cuts of around 20 per cent announced by Healey in December 1976 (National Archives, 2020). Healy arrived at Labour's conference and told the NEC: 'I do not come here with a Treasury view' and 'I come from the battlefront' (Castle, 1993, p 499).

The loan enabled the government to continue deflationary policies, although such cuts (the *Daily Mail* used the term 'austerity' to describe the plans; see Castle, 1993, p 500) were not uncontested – Crosland argued that with unemployment standing at more than a million, 'there was no economic case for the cuts'; the economy had sufficient capacity to increase exports and cuts of this magnitude would only serve to increase unemployment. Crosland saw that the 'only serious argument for cuts was one in terms of international confidence' (Burk and Cairncross, 1992, p 86). The Cabinet failed to support the decision in November as senior figures preferred to take a protectionist approach. Another critic of the loan, Tony Benn (1996, p 379), outlined his concerns a week later on 1 December. He again sought to distance himself from the Treasury, by likening the crisis to that of 1931, stating that 'in 1931 the chancellor warned the cabinet that import duties and revenue tariffs were not acceptable, and that if we came off the gold standard, the standard of living of workmen would fall sharply. Yet two months later, both were done. Someone from that Labour cabinet subsequently said that we were never told we could do it.'

The loan further changed the rhetoric of the government; Callaghan (1976), speaking in Blackpool at the Labour Party's annual conference, outlined the governments shift away from unemployment towards inflation as the key macroeconomic indicator, telling delegates:

'We used to think that you could spend your way out of a recession, and increase employment by cutting taxes and boosting Government spending. I tell you in all candour that that option no longer exists, and that in so far as it ever did exist, it only worked on each occasion since the war by injecting a bigger dose of inflation into the economy, followed by a higher level of unemployment as the next step, higher inflation followed by higher unemployment. We have just escaped from the highest rate of inflation this country has known; we have not yet escaped from the consequences: high unemployment.'

This followed what could be seen as a retreat from the post-war economic settlement announced by Healey in 1975 (quoted by Bogdanor, 2016), who when faced with rising unemployment argued: 'I do not believe that it would be wise to put unemployment as the central problem.' Such an approach was a shift away from Keynesian understandings, which suggested that rising unemployment should be combatted by fiscal stimulus. This was for Bogdanor a 'fundamental change [which] it is worth emphasising, came about not under Margaret Thatcher or her Government from 1979, but under a Labour Government, with Healey as Chancellor, a Government of the left'.

In the autumn of 1978, the voluntary nature of the social contract was removed as Callaghan announced a new phase IV, which would see wages settlements capped at 5 per cent. This figure was not discussed with the unions, and such a move was seen as electioneering, rather than a serious offer to the unions; even some Cabinet ministers saw this as widely unrealistic/ unenforceable (Thorpe, 1999, p 145). Instead, it was seen as paving the way for an election in the autumn of 1978, which in turn would lead to a new, higher, pay norm being established, assuming Labour won the election.

The postponing of the election, from autumn 1978 to the spring of 1979, gave scope for unions, government and private companies to test the limits of the 5 per cent pay norm. In December, and following a three-week strike, Ford settled a pay claim at 15 per cent. Parliament refused an opposition proposal by 285 votes to 283, which would have granted the government powers to impose penalties on the company. As Hattersley noted in his speech to Parliament, rejecting the proposal, this was not the first pay deal to break the norm. However, the vote should not be seen as a desire to keep the government's industrial relations policy intact. It was Ford's size, rather than the principle of the wage restraint that led the Conservative opposition to propose the amendment (HC Deb, 1978; Butler and Kavanagh, 1980, p 120).

The Ford workers' pay settlement led to high wage claims, and industrial action aimed at achieving them, in other sectors. The failure of the pay policy, and in particular the inability of the government to impose sanctions on Ford led public sector workers, whose wages had lagged behind their private sector counterparts, to push for increased wages. 'Oil- and petrol-tanker drivers threatened to strike over a 25 per cent pay claim but settled for 20 per cent. And, on 3 January 1979, lorry drivers struck ... they settled for a 21 per cent pay rise.' Such settlements destroyed the notion that a 5 per cent pay cap was workable, even 'before public-sector workers struck on 22 January in favour of a £60.00 per week minimum wage' (Artis and Cobham, 1991, p 15; Taylor, 2001, pp 122–123).

The 'Winter of Discontent', as the period became known, was not a unique event (or even a series of events) located only in the first few months of

1979, but a product of the economic failings of the decade (Hay, 2010). And arguably, just as the causes of the Winter of Discontent were not primarily in the first few months of 1979, the effects were possibly felt most in the 1980s. The Winter of Discontent 'destroyed the image that only Labour could deal effectively with the trade unions' (Taylor, 2001, p 123) and as Thatcher herself later admitted, without it, 'it would have been far more difficult to achieve [industrial relations reform] in the 1980s' (Thatcher, 1995, p 414).

Scholars exploring the political history or political economy of the period have also argued that the media reporting of key events, especially the Winter of Discontent, was inconsistent or biased against the trade unions (Minkin, 1991, p 122; Thomas, 2007). Hay (1996, pp 253–254) argues that perceptions of events came to dominate narratives of the events:

> If there is indeed such a thing as a collective British political imagination then it is surely to be found in the mythology which surrounds the 'Winter of Discontent'. Moreover, if this collective imagination resides anywhere then it surely lingers in the enduring popular resonances and connotations of a new political lexicon spawned in the winter of 1978–9. This discursive regime enlists characters as diverse as Richard III, 'Sunny Jim' Callaghan and St Francis of Assisi in the recounting of the tale; of how the country was 'held to ransom'; of how 'the dead were left unburied' and of how the 'bins were left unemptied' during a 'winter of discontent' in which 'Britain was under siege' from 'militant trade unionists' and their 'communist leaders' while the Prime Minister disdainfully 'abandoned the sinking ship', jetted to Guadeloupe, 'sunned himself' and complacently returned to pronounce 'crisis, what crisis?'

The 1970s became synonymous with industrial disputes and unrest. One former Labour MP, Woodrow Wyatt (1977), argued that such narratives represented increasing union militancy and unrealistic assumptions/demands demonstrated the existence of a Marxist or ultra-left coup within trade unions and even the Labour Party/government. Giles Radice disputes these points. He says that presentations of the trade unions and their aims were at odds with reality. Radice (1978, p 19, emphasis in original) argues that ulterior motives and 'flimsy reporting by the mass media' may have led some to make the same conclusions as Wyatt. Radice contests that the media too frequently, uncritically, often portrays 'claims or stoppages as the fault of the unions. So much so that a reader or viewer could not be blamed if he received the impression that ... *any* use of union power was to be considered irresponsible.'

Others such as David Owen, who would leave the Labour Party in the split of 1981, further saw the nature of corporatism and the tripartite relationship as problematic, with decisions being made by unelected pressure groups such as the Confederation of British Industry (CBI) and trade unions. These anti-democratic practices were the new enemy of the socialist. Such groups were insensitive to individual cases and the size of such groups 'discouraged the initiative and innovation so needed by Britain' (Foote, 1997, p 248). Owen critiqued the party for adopting 1940s' solutions – expansion of state ownership and planning – to such problems.

Labour's ideology

The period between 1964 and 1979 represented a reaction against the prevailing revisionist social democratic thought within the Labour Party, while at the same time trying to reconcile the collapse of the Keynesian-informed post-war settlement, in the 1970s. However, such reactions were tempered by pragmatic governments following election victories in 1964 and 1974, which oversaw a breakdown of the post-war settlement. Labour's defeat in 1979 left others, outside of the Labour Party, to establish a new framework or paradigm for the British economy in the 1980s. Such moves were led by the Conservative right who, as early as the mid-1970s, were turning to economists such as Milton Friedman, and calling for reductions in the money supply, cuts to public spending and increasing flexibility in labour markets (Holland, 1987, p 1).

Revisionism was in retreat during the first Wilson government and opposition after the 1970 general election encouraged the party to shift leftwards, emphasised through only two members of the NEC, Shirley Williams and Denis Healey, being associated with the right of the party (Jones, 1996, p 65). Hatfield (quoted in Jones, 1996, p 67) argued that Labour's policy makers shared the belief that 'successive Labour Governments had failed, and would continue to fail, unless there was a fundamental change in the balance of public and private sectors of the economy'. *Labour's Programme* of 1974 (Labour Party, 1974) is described by Jones (1996, p 68) as the most left-wing document published by the party since *For Socialism and Peace* in 1934 (Labour Party, 1934). It amounted to 'a clear repudiation of a revisionist social democratic approach to economic strategy'. The document lamented the slow progress made in the 1960s and claimed that such measures were limited to masking 'the unacceptable face of a capitalist economy and cannot achieve any fundamental changes in the power relationships which dominate our society'. The document, instead, sought ' "to bring about a fundamental and irreversible shift in the balance of power and wealth in favour of working people and their families" … words originally proposed by Tony Benn and destined to become "the battle cry of the left"'.

Another example of the challenge of earlier revisionism was Crosland (1975a, p 15) whose essay *Socialism Now* can be seen as an updating of his earlier revisionist works. In this he argued that revisionists need not revise their definitions of socialism. For the revisionists, socialism was still 'basically about equality'. However, such understandings drew on notions of equality of outcome and rejected 'a simple – not that it has proved simple in practice – redistribution of income'. The equality that was proposed by Crosland was a 'wider social equality embracing also the distribution of property, the educational system, social-class relationship, power and privilege in industry – indeed all that was enshrined in the age-old socialist dream of a more "classless society"', although Crosland did not stray from his previous assertions 'that capitalism in itself was no longer an enemy for socialists. While capitalist industry had certainly increased in size, he did not detect any increase in capitalist power' (Foote, 1997, p 235). Such understandings were consistent with those of previous Labour politicians and thinkers; here socialism – which still had at its heart an ethical, rather than economic, drive – did not need to replace capitalism but could be established alongside and within the existing structures.

Stuart Holland also acknowledged that the prevailing multinational economy had led to the erosion of basic Keynesian assumptions. Rather, it had generated an intermediate or meso-economic sphere. Some companies had been allowed to grow to the extent that they were able to undermine state control. The British government especially, for Holland, was unable to control the power they exerted, and policies such as state subsidies actually increased the power the companies possessed. Holland further criticised attempts to encourage regional investment as simply giving money to such firms 'who would set up branches in deprived areas, often without creating much employment as they were mainly capital-intensive projects. The result was merely to worsen the regional problem of unequal distribution of resources in the economy' (Foote, 1997, p 308). The rise of the meso-economy challenged the assumptions made by Crosland and others of a democratic economy, but also challenged capitalist theories whereby the labour market would be able to correct itself with firms moving to areas of high unemployment (see for example Holland, 1976).

Holland further argued that Labour should not view the public sector as failing. Rather, he identified the problems of the 1964–1970 government as 'having failed to grasp that social distribution depended on socialist transformation, it was forced to cut back on the very social expenditure supposed to alleviate injustice and inequality' (Holland, 1975, p 51). If, then, the 1960s and 1970s were displaying the ends of the Keynesian post-war settlement, the Labour Party largely failed to offer a coherent new paradigm to replace it. Those opposed to revisionism, such as Holland and Crosland, may have fed into debates in opposition, in both 1970–1974 and the early 1980s, but failed to command a majority in the party when in government. In government, Labour's right wing, exemplified by Jim Callaghan and Denis Healey, sought to offer pragmatic approaches. Stewart (1977, p 246) argues that democracy or democratic tendencies moderated both Labour's left and right when in government in the 1960s and 1970s and pushed the party to adopt a more pragmatic approach. Stewart argues that in office the party was unable to conclusively reshape the 'organisations of society' to overcome the 'fatal contradictions' of a mixed economy. Although agreement between Labour and the Conservatives was broadly reached on the stated aims of the post-war consensus – full employment, stable prices and higher living standards – the means of achieving these faced strong democratic resistance. The plans of Labour's left in particular faced resistance not only from across the political spectrum but also from within the Labour Cabinet.

Wickham-Jones (1996, p 2) similarly summarises the period between 1964 and 1979, ideologically speaking, as 'one of profound crisis and seemingly irreversible decline for the party'. This period 'indicated to many the exhaustion of the party's Keynesian welfarist policy programme. Both governments had departed from their original social democratic trajectory and resorted to deflationary economic policies.'

The Labour government of 1974–1979, in its response to the IMF crisis and failure to extend the social contract beyond 1978, saw a retreat from the socialist path, and helped lay the ground for the monetarist revolution of the 1980s, associated with the Thatcher governments. In turn, this led to key divisions within the party that dominated the fall of the Callaghan administration and the early 1980s (see the next chapter).

Labour's responses to the crises

Harold Wilson adopted a technocratic approach to government and governance. He was a pragmatic leader who claimed that his leadership represented a 'theology' and avoided 'old arguments over Clause Four or nuclear disarmament', which had dominated Gaitskell's leadership (see the previous chapter). Wilson sought to reform the machinery of government. Upon being elected in 1964, the government, as part of its modernisation programme, created four new departments: the Department of Economic Affairs, the Ministry of Technology, the Ministry of Overseas Development and the Ministry of Land and Natural Resources (Clifford, 1997, p 94).

Wilson placed a strong emphasis on scientific modernisation and declared that socialism 'was "about science"'. However, far from adopting an objective scientific approach, Morgan (2004, pp 42–43) argues that the crises were closely identified with Wilson and exacerbated by his agency, for example defining the 1966 seamen's strike as a 'left-wing conspiracy' or his infamous television broadcast asserting that 'the pound in your pocket has not been devalued' following devaluation in 1967.

Each crisis, along with wider economic problems, inhibited the Wilson governments from implementing certain policies. The new institutions established by Wilson did not overcome the power of the Treasury. In addition, wider failures of the Department of Economic Affairs and the National Plan (See Clifford, 1997) were largely attributed to the balance of payments crisis and devaluation (in particular the conflict between the National Plan and maintaining the value of the pound – on this issue see Pimlott, 1993, p 363) and subsequent austerity measures. Wilson (quoted in Clifford, 1997, p 108) remarked that '[planning] never had a proper chance: the fragile economic conditions which made it an attractive option, combined with precarious politics of 1965–66, prevented the subordination of other aims that would have been necessary to make it work'.

Brittan (1977, pp 285–286) further notes that the political constraints of the parliamentary system and the election results of the 1970s encouraged the Labour Party to adopt a pragmatic, rather than ideological, understanding of events and crisis prevention. Maintaining Labour's fragile governing position was given priority over ideological concerns. Many ministers defended policies on 'the grounds of political necessity' and ministers privately feared that changes in policy would risk splitting the wider Labour movement, an attitude that 'was determined by the desire to keep the TUC sweet for incomes policy'.

In contrast to the private musings of ministers, Callaghan's speech (1976) at Labour's 1976 conference in Blackpool was designed to establish a new framework for understating the economy, prioritising inflation over unemployment as the key macroeconomic target, although its central argument – the need for an incomes policy – remained firmly in place. It can be seen as the ending of the post-war consensus and an attempt to build a new consensus, emphasising inflation as the key macroeconomic indicator over unemployment.

However, although Callaghan is often cited as leading this shift – not unsurprisingly as he was the most high-profile figure to suggest that unemployment is no longer the primary focus of the government – such arguments were being discussed earlier in the decade. Speaking to Trade Union Public Services International, Crosland (1975b, p 246) noted that 'the most fundamental question concerning the distribution of income is not necessarily the distribution of income to various groups but the question of the growth of Gross National Product, because without a dynamic growth-rate there cannot really be significant redistribution'.

Policies of delaying an election that was widely expected to be called in the autumn while simultaneously rigidly advocating a pay norm well below the running rate of inflation were thought to offer the best chance of returning a majority Labour government. Such attempts, however, were seen as unworkable. Ministers and trade unions alike did not expect the pay norm to last long into any future government, leaving the policy lacking credibility. In this regard, it facilitated – if not encouraged – industrial action in the Winter of Discontent, which in turn weakened the party's position by the time of the 1979 general election, affording the Conservatives a landslide victory.

Labour's understanding of socialism

Harold Wilson argued that socialism could be achieved by employing technocrats and professionals 'who would bring purpose to Britain's stagnating economy and society. Only they could competently apply the latest statistical and analytical techniques to the problem of economic expansion' (Foote, 1997, p 231). For Wilson, socialism was not to emerge out of a crisis of capitalism, rather its implementation relied on a solid economic foundation. Such an understanding meant that socialism could be implemented through parliamentary means, largely at a time of the government's choosing, if wider conditions permitted.

Rather than being afforded such economic conditions, Wilson's personal secretary, Marcia Williams (1975, p 25), lamented Wilson's inheritance in 1964. 'We had a tiny majority and an enormous economic problem, much worse than anyone had anticipated – two problems which seemed incompatible with an effective socialist government.' Such constraints, Williams argued, were incompatible with socialist planning and policies. A similar view was expressed by Castle (1995, p 38) who argued that the 'dash for growth' of the Conservative Chancellor Reginald Maudling left the incoming administration facing a 'record balance of payments deficit'. Along with the 'outrage' of the City of London over Labour's redistribution plans, key members of the Cabinet – Wilson, Jim Callaghan and George Brown – accepted that 'the defence of the currency must always have overriding priority, [with] devaluation being ruled out, deflation became the only alternative'. Here, in much the same way as Labour bowed to the pressure of the Treasury in 1931, Castle noted that the government sought to uphold the existing economic system and '[t]he cut backs began'.

The Wilson government succumbed to a paradox. Although socialism seeks to replace the key tenants of the capitalist economy, crises in capitalism or aspects of capitalism did not necessarily entail that socialism would be easier to implement. Here socialism was seen as extending from within a strong economy; it was something to be pursued only when the economic (capitalist) conditions were stable enough to allow. Wilson and Callaghan very much worked within the structural constraints of the capitalist framework; in doing so they maintained its centrality to the economy, sometimes at the direct expense of the left's socialist model (for example, in the hard-line discussions with the trade unions in 1969 and 1978/1979).

Crosland (1975a, pp 18–19) outlined similar arguments in *Socialism Now*. He argued that although the first Wilson government made 'solid progress … on a number of fronts', these were tempered by external events and an overemphasis on the balance of payments at the expense of delivering a socialist economy. Upon leaving office in 1970, unemployment and inflation were both higher than in 1964 and the growth rate was 'particularly lamentable', growing at an average of just 2.3 per cent per year, compared with 3.8 per cent in the previous six years. But for Crosland, and others, the sacrifice of growth to focus on the balance of payments represented the 'central failure [that] bedevilled all the efforts and good intentions of the Labour Government. It constrained public expenditure. It antagonized the Trade Unions and alienated large groups of workers.'

Such positions were attacked by the New Left. The New Left questioned the ideas of the mixed economy on Keynesian principles as unemployment and inflation began to increase simultaneously. The economic failures of Labour governments in the 1960s saw the first cuts to the welfare state and the unsuccessful 'attempt to bring collective bargaining under state control' through *In Place of Strife* (Foote, 1997, p 297).

Others argued that Crosland offered too narrow a definition of socialism. Barratt Brown (quoted in Foote, 1997, p 304) critiqued Crosland's understanding, arguing that socialism was not 'primarily about equality … [but] about the eradication of class, about social control and production for use, instead of profit, for socially formulated needs in place of privately managed markets'.

The experience of the late 1970s demonstrated, particularly after the negotiation of the IMF loan, that just as in 1931, neither the institutions of the British state nor the Labour Party were willing or able to entertain a feasible alternative to the existing capitalist structures. The Labour governments of the 1960s and 1970s were unable to radically seek to alter the existing economic model, in part due to the crises of the 1960s, but later due to the dominance of social democratic thought within the leadership of the party. The 1970 manifesto only references socialism under the heading 'Britain in the world community' (Labour Party, 1970) and in the 1979 manifesto the term 'socialism' does not feature at all, rather the manifesto defines the party as 'a democratic socialist party and proud of it'. The same manifesto, drawing on the ideas of Callaghan and Healey earlier in the decade, maintains that inflation, rather than unemployment, is the key priority of the party; 'nothing so undermines a nation as inflation. Not only does it make the family's task of budgeting more difficult, it is a threat to jobs and a standing invitation to our overseas competitors to invade our markets' (Labour Party, 1979).

The Labour Party and the trade unions

While the British political system is designed to promote strong, single-party governments, the 1960s and 1970s presented a challenge to this understanding. In the 11 years between the start of 1964 and the end of 1974, the British electorate voted in no fewer than five general elections (to contextualise this, the fifth general election after October 1974 occurred more than two decades later, in 1997) and 1974 became the first year since 1910 to see two British general elections, which was also set against the backdrop of a crisis following the House of Lords' rejection of the Liberal budget of 1909 (for a discussion of the 1909/1910 crisis see Murray, 1973).

Contemporaries such as King (1975; see also Brittan, 1977) have argued that the post-war settlement by the 1970s had led to a battle between vested interest groups and democratic government. Such a battle may have ended dramatically in 1979 but certainly had its origins in the 1960s. The unions were disappointed by Wilson's commitment to and prioritisation of economic orthodoxy; the postponement of devaluation could be seen as a prioritisation of capital over labour or the working classes, the ultimately fruitless attempt to maintain the value of sterling required in part perusing wage deflation and came at the expense of the government's commitment to full employment. The period following devaluation also saw wage restraints, in 1968–1969 (Artus, 1975, p 631).

Linked to this, Wilson's direct condemnation of the seamen's strike of 1966, as being led by a 'tightly knit group of politically motivated men', caused much astonishment within the Cabinet and highlighted a direct tension between the Labour Party and some unions. Wilson's understanding of the strike was linked to higher issues: 'he realised it might be necessary to confront and face down some major unions if his [incomes] policy were to work and he wished to convince both the British public and the international bankers that, if need arose, a Labour government could be as tough as any Tory' (Zeigler, 1993, p 251).

Wilson's willingness to appear tough on the unions mirrors what Fielding (2003, pp 23–24) identifies as Labour's transition, when in government, from a class-based party to a national party (Fielding notes that attempts were made to reverse this trend in opposition, principally through *Labour's Programme* – Labour Party, 1974 – but this was never implemented). Throughout this period, the unions were diminishing in their ability to guarantee Labour election victories (due in part to the inability of trade union leaders to compel members to vote in a particular manner). Labour needed to appeal beyond this narrow interest if it was to avoid the problems of minority administrations. Central to this were wider (public) understandings of crises and in particular the relationship between the party and what were presented as increasingly extreme trade unions.

Castle (1993, pp 403–404) further notes that the late 1960s saw a number of left-wing leaders assume leadership roles in the trade union movement: Frank Cousins, who had held cabinet positions in Wilson's government but resigned over the government's decision to freeze incomes and prices, became General Secretary of the Transport and General Workers' Union; Jack Jones, head of the dockers; and Hugh Scanlon, President of the Amalgamated Engineering Union. The latter two were both described as communists by others within the party, although Castle rejects labelling Jones as such.

In response to this, the government's decision to create a commission to explore industrial relations and hastily publish a white paper, *In Place of Strife* (Castle, 1969), further stoked tensions between Wilson's government and the unions. This led to a rebellion within the Cabinet, led by Callaghan, which isolated Prime Minister Wilson and architect of the white paper, Castle. One estimate suggested if the bill had been brought to the House of Commons, as many as 150 Labour MPs could have rebelled. The bill was humiliatingly withdrawn but demonstrated the key tensions within the PLP and between the party and the trade unions (Morgan, 2004, p 44).

In 1974, Labour was returned to power on the promise that it, and it alone, could work with the unions. There were early indications that this could strengthen the relationship between the unions and the party. The miners' strike was settled, with the miners 'handsomely rewarded', and much of the unpopular legislation of the Heath government was overturned (Bell, 2004, p 247).

Wider perceptions of the trade union movement in the 1960s and 1970s were heavily linked to notions of increasing strength. Union membership had been rising since the end of the Second World War and the 1970s especially saw a greater willingness to undertake industrial action (Kirkland, 2017). Such actions were seen as tipping the balance of economic planning away from governments and democratic processes towards the trade unions. Trade unions not only increased the numbers of members they had, from 10 million in 1964 to more than 13 million in 1979, but also became increasing concentrated. In 1964, there were 641 unions; by 1979 the number had fallen to 454. The largest organisations accounted for almost half of the unionised workforce and 64 per cent were members of TUC affiliates. As the unions appeared to increase in strength, it was argued that industrial action was pitted against democratic interests to the extent that a 'plausible case could be made that strikes had brought down two elected governments, those of Edward Heath in 1974 and Jim Callaghan in 1979' (Howell, 2007a, p 131). Such increases in power, however, meant that unions 'soon became the scapegoats for Britain's poor economic performance … the press and media writers led the campaign against them. The sharp increase in industrial strife in the late 1960s and 1970s finally turned public opinion against them' (Aldcroft and Oliver, 2000).

Hayter (2005, p 10) argues that the 1970s in particular led to a fragmentation of the relationship between the trade unions and the Labour Party. Despite being the principal dissenter in the overturning of *In Place of Strife*, Callaghan 'and union leaders assume[d] a government-Trade Union Congress dialogue would carry the unions with it. But ... union leaders could no longer carry their members.' Such problems led Callaghan (quoted in Hayter, 2005, p 10) to describe the unions as 'completely leaderless' during the Winter of Discontent. Those on the left of the party saw this as an example of the party leadership losing touch with the membership and used this breakdown to challenge the wider internal structure of the Labour Party through the Campaign for Labour Party Democracy.

Labour's 1979 manifesto set out its first priority as curbing inflation and prices, echoing the move to monetarism that Callaghan signalled in 1976. Here the commitment to 'full employment' was only third on the party's aims for the next government, behind controlling inflation and 'putting into practice the new framework to improve industrial relations' (Labour Party, 1979). The manifesto commitment to bring inflation down to 5 per cent by 1982 could be set against the government's decision to limit pay increases to 5 per cent in the autumn of 1978, an acknowledgement that such proposals would result in real-terms pay cuts, prompting/encouraging the unions to undertake industrial action in defence of their members.

The unions were certainly portrayed as frustrating the actions of the government. Denis Healey (quoted by Pym and Kochan, 1998, p 217) would later recall that 'we had the disadvantage of very powerful unions with strong political clout in the party ... I spent half my time (as chancellor) on wages policy'. Another former Labour minister, the former Secretary of State for Transport, William Rodgers, saw the subsequent election loss as a result of trade union activities (Rodgers, 1984, pp 172–173). This view was shared through the discourse of both the left and right within British politics, and outside of politics, images of rubbish lying uncollected in the streets (for example Leicester Square, London) and reports of dead bodies lying unburied, due to a grave diggers' strike in Liverpool, became synonymous with the strike action and wider economic problems of the 1970s (Sandbrooke, 2012, p 4). Rodgers (1984, p 178) notes: 'The reporting of the strike by newspaper, radio and especially television was dramatic and had much more impact on opinion than the public's own direct experience of the strike.'

The problem or difficulty with the analysis offered by the Labour Party and former ministers is that it misunderstood – if not wilfully ignored – the differences in the objectives of the Labour Party and the trade unions. As previous chapters have demonstrated, although the party was built from the unions, this did not equate to both sharing the same goals. The failings of the social contract demonstrated this to both sides. For the unions in particular,

Callaghan's shift to focus on inflation symbolised that the government could not uphold its end of the bargain. For both groups it demonstrated a weakness in the historic alliance – what Hobsbawm (1978) identified as 'the forward march of Labour halted'. Despite the trade unions being numerically stronger than at any point in history, and willing to work within the constraints of a social contract, the government was willing to pull the rug from under them and seek to impose a pay norm that was significantly lower than inflation. As Bogdanor (2015) notes, the 1979 election ended 'the whole idea of consultation with the trade unions ... and the whole idea of an organised working class working with the Labour Party went as well. It was a crisis for labour, and socialism no longer seemed, as it had for much of the twentieth century, the wave of the future.'

Conclusion

The 1980s are often regarded as a turning point in British politics. Yet this change had its roots firmly in the late 1960s and the 1970s. On Labour's return to government in 1964, the tripartite relationship established in the immediate post-war period remained strong but by 1979 this had broken down. Labour's commitments to employment were weakened by the transition to monetarism in 1976. The conditions imposed by the IMF loan in 1976, along with the decision not to devalue the pound upon coming to office in 1964, further demonstrated that when in direct conflict, the priorities of capital trumped those of organised labour or the working classes.

This links to previous arguments and themes explored within this book: that the implementation of socialism – to which Labour leaders in the 1960s and 1970s, rhetorically at least, were still very much committed – was not seen as emerging out of the failures of the capitalist system. Any such failures had to be fixed or patched up first to allow for socialism to develop from a strong economy. Second, the experience of Labour in the 1960s and 1970s demonstrates that when in government the party was unable to effectively challenge economic orthodoxies or structures. The 1970s witnessed much discussion about Britain being the 'sick man of Europe', beset by problems of high inflation and low economic growth. Such understandings underpinned much of the Labour Party's economic policies; the balance of payments – an indicator that received little attention a decade later – was seen by politicians to affect the course of government. The IMF loan pushed the party to adopting a monetarist position on macroeconomic policies and eventually led to a Labour Prime Minister advocating wage increases significantly below the rate of inflation.

Wilson's attempts to reorganise economic planning, through the creation of the Department of Economic Affairs, failed to offer a challenge to the power of the Treasury (which Gordon Brown would later reform in 1997 – see

Chapter 7). Socialism came in the form of ethical socialism (for example, the creation of the Open University), and very much emphasising individuals' agency rather than amending the relationship between capital and labour. Even support by Castle, the most prominent woman in the Labour Party at the time, for the Equal Pay Act 1970 could also be seen as a pragmatic means of resolving the Ford sewing machinists' strike of 1968, or attempts to avoid a parliamentary rebellion/defeat, rather than an ideological attempt to reduce inequalities between men and women (Castle, 1993, pp 408–412, 427; Cohen, 2012).

The Callaghan government, just as in 1931, was beset by external crises, which both led to the fall of the Labour government and generated ideological splits within the party. Both Wilson and Callaghan upheld contemporary orthodoxies (for example, maintaining the value of sterling or cutting inflation) at the expense of economically socialist policies. Callaghan, like MacDonald before him, was constrained by parliamentary arithmetic (and having only a minority administration following by-election defeats in 1976 and 1977). Although the (memories/mythology of the) Winter of Discontent would ultimately come to symbolise the overextended nature of the British state and lead to an examination of the relationship between the Labour Party and the trade unions (see the next chapter), such revisions ultimately overlooked the fact that for four years the social contract – something that would not be attempted again – did prove effective in lowering the rate of inflation.

The Advent of New Labour

Introduction

Electoral defeats in 1931 and 1951 had left the Labour Party out of government for prolonged periods of time, a trend that was reversed following just the four years spent in opposition following defeat in 1970. The end of the 1970s, however, continued this trend. The 1979 general election was fought amid an economic crisis, and one that came to be viewed as a turning point in British history. It also represented a turning point for the Labour Party. Having been in office for 11 out of the previous 15 years, election defeat in 1979 left the party out of office for just over 18 years. Such was the scale of Labour's election results and polling throughout the 1980s that commentators towards the end of the decade asked the question: 'Can Labour win?' (Harrop and Shaw, 1989).

Electoral defeats in the 1980s – including the landslide victory for the Conservative Party in 1983 – led Labour to undertake a further period of revisionism, exploring questions of socialism and the relationship between the party and the trade unions, to the extent that in the 1990s, under the leadership of Tony Blair, the party rebranded itself as 'New Labour'. Much of this process began under Neil Kinnock, who assumed the leadership in 1983, including reforming the relationship between militant groups and branches of the trade union movement and the wider Labour Party.

Central to Labour's crisis was its relationship with the trade unions; the unions were blamed, both implicitly and explicitly, for Britain's economic problems of the 1960s and 1970s (see the previous chapter) and their ties to the party, along with the ideological stances of some leaders were seen by modernisers as barriers to reforming the Labour Party. As Hay (1999, pp 38–39) notes, the Winter of Discontent became a focal point for Conservative-leaning newspapers in subsequent elections, up to and including 1997. It was also clear that appealing only to the union vote was insufficient in obtaining a parliamentary majority. A growing number of union members voted for the Conservative Party throughout the 1970s and, despite union density peaking in January 1979, the election four months later swept Labour leader Jim Callaghan from power (Skelton, 2013). Finally, as the debates over internal democracy in the Labour Party gathered momentum, proposals for 'one member, one vote' (OMOV) in the 1990s and increasing incentives for individual members (for example, increased power in leadership votes) came at the expense of weakening the formal ties between the unions and the party.

This chapter explores how the Labour Party responded to the crisis of successive electoral defeats. It asks how it overcame divisions to forge a new electoral coalition and regain voters' trust, especially with regard to economic management. It explores how the party was able to overcome the crisis, through a process of modernisation, albeit at the cost of 'accepting much of the social, political, economic and ideological legacy of eighteen years of Conservative rule as unchallengeable' (Davis, 2003, p 53). In doing so, it highlights some similarities and differences between Labour's revisionism in the 1950s and 1980s/1990s before assessing Labour's transition in terms of its commitments to socialism (drawing on the work of Anthony Giddens and Tony Blair) and its broader relationship with the trade unions.

From government to opposition: an electoral crisis

Following electoral defeat in 1979, Callaghan resigned from the party leadership and was replaced by Michael Foot in 1980. This was the last leadership election determined solely by Labour MPs. Foot was initially reluctant to stand, leaving Peter Shore and John Silkin as the main centre-left challengers. He was later persuaded to do so after being convinced that Shore could not win and a failure to enter the contest would lead to Denis Healey being elected. Neil Kinnock ran Foot's campaign and Foot beat Healey in the second round by 139 votes to 129 (Gouge, 2012, p 127).

Foot's premiership saw the party shift leftwards and resulted in high-profile splits, most notably the Limehouse Declaration of 1981. Four Labour MPs, including three former ministers, left the party to form a new Social Democratic Party (SDP) (which would later merge with the Liberals to form the Liberal Democrats). The prospect of a split emerged following the 1979 defeat and was first sounded to the public by Roy Jenkins (quoted by Williams and Williams, 1989, p 108) in 1979 who, in the Dimbleby lecture series, told BBC viewers that the Labour Party was likely to shift leftwards and argued for a 'strengthening of the radical centre'. Jenkins argued that the response 'should not be to slog through an unending war of attrition stubbornly and conventionally defending much of the Old Citadel as you can hold but to break out and mount a battle of movement on a new and higher ground'. He claimed that doing so could incorporate those who were currently 'alienated from the business of government, whether national or local, by the sterility and formation of much of the political game'.

Twenty-eight Labour MPs and one Conservative MP would defect to join the SDP, as the new party surged in the opinion polls. The SDP sought to challenge the Labour Party as the main opposition party. Labour achieved a mere 27.6 per cent of the vote in the 1983 general election, and just managed to retain its second place ahead of the SDP–Liberal Alliance (25.4 per cent). The SDP–Liberal Alliance came within 700,000 votes of 'displacing Labour in the popular vote'. Labour lost 119 deposits, compared with the 10 lost by the SDP–Liberal Alliance and 'in many ways was on the verge of dissolution into a regional party far removed from competition for national office' (Wickham-Jones, 1996, p 3). The same regional concentration, however, enabled Labour to maintain a clear second place in terms of parliamentary seats, winning 209 seats against the SDP–Liberal Alliance's 23.

Defeat in 1983 became the focal point for Labour's inability to win, as the party recorded its worst polling since 1935. Others painted an even bleaker picture. In the Fabian tract *Can Labour Win Again?*, one Labour MP argued that it was easy to overstate the party's electoral success in the 1970s. Power was obtained in 1974, according to Mitchell (1979, p 1), 'almost by accident' and in many ways Labour 'hadn't won the 1974 election. We'd simply proved better at not losing it than an incompetent Tory government.'

The 1983 election manifesto was a product of the hard-left taking an anti-Europe stance, promising large public investment in areas such as transport, housing and energy, to formulate a national economic assessment in conjunction with the trade unions and to nationalise everything the Conservatives privatised since 1979 (Labour Party, 1983). Electoral defeat led to a rejection of ideas that had first emerged in the 1930s, such as the extension of nationalisation under policies of corporate socialism, as the party sought to avoid the 'extremist label which the majority believed to be responsible for bringing Labour to the brink of political dissolution' (Foote, 1997, p 324).

Such emphasis on electoral considerations is further borne out by Hayter (2005, p 2), who argues that these sustained party divisions in the 1980s: 'the [Labour] right ... wanted no such compromise with the left, largely because polling evidence showed the electorate's rejection of the left's policies and behaviour'. Such beliefs were compounded as the 'SDP notched up by-election victories and the [right] foresaw the possibility of being eclipsed by them in the general election [of 1983]'.

The 1983 election result and the resignation of Foot that followed left a limited number of potential leaders from the left of the party. Tony Benn, who had challenged incumbent Denis Healey for the position of deputy leader in 1981 and would have been a contender for leader, lost the constituency of Bristol East after his seat of Bristol South East was abolished in boundary changes, and Benn lost out to Michael Cocks for the party's nomination in Bristol South. Although he was returned to Parliament a year later, successfully winning the seat of Chesterfield, this left Neil Kinnock as the left-wing's frontrunner in the 1983 leadership contest. Kinnock was seen as a 'candidate from the left, although no longer hard left' whose nomination formed a 'dream ticket' with Roy Hattersley from the right of the party. Kinnock was presented as the unity candidate and won '71 per cent of the party's vote; winning in every section of a college of unions, MPs and party members' (Griffiths, 2012, pp 142–143).

Kinnock's transition to leader was not universally welcomed within the party, especially those on the left. Benn (1996, p 550) in his diaries records that on the Sunday following the election defeat, one newly elected MP, Tony Banks, had offered to resign his seat to pave the way for Benn to return to the House of Commons and stand in the leadership election. A similar idea was floated by Stuart Holland, but Benn dismissed both notions.

By the mid-1980s, the Labour leadership increasingly recognised fears that the party had become too associated with the hard-left, some of whom may have 'infiltrated' the party from outside. Kinnock (1985b) was determined to take on such militants. In his 1985 conference speech in Bournemouth, he sought to distinguish between the 'traditional left' of the party and what were seen as highly organised sects such as the Militant Tendency, which were regarded as Trotskyist in their ideology. A Militant-Tendency-led Labour group had recently taken control of the city council in Liverpool, refusing to implement funding cuts imposed by the Conservative government.

In his clearest denouncement of the 'Militant' approach, Kinnock used his Bournemouth speech to denounce both abstract ideology and policies that ignored the political reality of a Conservative government: "If Socialism is to be successful in this country, it must relate to the practical needs and the mental and moral traditions of the men and women of this country." He went on to tell delegates that they must do more to engage with the experiences of their "neighbours, workmates and fellow countrymen and women", denouncing those focused too heavily on abstract debates and arguments:

'implausible promises don't win victories. I'll tell you what happens with impossible promises. You start with far-fetched resolutions. They are then pickled into a rigid dogma, a code, and you go through the years sticking to that, out-dated, mis-placed, irrelevant to the real needs, and you end up in the grotesque chaos of a Labour council hiring taxis to scuttle round a city handing out redundancy notices to its own workers. I am telling you, no matter how entertaining, how fulfilling to short-term egos – you can't play politics with people's jobs and with people's services or with their homes. Comrades, the voice of the people – not the people here; the voice of the real people with real needs – is louder than all the boos that can be assembled. Understand that, please, comrades. In your socialism, in your commitment to those people, understand it. The people will not, cannot, abide posturing. They cannot respect the gesture-generals or the tendency-tacticians.'

The speech was widely seen as a turning point in the willingness of the leadership to publicly condemn those on the left of the party and explicitly challenge the relationship between Labour and the trade unions. Yet recovery was by no means an easy or even process. Further electoral defeat in 1987 encouraged Kinnock to increase the pace of modernisation. The party's conference in Brighton later that year saw Labour commit to 'a rigorous review of its main policies'. Kinnock called on the party to 'match new times, new needs, new opportunities, new challenges' and a year later in Blackpool Kinnock 'argued that Labour had to come to terms with the market economy' (Diamond, 2004, p 222).

Following defeat in the 1987 general election, Kinnock announced seven 'policy review groups', which would report to the 1989 party conference (Thorpe, 2015, p 230). This review represented a new approach to internal decision making, as it elevated the shadow cabinet and PLP to a position of partnership with the NEC and increased the policy contribution from the right of the party. By 1992, four reviews had been established and these formed the basis for the 1992 manifesto. These reviews 'completely repositioned the party's stance on the market and working with industry, high taxation and uncontrolled public expenditure, trade union responsibilities and defence' (Hayter, 2005, p 192). Labour's 1992 manifesto included plans for a small business 'tax incentive' and proposals to allow the privatisation of British Rail and appealed directly to private businesses, claiming that 'it is the government's responsibility to create the conditions for enterprise to thrive'. Akin to this, the party promised 'sustained and balanced growth, with stable exchange rates, steady and competitive interest rates and low inflation' (Labour Party, 1992).

Further election defeat in 1992 – the party's fourth consecutive loss – led some to question whether this was 'Labour's last chance?' (Heath, Jowell and Curtice, 1994). It ensured that the period from 1979 would be a longer period of opposition than either 1931–1945 or 1951–1964. Although the party had made up considerable ground under Kinnock, the inability to regain economic credibility was seen as key to its defeat. The campaign itself, culminating in a high-profile rally in Sheffield three days before the election, was also accused of alienating voters with its 'triumphalist' tone. As Jim Parish (1999), the senior campaigns officer for the Labour Party, points out, however, Labour's poll ratings were in decline even before the rally. A fall of six to seven percentage points in the polls was, according to Parish, 'known in Sheffield that night'. For Parish it was Labour's economic policies and lack of trust on the economy, rather than Kinnock's performance at the rally, that were the reasons for defeat in 1992.

Heffernan and Marqusee (1992, p 1) offer a critical account of Kinnock's legacy. They argue that 'Labour woke up on the morning of the 10 April 1992 to find itself bereft of policies and ideology, financially bankrupt and stripped of one third of its membership'. The party had further lost its working-class roots and was 'infected with a culture of careerism that combined, in unhealthy measure, forelock-touching and back-stabbing'. However, the authors point to structural factors to explain this, noting that Labour's defeat was in 'part symptomatic of a worldwide crisis of socialism, which would have caused serious difficulties for Labour under any leadership'. Yet, aside from the international pressures, such as the collapse of the Soviet Union, long-term domestic factors, such as the legacy of the last Labour government, also played an important role. The defeat was 'the result also of a string of industrial defeats stretching back over a decade, and reflected in the prolonged shrinkage in trade union membership and influence. Britain's economic decline had removed the material basis for Labour's previous achievements in office.' The authors conclude that Labour's response must reflect these changes and offer something new, based on the prevailing economic settlement of the 1980s.

Kinnock can be seen as a failure in comparison to previous longstanding leaders. Gaitskell, although unable to win an election, held a consistent set of beliefs. Wilson, although accused of holding few principles, won four general elections. Kinnock, who led the party for eight and a half years, can be 'seen as lacking both principles and the ability to win' (Fielding, 1994, p 589).

Others emphasise the time-sensitive nature of Kinnock's tenure as Labour leader. Griffiths (2012, p 142) argues that we should refrain from viewing the past 'through the changing lens of the present' and asserts that the party that Kinnock left to John Smith was much changed from the one he inherited in 1983. Kinnock inherited a party that achieved just 27.6 per cent of the vote in 1983; eight years later, although falling short of government, it gained 34.4 per cent and in over the course of the 1980s saw off the challenge of the SDP (Butler and Kavanagh, 1992, pp 284–285). By 1992, Labour was 'less divided, with a set of policies more attractive to the wider electorate, better presented and on the cusp of regaining power after over a decade out of office'.

Following Kinnock's resignation as leader, there was still a long way to go before the party was seen to be electable. After John Major's victory in 1992, Thatcher (1993, pp 3–4, emphasis added) wrote: 'On 28 March 1979, James Callaghan's Labour Government, the last Labour government and perhaps the *last ever* fell from office.' Dismissing this as simply political point scoring is too simplistic and overlooks the feeling within the Labour Party. Stuart (2012, p 156) notes the 'the utter sense of demoralisation that befell ordinary Labour members following their party's fourth successive electoral defeat. There was a general feeling of hopelessness, that if the Labour Party could not win in 1992, when would it ever regain power?'

Kinnock certainly saw his leadership as a reformist one, and recognised that reforms would come at the expense of existing relationships and norms. Electability was central to this understanding. Kinnock (quoted by Stuart, 2012, p 157) set out his view of the responsibility of the Labour leader: 'It is important that the Leader likes (or loves) the party enough to maximise its chance of winning. Sometimes the affection can only properly be transmitted through a firm grip on the back of the party's neck.'

Following Kinnock's resignation, Labour elected John Smith as leader in 1992. Smith, according to Stuart (2012, p 155), has been both revered and forgotten, depending on the perspective of those analysing his leadership. Smith's leadership, although only lasting two years, is often seen as one whereby 'the process of modernisation ground largely to a halt'. However, this is often due to the presentation of 1994 and the election of Blair as a 'year zero' and the redefinition of the Labour Party as 'New Labour'.

Outside of the agency of the leader, wider structures also influenced party politics. One such structural consideration was Britain's withdrawal from the European Exchange Rate Mechanism (ERM) in 1992. This mechanism was designed to stabilise European currencies, ahead of further integration that would involve moving towards a shared currency. However, inflationary pressures meant the Bank of England was unable to prevent the pound from falling below set limits. In part this was due to political pressures against raising interest rates to match the direction of Germany's interest rates, in late 1991/early 1992, and fears over the UK housing market (Cobham, 1997, pp 220–223). Investors speculated against the pound in the summer and autumn of 1992 and by Wednesday 16 September the Bank of England was reportedly buying £2 billion worth of sterling per hour, although this was insufficient to maintain the value of the pound. By the evening of 16 September, the UK was forced into leaving the mechanism, allowing devaluation and further increases in interest rates. The overall cost to the UK was estimated at £3.3 billion (Inman, 2012).

The ERM crisis helped improve public perceptions of the Labour Party, but also helped signify changes in Labour's European position. Labour's relationship with Europe in the 1970s and 1980s was fractious, from the Wilson government's referendum on renegotiated terms of entry to Callaghan's and Foot's opposition to monetary union, and the 1983 manifesto commitment to withdrawal from the EEC. During Kinnock's tenure, Labour shifted towards a more pro-European stance, although this transition was slow, and driven by pragmatic considerations, such as the need to prepare for the 1984 European parliamentary elections. Kinnock (quoted by Holden, 1999) believed that 'Britain's future like its past and present, lies with Europe' and argued for reform of the EEC. Along with the decline of the left of the party, such engagement pitted the party against the more radical elements of the Conservative Party, Euro-sceptics under Thatcher and the rebellions

Major faced over Black Wednesday and later the Maastricht Treaty. Labour's pro-European stance became 'a key element in [its] move back towards the middle ground of British politics' (Daniels, 1998, pp 79–80).

A more direct cause of events on 16 September 1992, however, was that the Conservative Party had lost its reputation for economic management, and this propelled Labour ahead in the polls – a position it would not relinquish in the run-up to the next election (Clarke, Stewart and Whiteley, 1998, p 561; McAnulla, 2012, p 168). Importantly, this shift – in which voters saw Labour as a more competent manager of the economy – came not as a direct result of Labour's transition (although this was important in maintaining its position) but of external events.

Hay (1994, p 707) rejects this 'modernisation thesis', arguing that New Labour had accepted a post-Thatcherite, but nonetheless Thatcherite, settlement. Although he notes there was no intention or demand to return to the 1970s and memories of an overloaded state, this did not mean that Labour had to accept all the component parts of Thatcherism. Hay argues that the 1990s also presented economic challenges. He notes that if we accept the narratives that the 1970s saw an ungovernability crisis and an overloaded or over-extended state, then the 1990s witnessed 'a crisis of an underextended, retrenched and debilitated state stripped of the strategic capacities for economic intervention'. There was, as Hay noted, scope for Labour to offer a 'rejection of Thatcherite neo-liberalism and the construction of a "developmental state" capable of providing the modernizing role that the free play of the market has consistently failed to deliver'. As the next chapter describes, following election victory in 1997, Labour saw a limited role for state planning and sought to incorporate high levels of public spending with notions of free-market efficiency.

Labour's ideology

Following the sudden death of John Smith in 1994, the Labour Party elected Tony Blair as party leader, beating John Prescott (who became deputy leader) and interim leader Margaret Beckett. Blair won an overall majority on first preferences, gaining a majority in each of the three sections of the electoral college – MPs and Members of the European Parliament (MEPs), individual members and trade unions (Alderman and Carter, 1995, p 448).

Blair (1994a, pp 2–3) set out his understanding of socialism in a 1994 Fabian pamphlet. He argued that two strands of socialist thought had dominated Labour Party thinking. One argued that socialism was a series of 'values or beliefs' whose understandings of class divisions within society were not time dependent. Blair posited against this second strand, a 'quasi-scientific' understanding of socialism, which emphasised economic determinism, drawing on the work of Marx. In doing so, Blair tied these strands to wider geopolitical developments, arguing that the first strand is representative of the European social democratic traditions while the second ultimately failed following the collapse of communism and the Soviet Union.

Blair, and New Labour, drew heavily on the work of Anthony Giddens. Blair drew on Giddens' concept of the 'third way' to shift the Labour Party's economic ideology towards the political centre, drawing on theories such as the median voter theorem. This suggests that in a two-party system, such as the UK, parties that are able to position themselves closest to the centre ground are more likely to win elections (Downs, 1957). In this respect the third way can be seen as an ideological response to the electoral defeats (and crisis) of the 1980s and early 1990s. Blair was not a key architect in the intellectual design of the third way (hence Beech and Hickson, 2007, include Giddens and Brown but not Blair in their list of key thinkers) but nonetheless incorporated much of Giddens' understanding into Labour Party policy. The third way was seen as a modernisation project for the Labour Party – a further wave of revisionist thinking.

The term 'third way' stemmed from Giddens' (1994) publication *Beyond Left and Right: The Future of Radical Politics*. This represented an attempt to move beyond socialism and capitalism, which Giddens saw as two failed economic systems. He sought to untie these through combining conservatism and radical politics, noting that the preservation of certain institutions was no longer the monopoly of the political right. Giddens (1998, p vii) later noted that 'the term "third way" is of no particular significance in and of itself' and had been used previously to denote a plethora of different ideologies. Attempts to define the precise meaning of the term were more problematic. The term was associated with modernity. Blair (1998) argued that the term was the 'best label for the new politics which the progressive centre-left is forging in Britain and beyond', yet Gamble (2005, pp 430–431) notes that the term was used less frequently after the Democrat US President, Bill Clinton, left the White House, and argues that the term could also be used to define a precise electoral strategy.

As Crosland (see Chapter 4) had argued in the 1950s, Giddens (1994, p 139) made the case that existing understandings of policies and orthodoxies needed to be reviewed in light of societal developments/trends, such as globalisation (not dissimilar from Holland's understanding of the meso-economy; see Chapter 5) and the collapse of communism in Eastern Europe, which he considered a challenge to other strands of leftist ideology, such as socialism. When assessing the welfare state, he argued that the promise of 'full employment' within the post-1945 settlement rested on a particular understanding of male employment, and the goal of full employment 'belonged to a time when gender identities had not yet been reflexively challenged and when "non-standard" work, including domestic work, in official definitions of things didn't count as work at all'. Giddens (1994, pp

143–144) also argued for a reassessment of how social class was understood. For Giddens, social class had become more individualistic in nature, and the constraints and opportunities associated with social class were being experienced less and less through a collective lens. In addition to this, an individual engaged with the class system not simply as a producer but also as a consumer. Here an individual's lifestyle and tastes were seen as 'markers of social differentiation' in the same vein as their 'position in the productive order'. Equally, class was becoming more transient, with children not following their parents (fathers) into a particular occupation. Class was seen as less of a 'life-time experience' as people moved freely between careers. Giddens differentiated here between blue- and white-collar workers and noted that unemployment was not something that only 'affect[ed] those at the lower end of the class scale'. He also pointed to the 'new poor' – those who had 'a weak situation in the labour market, or [were] excluded from it altogether'.

Just as previous leaders benefited from wider changes, beyond their control, so too did Blair. The economy had by 1997 become a valence issue. Improving economic conditions was no longer sufficient to guarantee the success of an incumbent government, as the Conservatives discovered. Although economic indicators were, by 1997, heading in the right direction, individuals perceptions were slow to mirror such events. The recovery was also slow to take hold – unemployment did not fall below 8 per cent until 1996, and even in 1997 house prices were declining or slowly rising. As a result, 'voters felt less secure and optimistic than during previous economic recoveries. Further it was recognised that the Conservatives had broken the promises on tax made at the election, and that recovery had only commenced once the government had been forced to abandon its initial policies.' Other factors, such as sleaze and scandals, also impacted on individuals' perceptions and the government soon 'began to attract a reputation for incompetence' (Butler and Kavanagh, 1997).

Sanders (2004, p 310) notes that the economic indicators that determine voting intentions also changed over the 1990s, making links between economic performance and voting intentions more volatile and difficult to gauge. Initial studies, in the 1950s and 1960s, suggested that support for the governing party was strong correlated (negatively) with unemployment. Later studies suggested that inflation was the significant predictor of incumbent support. In the mid-1990s, 'aggregate personal expectations was a significant predictor of aggregate perceptions of governing party. By the late 1990s [however], this relationship, too, had disappeared.'

New Labour offered voters economic competence. Blair and Gordon Brown (the latter widely seen as the prospective chancellor) had to convince voters of their ability to manage the economy. Hay (1999, p 181) notes that '[the party's] manifesto and supporting documents contained, at best, a submerged radicalism couched within the rhetoric of competence, consensus and conciliation'. The 1997 Labour landslide victory provided a challenge in this context. The election results represented a clear mandate for change, an opportunity to reshape British capitalism and deliver a radical programme. Tony Blair and New Labour had an 'unprecedented opportunity' to create a new policy paradigm, but it was 'only by making a break with neo-liberal orthodoxy that New Labour in government can deliver the economic competence it so avidly espoused in opposition' (Hay, 1999, p 182).

Writing in 1997, Kenny and Smith (1997, p 220) argued that perceptions of Blair were mixed: 'the range of judgements about him are striking: he has been presented as a one-nation conservative, a moderniser completing the "mission" of previous leaders like Gaitskell and Kinnock, and a Labour politician still committed to the traditions of "labourism"'. Such perceptions were fostered by a leader and leadership team seeking to overcome the tribal distinctions that had kept the party out of power for almost two decades. Blair and others were comfortable using the language of socialism and equality, but only with the caveats of redefining crucial elements of these terms. For example, equality was to be transformed into not determining or controlling outcomes, but ensuring that everyone was presented with the same opportunities in life.

Labour's election victory in 1997 confirmed that the party had overcome the electability crisis of the 1980s. But, as the next chapter demonstrates, the modernisation of the party also led to significant changes in economic assumptions/policy. The party that found a way into Downing Street held a different economic policy/outlook to the party that was removed from office 18 years earlier. It was a party with a much broader commitment to private industry and the role of the market, which redefined equality away from equality of outcome to equality of opportunity and that had redefined its relationship with the trade unions.

Labour's responses to the crisis

Labour's election defeat in 1979 saw the rise of the left of the Labour Party. However, as Joyce (1999, pp 255–256) points out, this was far from 'total control' and the period was marked by internal divisions beyond the split of 1981. Although Michael Foot won the leadership contest of 1980, the shadow cabinet, which was elected by the PLP, did not see a similar swing to the left; ten out of the 12 MPs who were elected had served before and the two new members (replacing Foot and David Owen, who would later defect to join the SDP) were Gerald Kaufman (who was famously to declare the 1983 manifesto to be 'the longest suicide note in history' (Bull, 2000 p 3) and Neil Kinnock. Both men were more successful in the election than Tony Benn, who was only appointed to the shadow cabinet following the defection of William Rodgers.

Equally, the election for the NEC in 1981 saw the defeat of five left-wing candidates, while Healey narrowly beat Benn in the election of deputy leader the same year. The left were able to make some constitutional changes, but these were only done through the support of the trade unions, which were keener to 'make a pointed gesture to Callaghan' than pursue any ideological purpose safe in the knowledge that a 'general election was a long way off' (Hayter, 2005, pp 12–13). However, they were unsuccessful in others, principally the 'desire to take the drafting of the party election manifesto out of the hands of the leadership'. The proposal was important to the left, as a safeguard against a right-wing leadership imposing its views on party members. Giving sole responsibility to the NEC over the party manifesto would, according to Patricia Hewitt (quoted by Hayter, 2005, pp 12–13), have removed 'the divide between the policies that we as a party decide on, the policies on which we fight the election, and the policies which the Labour government implement in office'.

The splits within the Labour Party during the 1980s pose questions about whether or not the crisis explored in this chapter was born out of ideology – or at least perceptions of Labour's ideology. Hayter (2005) notes that for much of the early 1980s, internal party divisions rested on differing narratives of the last Labour government's record. Those who split from the party in 1981 used understandings of the last Labour government to present Labour as holding a more extreme ideological position, certainly when compared with the new SDP. At the same time, those on the left of the party blamed the last Labour government for watering down commitments to socialism and weakening the links between the party and the trade unions, although the imposition of Phase IV of the Social Contract.

Several differences can be drawn between the splits of 1931 and 1981. In many respects, Labour was in a far better position following the 1981 split; the party had not been propelled from office, and the defectors had not directly strengthened their main political opponents, the Conservatives. Although the SDP–Liberal Alliance demonstrated a threat to Labour in the 1980s, as Foote (1997, p 255) notes, this was 'short lived'; Kinnock's reformist agenda 'destroyed their electoral chances and led to their absorption into the Liberals'.

Kinnock's attacks on the militant factions – most famously in his 1985 conference speech – provide some evidence of the success of pursuing such a reformist strategy. The language used within manifestos also changed; in his 1983 foreword, Foot referenced Labour's 'democratic socialism' and likened the party's positions in 1983 to those of 1945, claiming that the manifesto set out a 'programme of socialist reconstruction' (Labour Party, 1983). Kinnock in 1987, by contrast, refrained from such language, using the term 'socialism' only once – in reference to 'democratic socialism' – and made no mention of Labour's politics prior to 1979. Rather, Kinnock (1987) presented the manifesto through the lens of electoral calculations, stating that:

> There is no other way to prevent thirteen years of Thatcherism. No party other than Labour can possibly win enough seats to form a government. The Liberals and SDP know that. Their hope is to profit from confusion ... [and generate] a hung parliament and have power far beyond their responsibility.

Although initially reluctant to engage with explicit debates surrounding ideology, Kinnock, following defeat in 1987, asked Roy Hattersley to outline Labour's aims and values, which were published in a document entitled *Statement of Democratic Socialist Aims and Values* in 1988 (Labour Party, 1988). The rationale for this was to pre-empt an alternative ideological framework being developed by Bernard Crick and David Blunkett and 'because of the perceived need to provide some kind of statement for the ... policy review' started in 1989 (Beech and Hickson, 2007, p 235).

Kinnock, and Blair, sought to reform the old established ideology of the party. Both men embarked on a 'reform or die' leadership style (Stuart, 2012, p 157) that had at its heart a focus on electability and was similar to New Labour's commitment to economic credibility. In economic policy this reformism represented a shift towards the centre ground. As Diamond (2021, p 24) notes: 'New Labour transcended the ambiguity of ideology and identity that bedevilled the post-war party, fashioning a more persuasive political and policy strategy.'

The third way and the guiding principles of New Labour were not devoid of ideology but rooted in finding a new ideology, one that could unite different factions by encompassing the best elements of socialism and the neoliberal economic reforms of the previous two decades. This was not confined to a redefinition of socialism. The challenge for New Labour, according to Gordon Brown (2003, p 270), 'while remaining true to our values and goals, [is] to have the courage to affirm that markets are a means of advancing the public interests; to strengthen markets where they work and to tackle market failures to enable markets to work better'. Labour could not simply revert to anti-market positions, but had to 'assert with confidence that promoting the market economy helps us achieve our goals of a stronger economy and a fairer society'.

In outlining the ideological underpinning of the third way, Giddens (1998, p 38) emphasised the continuing evolution of ideologies and ideas. Historically, 'the distinctions between left and right were often ambiguous and difficult to pin down yet [they] obdurately refuse to disappear'. Comparing free-market philosophies in the 19th and 20th centuries, he proceeded to note that 'the same ideas have been regarded as left-wing in certain periods and contexts and right-wing in others'.

It is worth noting that the term 'ideology' was used pejoratively by the Labour Party, which preferred instead to define itself through the lenses of 'ideas' and 'values'. Labour's 1997 election manifesto stated:

> We will be a radical government. But the definition of radicalism will not be that of doctrine, whether of left or right, but of achievement. New Labour is a party of ideas and ideals but not of outdated ideology. What counts is what works. The objectives are radical. The means will be modern. (Labour Party, 1997)

Labour's understanding of socialism

Successive electoral defeats after 1979 left Labour with key questions surrounding its ideology and appeal to traditional supporters. The party could no longer be confident that it was on a linear trajectory with socialism the end destination (see Hobsbawm, 1978; and the previous chapter). The momentum gathered in the immediate post-war period and election victories seemed to have dissipated and questions were being asked about whether Labour could ever form another government. Diamond (2021, pp 370–371) notes that the party faced a number of 'awkward questions' in the 1980s:

> What were Labour's principal political ideas? Was it any longer a socialist or social democratic party? Was Clause Four of Labour's constitution still relevant in the post-Thatcher age? Did social democracy have a viable future anywhere in the world? What precisely was the social democratic governing prospectus after the breakdown of Keynesian orthodoxy and corporate socialism? If Labour owed more to methodism than Marx, how could the party's ideological identity advance in a more secular society? Should Labour even continue to view itself as an ideological movement? Ought it instead to pursue pragmatism and technocracy?

These were not new questions, and as previous chapters have highlighted, have been asked, in various guises, at various points in Labour's history. Others, such as Crosland and Holland, had previously pointed to contemporary changes that challenged Labour's existing understandings and ideology.

Blair and Kinnock both distinguished between the scientific understanding of socialism and Marxism and its values. In his 1985 conference speech, Kinnock famously talked about the problem of militant sects within the Labour Party. He later equated some within the party with the public-school boys within the Conservative ranks. In doing so he set out a distinction between winning elections and holding an inflexible ideology, whereby it did not matter whether the party was victorious in elections, but how it 'played the game'. When the inevitable defeat comes, such 'game players' seek to blame others 'for not showing sufficient revolutionary consciousness, always somebody else, and then they claim a rampant victory. Whose victory? Not victory for the people, not victory for them' (Kinnock, 1985b).

Here the distinction between a scientific (or scientifically informed) ideology and values are important. Kinnock asserted, as did Blair and other New Labour figures later, that there existed more than one route to socialism while maintaining that without winning elections, such values/policies cannot be implemented.

Kinnock's own path into socialism demonstrates some of these themes. Jones (1994, p 568) quotes him as stating that he 'didn't come to [socialism] intellectually. I came to it pragmatically.' Kinnock's rooting in socialism stemmed from Bevan, with his only intellectual understanding developed from Tawney who he read at university. This was also reflected in the pragmatism that Kinnock displayed; although initially adopting a traditional view of socialism, which placed economic ownership at its heart, by the time he was elected leader he demonstrated a reformist approach that appealed to the soft-left and centrists in the party. He established three policy areas that were in need of alteration or modernisation: the EEC, nuclear defence and the 'general policy on nationalisation' (Jones, 1994, pp 568, 573).

Blair described himself as subscribing to a form of socialism, although was consistently clear to distinguish this from other, historic, forms of socialism. He was keen to suggest that his was a different kind of socialism than the rigid economic determinism of Marxism. In his first conference speech as Labour leader, Blair (1994b) told delegates to stop apologising for using the term 'socialism', noting that the socialism espoused by the Labour Party was markedly different from that of Marxism or simple state control. Rather, for Blair, socialism was:

> rooted in a straightforward view of society, in the understanding that the individual does best in a strong and decent community of people with principles and standards and common aims and values. We are the party of the individual because we are the party of community. It is social-ism, and our task is to apply those values to the modern world.

Blair, and other proponents of New Labour, redefined terminology such as 'socialism' and 'equality'. The latter shifted from traditional equality of outcome to equality of opportunities. This was controversial, as Beech and Hickson (2007, p 262) note, such understandings of equality, and in particular the emphasis on equality of opportunity at the expense of equality of outcome, appeared to water down Labour's commitments to social democracy to the extent that it could be asked 'whether social democracy is still their political doctrine or whether it has been replaced by a more modest commitment to social reform'.

This understanding of socialism drew on the traditional debates within socialism, Marxism and Fabianism. Kinnock and Blair were asserting that socialism is not rooted in, but detachable from, utopian understandings. Such notions have a long history and were prevalent in the early Labour Party, stemming from Marxists and Fabians alike (Leopold, 2007). Here, Blair and Kinnock defined their ideology as socialist, as demonstrated by their values. For Blair (1998, quoted by Diamond, 2021, p 108), the third way was 'about traditional values in a changed world. It draws vitality from uniting the two great streams of left-of-centre thought – democratic socialism and liberalism – whose divorce this century did so much to weaken progressive politics across the west.'

Such understandings, however, often overlook the means of achieving these values. As the next chapter demonstrates, Blair's and New Labour's values saw (or at least allowed) a larger role for the market and capitalist structures than Labour's historical understandings, which were developed out of a critique of those structures.

The contemporary international context is also important. Diamond (2021, p 108) argues that Blair drew on the experiences of the Australian Labour Party as well as the Democrats in the US. While it has been appropriate to distinguish between varieties of capitalism (see for instance Howell, 2007b), less emphasis – at least in understanding the Labour Party – has been placed on understanding different forms of socialism, rather than binary debates around whether or not someone or a policy is socialist 'enough'. It was politically useful for Labour politicians, concerned with winning elections, to distinguish themselves from other radical governments. The collapse of the Soviet Union in 1991 was defined in terms of the success of liberal capitalism. It is in this context that the Labour Party opted to align itself with social democratic parties (such as the Democrats in the US) rather than the collapsing regimes in Eastern Europe.

Socialism, for Blair and other New Labour figures, was not exclusionary. Socialism here was not defined by who or what they opposed; it was not a rejection or critique of capitalism or the market economy. Alongside these changing definitions, New Labour incorporated and sought to attract new groups, previously seen as the enemy:

Labour under its new leader proclaimed itself to be the party of business, of low taxation and of 'zero tolerance' in law and order. Its many-sided 'values' (ideology would be too strong a term) could embrace the welfare of the European Social Chapter and the deregulated economics of the American way. (Morgan, 2004)

The Labour Party and the trade unions

The electoral coalition Labour had previously relied on to deliver its success had by the end of the 1970s diminished. Hobsbawm (1978), in his lecture 'The Forward March of Labour Halted', noted that the working class were no longer a homogenous group, or the most numerically numerous group in Britain. Changes such as automation, female employment and immigration ensured that contemporary understandings of the working classes had to be differentiated from those advocated by Marx and Engels.

Such trends had developed over the previous decades; in the mid-1960s, discussions grew about the nature of working-class voters (see for instance Nordlinger, 1967; McKenzie and Silver, 1968). Marx himself talked about the false consciousness of the working class. Runciman (1966) argued that working-class Conservative voters perceive themselves to be middle class, seeing voting Conservative to be in their interests, despite a lack of empirical data to differentiate themselves from working-class Labour voters. And Parkin (1967, p 278) noted that about one third of the manual working class 'regularly [vote] Conservative'.

Historically, despite not wishing to play a 'revolutionary role', a majority of the working class were willing to vote for left-leaning parties that 'promised far reaching changes' (Miliband, 1994, p 133). The experience of the 1980s demonstrated that this link was further diminishing; indeed members of the working class were increasingly inclined to vote for the Conservatives under Thatcher. One-nation Conservative policies such as the Right to Buy appealed to such voters by offering them a stake in society. Between 1979 and 1992, more than a third of working-class voters cast their ballots for the Conservatives – a figure that fell to just over 20 per cent in 1997 and 2001 (Clarke, Sanders, Stewart and Whiteley, 2004, pp 45–46).

Such changes within Labour's electoral coalition filtered into the relationship between the party and the trade unions. Maintaining close relationships was important in the 1974 elections as these relationships demonstrated that the party could achieve what Heath could not: namely restoring industrial peace. Unions weakened throughout the 1980s as their membership haemorrhaged, partly due to changes in the workforce and a move away from traditional manufacturing. In addition, the salience of industrial relations plummeted in the 1990s. Such changes meant that by 1990 the close union–party link 'was increasingly depicted as anachronistic' (Alderman and Carter, 1994, pp 321–322).

However, this did not translate to widespread reform. Kinnock's proposed reforms – including proposals for OMOV a decade before Smith was able to partially introduce the system – were defeated by the NEC. Kinnock (1994, p 538) argued that this conference defeat – by 4 million to 3 million votes – was a product of the relationship between the Labour Party and the trade unions, arguing that it 'provided an extra pinprick to the barbed wire jacket that I felt myself to be wearing throughout the conference and indeed the whole 12 months of the miners' strike', which Kinnock (1994, p 542) later referred to as 'the lost year'.

By the mid-1980s, the unions had become synonymous with extremism within the Labour Party, encouraged by the rhetoric of the party's leadership. Throughout the miners' strike, Benn argued that the Labour leadership failed to support the miners or the wider working class. Kinnock's 1984 speech, during the miners' strike, criticised the policies of the government, blaming Thatcher for prolonging the strike and not offering miners sufficient options. But a year later, Kinnock spoke critically of the strike, attacking the miners' leaders in particular. This was part of what Benn saw as a 'an attempt to destroy the left' of the Labour Party and distance the party from the unions (Benn, 1996, pp 579–580; Kinnock, 1984).

Linked to this were plans to dilute the formal powers of the unions within the party, such as the block votes in leadership contests to OMOV, which would be used for the first time in 1994. In reviewing the results of the 1994 election contest, McSmith (1996, pp 338–339) argued that trade unions leaders were less powerful than in previous contests, concluding that the powers of the trade unions in the ballot was minimal, arguing that although many trade union leaders expressed a preference for a particular candidate, 'the impact was minimal. Union levy-payers, like the ordinary party members, voted on the strength of what they saw on television and read in newspapers, not in accordance with recommendations from their union leaders.'

Wickman-Jones (2014) argues that such interpretations over-exaggerate the extent to which the trade unions were marginalised within the 1994 leadership election. Certainly this did not represent the end of perceived union influence in leadership elections as the election of Ed Miliband in 2010 demonstrated (see Chapter 8).

New Labour, under Tony Blair, extended the loosening of the ties between the party and the unions, started by Kinnock and Smith (Dorey, 1999). Changes to Clause IV of the constitution, Labour's traditional commitment to nationalisation, helped instigate a new relationship between the Labour Party and the trade unions. Blair was able to do what Gaitskell failed to do in 1960, and rewrite Clause IV, which, as McIlory (1998, p 540) notes, offered a dedication to

'the enterprise of the market and the rigours of competition' equated accountability with ownership as instruments for control of essential utilities. It announced the triumph of private capital over the mixed economy. Privatized industries would not be renationalized but would be regulated to encourage competition with only a one-off windfall tax on profit. (McIlory, 1998, p 540)

The rewriting of Clause IV weakened the link between the unions and the Labour Party as it weakened (if not abolished) Labour's commitments to nationalising industries. This was not simply a policy that went against the traditional ideology of labourism and most trade unions but meant that unions could no longer expect to be incorporated into governance structures as they had been historically. It was furthermore a shift away from ideologies of community, towards those of individualism. Blair (1994a) previously argued that Labour's socialism should be defined as 'a set of principles and beliefs, based around the notion of a strong and active society as necessary to advance the individual rather than a set of narrow timebound class or sectional interests or particular economic prescriptions'. This definition, and the rewriting of Clause IV, not only shifted the party away from historical policies such as nationalisation, but also reflected an acceptance of the limitations of the state's capacity with regard to economic planning.

Conclusion

The Labour Party that returned to office in 1997 was markedly different from its predecessor that left Downing Street in 1979. While there was some continuity in terms of New Labour's commitments to some of the end goals of ethical socialism, there were significant differences in how these could be achieved.

The revisionism of the 1950s, which had been weakened by electoral victories in the 1960s and 1970s (see the previous chapter), gained new momentum following successive election defeats in the 1980s. Giddens and other proponents of the New Labour project were able to fundamentally alter the party's understanding of the relationship between the state and market and achieve the reforms to Clause IV that Gaitskell failed to implement after the 1959 election defeat.

Such alterations were aided by large structural changes within the British economy (Hall, 1993). The collapse of the post-war consensus and policies such as privatisation and deregulation meant that the private sector came to be seen as the primary source of driving and sustaining British growth. Outside of supplying conditions for the market to function effectively, the role of capital was enhanced through reforms to financial markets and the banking system (Kirkland, 2017) and the state was seen to have a limited role in promoting growth.

Labour's transition from opposition to government incorporated and accepted these changes. Proponents of the third way, who argued in favour of combining the best elements of socialism and the free market, accepted a much more limited role for the state in economic planning. In contrast to the post-war consensus, a new consensus was emerging, one that prioritised the individual over the collective, and accepted a greater role for private enterprise. In accepting this post–Thatcherite consensus, Labour was able to demonstrate its economic credibility and doing so provided the foundations for the New Labour government of 1997.

7

New Labour and the Global
Financial Crisis

Introduction

The economic problems faced by the Labour government in 1974–1979
were often blamed on the Labour Party and particularly its relationship
with the trade unions. The Labour Party's key task between 1979 and 1997
had been rebuilding its economic credibility. Hay (1999, p 156) quotes a
former economic adviser to Neil Kinnock, John Eatwell, who noted in
1996 that 'credibility has become the keystone of policy making in the
nineties. A credible government is a government that pursues a policy that
is "market friendly"; this is a policy that is in accordance with what the
markets believe to be sound.'

The success of that modernisation was demonstrated in the landslide
election victory of 1997. Labour gained a total of 145 seats, taking its
overall total to 418, a majority of 179. For the first time since the 1970s,
Labour was in a position of government. However, the party inherited a
very different economic situation, one that had decoupled the link between
governments and markets. Froud, Moran, Nilsson and Williams (2010,
pp 25–26) point to four ways in which markets were 'insulated' from 'the
influence of democratic government': first through the changes in ownership
(for example, privatisation) of key industries; second through introducing the
discourse of the market in public service delivery; third through deregulation;
and finally through the creation of new 'regulatory institutions that were
designed to be non-majoritarian in character'.

Following Black Wednesday in September 1992, Labour overtook the
Conservatives as the party most trusted to run the economy. This accolade
was sustained through adopting much of the Conservatives' spending
plans in the early years of government (Pym and Kocham, 1998, p 216).
The Labour government 'consolidated and extended the financial growth
model which it inherited from the Conservatives, and which depended
on flexible labour markets, relatively low business taxes, the development

of a strong financial services industry and the development of strategies to make all citizens financial agents'. Labour even extended the model in some areas, noticeably by giving the Bank of England independence and the power to set interest rates immediately following its election in 1997 (Gamble, 2010, p 648).

This chapter focuses on Gordon Brown, incorporating his roles as Chancellor and Prime Minister. It covers the entire period during which New Labour was in office, culminating with the responses to the global financial crisis of 2007/2008. Focusing on Brown rather than Blair may appear odd (although the latter featured heavily in the previous chapter), but is in keeping with the wider literature exploring Labour's ideology. Beech and Hickson (2007) omit Blair from their book on Labour's thinkers, focusing instead on Giddens for his intellectual understanding of the third way, and Gordon Brown (even though the book was published before Brown became Prime Minister) for his views on Britishness. In a similar vein, Coates (2008, p 3) describes Brown as 'the architect of the domestic dimension of the "third way" project of which he is now [after becoming Prime Minister] the unchallenged leader'. This position was not unique to the 1997–2010 Labour government. As other chapters demonstrate, Labour leaders have not typically been key actors in shaping economic policy (MacDonald deferred economic policy to Snowden, see Chapter 3; Attlee devoted his interests primarily to foreign policy, see Chapter 4; and Corbyn relied on McDonnell, see Chapter 7).

This chapter highlights the crisis of 2007/2008 as the key turning point in the Labour government. For Brown, who became Prime Minister following Blair's resignation in 2007, this became a highly personalised crisis – not only was it the crisis that would define his premiership, but it was also one that opponents could personally assign blame to him for, given his decade-long tenure at the Treasury. As Moran, Johal and Williams (2010, p 96) note, Brown's time in the Treasury had been viewed as 'outstanding ... one acute observer ... described him as a "genius", who had apparently presided over steady economic growth, low interest rates, low inflation and low unemployment'. Brown was seen as central to Labour's electoral dominance for a decade. It was 'only after he became Prime Minister that an increasingly accepted revisionist account cast him as an incompetent who bailed out of the Treasury just as boom turned to bust'.

Although the origins of the crisis date from before Brown's tenure at either Number 10 or Number 11 Downing Street (for a discussion of the causes of the crisis see Martin and Milas, 2013; Kirkland, 2015), it struck at the core of the party's economic understanding, dispelling the myth or notion that it had found, by combining the best elements of the free market and socialist policy, a means of organising the economy that would lead to sustained economic growth and eliminate boom and bust.

The crisis of 2007/2008

Underpinning New Labour's economic approach was a belief or confidence in the market (or markets) to 'perform efficiently', through 'privatised Keynesianism'. This was based on 'increasingly extended investment chains and the opening up of these trade chains to riskier trades and traders' who were increasingly less interested in examining such trades, which combined safe loans with riskier unsecured mortgages in 'unspecified proportions', or the contents of such bundles being traded. Such risk was supplemented not only with a belief in the market but also an 'excessive optimism [of traders] that governments would not let the system fail and would therefore move in to compensate them for any losses they made through excessive trading' (Crouch, 2011, pp 99–101; Kirkland, 2015, p 516).

Such confidence was not unique to Britain. As Gamble (2009, p 1) notes, this confidence was shared in the US and across the Western hemisphere. Consumption was extended to the working classes as restrictions on borrowing decreased dramatically. Prices increased while savings declined. Offers of cheap loans and credit cards were made almost indiscriminately, with little thought given to how or whether this money could be repaid. 'Everyone assumed each bubble could be managed and burst at the right time by appropriate action by the authorities. What few people had recognised was that the activities of finance had transformed the entire economy into one giant bubble', with no consideration of what may happen if it were to burst.

In 2007, concerns over the repayments of loans and mortgages started to emerge in the US, with the subprime mortgage crisis. Interest rate increases left homeowners, particularly those on the lowest incomes, struggling to repay their mortgage. This led to an increasing number of defaults and foreclosures and a decline in house prices. It led to the bursting of not only the housing bubble, but also other bubbles built on consumer spending.

The effects of the crisis spread to the UK economy when banks stopped lending to one another. The most visual representation of this came in 2007 when, fearing a tightening of liquidity, depositors queued outside the bank Northern Rock to withdraw their money, leading to the first run on a British bank in 150 years. Northern Rock's demise was due not to risky lending in the US or elsewhere, but to the wider process of tightening credit. Northern Rock did not own subprime mortgages, rather it ran into difficulties through relying on short-term loans, from creditors who had financial interests in the US housing market. 'As credit conditions tightened – and, crucially, in the absence of any significant rise in the default rate on outstanding loans – it simply found itself unable to rollover the short-term debt on which it relied' (Hay, 2011, p 15).

The fear was that such liquidity problems would feed into the rest of the economy. As credit and lending dried up, so too did economic activity, leading to the UK's longest and deepest recession since the 1930s (Hay, 2011, p 16). Fears of contagion led to the government taking action to sure up not only Northern Rock but also other banks and building societies and even taking controlling stakes in or nationalising banks/building societies. In addition to Northern Rock, other banks and building societies requested financial assistance, such as Bradford and Bingley, Halifax, Lloyd's TSB and the Royal Bank of Scotland. In total, the government spent £133 billion to stabilise the banks (National Audit Office, 2020), with further assistance in the form of assurances under the notion of 'too big to fail'. It was argued that as banks had become so central to the economy, if they were allowed to collapse, the entire economy would suffer (Kirkland, 2017, p 140).

Notions of 'too big to fail' were used to defend actions to support certain banks; however, this logic was inherently flawed – a point noted by the-then governor of the Bank of England, Mervyn King, who in 2009 (quoted by Goldstein and Veron, 2011) said that 'if some banks are thought to be too big to fail, then … they are too big. … Privately owned and managed institutions that are too big to fail sit oddly with a market economy.'

The bailout of banks ensured that a crisis that was essentially a private (to the banking sector) crisis became a crisis that the state now accepted some responsibility for (see Blyth, 2013; Thompson, 2013, p 732). This led to an effective nationalisation of the crisis. The crisis was no longer contained in one sector of the economy or even in private institutions. Concern now grew at the level of national debt and spending. The bank bailouts were estimated to cost 54 per cent of Gross Domestic Product (GDP) (Acharya, Drechsler and Schnabl, 2011).

Although Brown won plaudits on the international stage for encouraging an interventionist response to the crisis, at home the bank bailouts and proposed tax increases (Brown proposed raising the top rate of income tax first to 45 per cent and later 50 per cent) led the right-wing press to suggest that these measures marked an end of New Labour. 'In November 2008, the Sun [newspaper] pictured a tombstone on its front page on which was carved "RIP New Labour". The accompanying story surveyed "The life and death of Blair's baby" which had, it claimed, finally succumbed to "socialism"' (Fielding, 2010, p 657). Such claims were denied by the party, especially Peter Mandelson, who Brown brought back to the Cabinet. Mandelson (quoted in Fielding, 2010, p 657) argued that Labour remained 'in favour of "people becoming very rich, as long as they paid their taxes"', although such claims held little success with the electorate.

The crisis of 2007/2008 was described by contemporaries through various lenses. It has been viewed as an international crisis (French and Thrift, 2009), or at least one whose roots can be traced to the US (Duca, Muellbauer and Murphy, 2010), and one that policy makers in Britain only had a little or an indirect influence on. The second narrative suggests that the crisis evolved from the accession of New Labour (Goodhart, 2008; Hodson and Mabbett, 2008); in particular, Gordon Brown's time as Chancellor, and the promising of the ending of boom and bust (Kavanagh and Cowley, 2010, pp 19–23). A third argument offers a slightly longer-term approach, whereby the crisis is seen as stemming from the ERM crisis of 1992 (Martin and Milas, 2013).

Later narratives distinguished between a debt crisis and a growth crisis. Hay (2013, p 24) notes that although the former has become the dominant discourse promoted by elites (politicians and the media), it is in fact a second-order crisis, which stems from the growth crisis. Hay contends that the combination of blame attribution alongside political considerations has led to a misdiagnosis, whereby the crisis of growth has been mislabelled a crisis of debt.

Conservatives were quick to blame the Labour government's prolific spending and link levels of debt to the prevailing crisis, but this was a confusion of cause and effect, according to Blyth (2013, pp 45–46), who says that 'some 35 per cent [of GDP] is the direct cost of bailing out the banks. ... To put it bluntly, the state plugged a gap and stopped a financial collapse. It did not dig a fiscal ditch through profligate spending.' Such nuances did not gain traction among the public or prevent the Conservatives' narrative of excessive spending becoming dominant (Kirkland, 2017). As the next chapter shows, Labour's inability to counter its critics' accusations of profligate spending were important in this regard.

Labour's ideology

The cornerstone of New Labour's rhetoric of economic competence was the implication that the party had moved away from the overloaded state of the 1970s. Tony Blair (2004, p v) argued that throughout the post-war period, voters 'never deserted Labour values, but sometimes doubted that the party could ever implement them'. In this respect, New Labour did not have to change drastically from the (ethical) socialism of the past, but through the language of competence placed greater emphasis on governance structures and their ability to deliver such ends. To achieve this, while still promoting a belief in the capacities of the state and public services, the party explored new means of funding such provisions.

As Chancellor of the Exchequer, Gordon Brown offered a new ideology to the role of the Treasury. Although a part of the Scottish Labour Party (traditionally seen as more left-wing than the English or national Labour Party) and having completed his PhD in Scottish history focusing on the socialist James Maxton, Brown also held a 'long-term interest in social democratic thought' and his ideology also drew on liberal thinkers such as Adam Smith. Brown exercised a more pragmatic approach, having never been a member of the left-wing group Campaign for Nuclear Disarmament, but a strong advocate of devolution (Beech and Hickson, 2007, pp 266–269; Griffiths, 2009, pp 54, 64).

In office, Gordon Brown advocated policies of prudence. He argued that all previous Labour governments entered office overburdened by spending commitments that were out of all proportion[to the fiscal health of the nation. Brown did not seek to reject the policies of previous governments outright, but in keeping with the tradition of New Labour argued that Labour had adopted '[n]ew economic approaches [that] have sought to learn from past errors'. Such approaches were rooted in the contemporary world, reinforcing the notion that contemporary economic policy should be guided not by ideology but by contemporary structures. The new approach '[was] designed to make sense of the new world of liberalised financial markets [and was] founded on the recognition that monetary and fiscal stability is the only sure foundation for growth' (Brown, 2001, p 31).

Brown (2001, p 32) argued that four lessons were central to this understanding. The first of these rejected assumptions of the 'Phillips curve', a key assumption of Keynesian economics, and acknowledged that as 'there is no long-term trade-off between inflation and unemployment, demand management alone cannot deliver high and stable levels of employment'. The second lesson was that economic rules could not assume 'a fixed relationship between money and inflation'. The third lesson emphasised the need for 'an institutional framework that commands market credibility and public trust'. And finally there was an acknowledgement that 'credibility depends on clearly defined long-term policy objectives, maximum openness and transparency, and clear and accountable divisions of responsibility' (Brown, 2001, p 31).

New Labour, however, did not wish to simply rip up existing understandings. Linked to Blair's understanding that voters supported the values of the post-war Labour Party, Brown (2001, p 30) acknowledged 'the high ideals and public purposes which ushered in the post war economic era' and praised economic institutions such as the IMF and World Bank. New Labour maintained traditional beliefs that the state could be used to mitigate some of the worst excesses of the market for those who benefited least from British capitalism. Policies such as the minimum wage were introduced and government spending increased every year from 1998. Although the state was not given free reign over the market. In aspects such as maximum wages or wage differentials Labour, prioritising notions of economic credibility, rejected notions of (or failed to correct) market failure(s). Brown, who according to Diamond (2004, p 226) 'redefine[d] Labour's "tax and spend" commitments prior to the 1997 general election', committed New Labour in office to fiscal rules, designed to combine a 'traditional focus on social redistribution' with the need to maintain Labour's economic credibility. Brown argued that the objectives of redistribution could be achieved through budget surpluses, brought about by financial stability and a growing economy. Brown readily acknowledged the limitations of state, or economic, socialism but wished to 'embrace the fundamental ideas of ethical socialism – including its emphasis on the need for society to act together on behalf of the individual, and to apply such ideas to the conditions of modern British society. Far from abandoning its past, Labour … returned to its traditional values' (Diamond, 2004, p 226).

Rather than portraying Labour's divisions as being between 'Old' and 'New' Labour, Diamond (2004) argues that a better understanding would differentiate between ideas of ethical and state socialism. The former does not see the capitalist market as necessarily opposing socialist goals of equality, and emphasises the ability of agents to improve their lives (for example through education), noting that this is not dependent on the state (Carter, 2003, p 7). Such understandings of ethical socialism allowed Brown to claim a historical link back to Tawney (see Chapter 2). Set against this are those, particularly on the left of the party, who advocate state socialism or an economic socialism derived from the work of Marx. Such views see the free market as opposed to the goals of socialism and emphasise the obstruction to socialism offered by existing market forces/structures. State socialism argues in favour of an expanded state – in the British context most predominantly through discourses surrounding nationalisation (see Chapters 3 and 4).

Gordon Brown, as Chancellor, advocated tougher regulation of financial markets (BBC News, 1998). He argued that this emphasis stemmed from the lessons of the Asian crisis of the late 1990s, yet he also admitted that the 2007/2008 global financial crisis occurred within 'a new and largely unregulated global financial system developed in the twenty years before the crisis' (Brown, 2010, p 78). This was a system where 'excessive financial remuneration was at the expense of the equity of capital that banks needed, we had created a wholly new economic phenomenon: capitalism without capital' (Brown, 2010, p 78).

Important in Brown's understanding of global structures is an implicit acknowledgement that New Labour, at least as much as Thatcherism or the economic policies of the previous Conservative governments, was complicit in the onset of the crisis. British governments had accepted light-touch regulation of the financial services industry, and sought to integrate this within global networks as it offered Britain a way out of the 'standard criticism[s] of post-war British economy policy' that Brown (2017, p 116) summarises as 'our economy was inflation-prone, slow growing and weighed down by unnecessarily high levels of unemployment, underinvestment poor infrastructure and hence, low productivity'.

In 1997, the financial and insurance sector contributed £118.5 billion (in 2019 prices) to the economy and represented 6.5 per cent of the total economy – figures that would rise to £189.6 billion and 8.8 per cent in

2007 (Hutton and Shalchi, 2021, p 5). By 2007, financial services accounted for 25 per cent of corporate tax revenues – money that New Labour used to fund 'ambitious programmes of welfare expenditure' (Hindmoor and McConnell, 2013, p 553).

Although the left criticised New Labour for rigidly following the path established by Thatcher and Major, this overlooks not only the structural importance of the financial services industry to the wider economy (not just in terms of the taxation revenue, but also in terms of employment and generating trade surpluses and foreign direct investment; see Hindmoor and McConnell, 2013, p 553), but also some of the institutional obstacles. One of these was the Treasury itself, an institution that was seen as obstructing the party in both the 1930s and 1960s (see Chapters 3 and 5). One of the first actions undertaken by Brown, alongside colleagues Ed Balls and Ed Miliband, was to change the style of working within the Treasury. According to Brown (2017, p 115), the way in which the Treasury worked in 1997 was 'unmanageable'. He set about reducing the number of people present at meetings. He also noted how he inherited a large office with a table so large that it was not conducive to conversation/discussion and took the 'first opportunity to move' offices to a smaller one down the corridor. These reforms reduced civil service access to Brown and emphasised junior members both within the Treasury but also within Brown's team, such as Balls and Miliband, both of whom were employed as special advisers. This led to tensions between Brown and the Permanent Secretary, Sir Terry Burns, who became 'semi-detached' from Brown. Burns had been responsible for many of the economic models introduced in the 1980s; however, 'Labour's men regarded the view implicit in these models that unemployment was a price worth paying for control of inflation as abhorrent, and they did not hold their tongue'. Burns resigned in June 1998 (Pym and Kocham, 1998, pp 204–206).

Brown's wider economic reforms were laid out in *Reforming Britain's Economic and Financial Policy*, which, according to its introduction, 'provides a comprehensive guide to the macroeconomic and certain key financial reforms implemented following the change of administration in May 1997'. The book starts by offering a critique of British macroeconomic policy over the past 30 years, following on from the critique of the relationship between inflation and unemployment outlined by Callaghan in 1976. It summarises two key lessons to be learnt from this period: first, that governments should 'adjust for the cycle and build in a margin for uncertainty'; and second, that they should 'set stable fiscal rules and clearly explain fiscal policy' (Balls and O'Donnell, 2002, pp 4, 22–23).

Brown sought to overcome these problems through employing a system of targets and rules. The first target was 'an underlying inflation rate – measured by the 12-month increase in the retail price index (RPI) excluding mortgage interest payments – of 2½ per cent'. And two rules: the 'Golden Rule', which stated that 'over the economic cycle the government will borrow only to invest and not to fund current spending'; and the 'sustainable investment rule', that 'over the economic cycle, public debt as a proportion of GDP will be held at a stable and prudent level'. The level of sustainable debt was defined as being under 40 per cent (Balls and O'Donnell, 2002, pp 71, 159, 167).

Although a measure of inequality, the Gini coefficient was higher at the onset of the crisis than it was in 1997 and the highest earners disproportionally increased their incomes over this time period; such trends were both global in nature and depressed by Labour's policies. Cribb (2013) notes that 'the changes made to the tax and benefit system under the Labour government between 1997–2010 meant that inequality was lower than it would have been under the system it inherited'.

Labour, under the ideology of the third way, pursued a scientific approach to understanding the economy. This differentiated the party not only from previous Labour governments (cf Wilson, 1964–1970) but also from public opinion, on a number of issues. For example, Brown's commitments to the 'Laffer curve', which posits that increasing the highest rates of tax leads to diminishing returns as there is less incentive to work/undertake economic activity and more incentives to pursue methods of tax avoidance, were, up until the crisis of 2007/2008, out of kilter with polling, which found that the level of public support for more taxation and spending was higher than for maintaining current levels (Vaitilngam, 2009).

New Labour, through the guise of the third way, acted more cautiously than previous Labour governments. It was keen to accommodate the capitalist structures inherited in 1997 and turned its back on the tax-and-spend plans associated with its predecessors. The party sought to reform 'rather than simply [fund] the existing welfare state, and eschewed any pretension to use taxation as a form of social levelling' (Coates, 2013, p 44). Over the period from 1997 to 2007, the British economy grew substantially; however, this growth was unequal and based on an easing of credit. Once this loosening tightened, Labour's electoral base was particularly exposed to rising unemployment and reductions in welfare provision and spending, necessitated by declining economic activity and falling tax revenue. According to Coates (2013, p 44), 'New Labour, far more than Old Labour, chose to ride the capitalist tiger without holding on to the reins even in the modest manner of its predecessors: in 2008 the tiger stumbled ... and in 2010 New Labour fell off'.

Labour's responses to the crisis

Rather than adopting an ideological approach, Labour was keen to demonstrate the scientific nature of its arguments. Drawing on the logic of 'there is no alternative', prevailing arguments of 'too big to fail' demonstrated – according to advocates – the need to bail out the banks. Alistair Darling's description of measures as 'temporary public ownership' was significant for two reasons. First, like the nationalisations of the Attlee administration, these were argued in terms of national importance and efficiency. The banks were 'too big too fail' and, like the industries nationalised after the Second World War, central to the contemporary growth model in the UK. Second, however, the nationalisation of banks was presented as a temporary measure – something that was born out of necessity rather than ideological grounds. Here this can be distinguished from earlier nationalisations, which were designed to help long-term planning. Private capital was not viewed as the problem, indeed the government actively sought private buyers to take over companies such as Northern Rock. Nor was the role of government, according to these narratives, to improve efficiency within these industries but simply to act as a safety net, preventing the collapse of the banking sector (and wider economy).

Darling (2012, pp 64–65) notes that neither he nor Gordon Brown wished to take Northern Rock into 'public ownership' as there existed 'the political difficulty of a Labour government nationalizing a bank'. Alongside the 'practical problem' of ensuring that decisions relating to loans did not become politicised, Darling notes that they were 'also conscious that Northern Rock shareholders would be ready to cry foul if we nationalized the bank without having established beyond doubt that there was no market solution'.

However, in contrast to Darling's assertions in 2008, the 2010 Labour manifesto (Labour Party, 2010) did describe the public ownership of Northern Rock as a 'nationalisation'. Although the manifesto was keen to stress the positive, progressive role of governments, it was also clear not to break with the prevailing economic orthodoxy. It maintained that the economy was best viewed through an individual lens, claiming that '[i]t isn't markets or governments that create wealth – people do, through their own effort and hard work'. It went on to promise reforms to the welfare system to 'end for good the concept of a life on benefits by offering all those unemployed for more than two years work they must accept' and guaranteeing 'that people will be better off in work than on benefit'.

Engelen et al (2011, p 189) compared the responses to the 2007/2008 crisis with previous economic crises in British politics and argued that politicians were happy to revert to technocratic or at least political independent voices. There were no scholars of thinkers such as Keynes or Beveridge to offer policies intellectual weighting. There were no expectations that: '(Andrew) Haldane [would] write Liberal or Labour party manifestos as Keynes or Tawney did, nor would we expect (Adair) Turner to write a report that sells more than 600,000 copies as the Beveridge Report of 1942 did. But the current complete disconnect between the technocrats and politics disempowers reforms.'

Brown (2010, prologue) argued that the decisions to recapitalise the banks represented not only the UK taking a different approach from the US or its European counterparts, but also was 'a government decision that turned the orthodoxy of the past thirty years on its head'. While the scale of bailouts was unique in a contemporary sense, it signified Labour's continued commitment to existing growth models, which was seen as the best means of providing economic growth that had enabled the party to increase public sector spending year on year from 1998/1999 (IFS, 2010).

In many respects, Brown's government had little room for manoeuvre. The crisis occurred after a prolonged period of economic growth, and assertions of Labour Chancellor Gordon Brown pronouncing the end of 'boom and bust'. Such rhetoric left the Labour Party, and in particular senior figures within the party, 'unprepared to acknowledge that, after 15 uninterrupted years of economic growth, it might be sensible to have some margin of error in its plans for the possibility of an economic downturn' (Dolphin, 2011, p 3).

However, one area in which Labour was able to challenge the status quo was through policies of quantitative easing. The government instructed the Bank of England to embark on £200 billion of quantitative easing in November 2009 (Bank of England, 2021), allowing the bank to purchase government bonds (debt). Former Monetary Policy Committee member, David Blanchflower (quoted in Partington, 2019), when reflecting on the crisis, argued: 'Two people saved the world. Bernanke saved the world on the monetary front and Gordon Brown on the fiscal front [by raising government spending to stimulate the economy].' Quantitative easing was required as the reduction in interest rates had failed to sufficiently stimulate the economy. Along with conventional economic thinking, interest rates were cut to stimulate money circulation (spending) and dissuade people from investing or saving money. However, there was only so far interest rates could go – between December 2007 and March 2009, the Bank of England cut interest rates from 5.75 per cent to just 0.5 per cent, leaving little room for further reductions (Kollewe, 2016).

Negative interest rates were applied in Sweden and Mervyn King suggested that the UK could follow suit in order to force banks to lend (Ward and Oakley, 2009). However, as a later Bank of England (2020) report focusing on the COVID-19 crisis of 2020 noted, negative interest rates could run the risk of both encouraging depositors to withdraw money from banks to store it 'under the mattress', further weakening banks' liquidity, while at the same time putting pressure on sterling. Such pressures encouraged the Bank of England to turn to quantitative easing. The initial £200 billion of quantitative easing was estimated to have increased GDP by between 1.5 and 2 per cent, enabling Britain to come out of its recession in mid-2009, while simultaneously increasing inflation by 0.75–1.5 per cent. This was the equivalent of a reduction in the 'Bank Rate of some 150–300 basis points' (McCafferty, 2017).

Quantitative easing, like the nationalisation of Northern Rock, was initially seen as a temporary or one-off event; it did not apply to normal policy times as building up large debts would further undo the economic credibility Labour had built up over the previous two decades. In many respects it was akin to Labour's wealth tax, which was proposed at end of the First World War (see Chapter 2) – designed for a particular purpose (alleviating the worst problems of a crisis), not to revolutionise the relationship between government and the private sector. It was designed very much within the wider context of economic credibility. It was designed 'as a short-term measure to support the economy through the global financial crisis', although it has since been incorporated into the macroeconomic tool kit, and since 2010 there have been a further five phases of quantitative easing, including within the COVID-19 crisis (Bank of England, 2021; House of Lords, 2021).

Throughout the global financial crisis, New Labour was keen to avoid associating itself with previous Labour governments, distinguishing its nationalisation and emphasising the time-limited nature of its Keynesian policies. Labour's goal throughout the crisis was not to pursue an ideological overhaul of the institutions of the capitalist state, but to strengthen the economic model that had produced high levels of growth over the previous two decades.

Labour's understanding of socialism

Brown (1999, pp 35–36) drew heavily on Crosland's understanding of socialism. He described Crosland's book *The Future of Socialism* as marking 'a decisive moment in the post war Labour history'. Brown argued that Crosland's legacy was threefold. First, 'he defined equality as the fundamental value that divides the Labour Party from the Conservative Party'. Second, Crosland, for Brown, offered a degree of pragmatism; he argued that Crosland emphasised values and in doing so understood that the socialist central focus should be on 'his or her essential values, not any particular method of achieving those values. Means may change from time to time, but essential objectives endure.' The third legacy, according to Brown, was that Crosland set out 'a socialist position that was both intellectually rigorous and practically credible for the world as it actually exists'.

Brown (1999, p 45), however, noted that some of the assumptions Crosland made – particularly regarding unemployment –were no longer applicable. He noted that when Crosland was first writing in the 1950s, commitments to full employment meant that the unemployment rate was around 1 per cent. Even in the 1970s, unemployment averaged 3 per cent but by the 1990s it was 5 per cent.

Brown's first act as Chancellor was to decentralise the Bank of England. The week of the election he informed Ed Balls that this decision would be taken the following week, rather than at an unspecified point in Labour's first term. This was, according to Brown, to maintain long-term stability. Although radical in its delivery, it overturned Labour's nationalisation of the Bank in 1946, although it was in keeping with the post-Thatcherite landscape/consensus that New Labour inherited, having been previously advocated by Conservative Chancellors Nigel Lawson and Norman Lamont. Brown (2017, pp 115–116) justified this decision as it would depoliticise the setting of interest rates, allowing these to be driven by long-term factors and not short-term considerations. This linked to wider notions of economic credibility; Brown (2017, p 117) continued, arguing that: 'By ... accepting operational independence of the Bank to decide interest rates, it would give both the public and the markets confidence that we had put in place a framework to ensure stability and keep inflation low.'

Labour's economic credibility was ensured partly from the fact that decisions were being taken away from elected politicians and directed to experts in the field. This increased stability within the markets, and subsequently made revolution or any paradigm shift more unlikely – the Bank of England was tasked with upholding the banking system in the UK, something that would appear at odds with introducing a new explicitly socialist system.

Labour, according to Gamble (2009, p 106), promoted the idea of a 'social investment state', only after it had enhanced its own economic credibility by giving the Bank of England autonomy and adhered to Conservative spending targets. Once credibility was assured, Labour was able to substantially increase public sector spending, allowing the party to win three successive general elections.

Drawing on ethical, rather than statist or economic, understandings of socialism allowed New Labour to advocate decoupling the state and the market. By doing so, Labour reduced both the scope, but also the need, of the state to introduce measures to overturn (or even correct) the market. Here policies such as granting independence to the Bank of England were in stark contrast to the ideas of those within the party who advocated state, or economic, socialism. It also challenged those looking at the party from the outside who expected Labour to extend the role, or functions, of the state. This was reflected in the following comment in *The Times* (quoted in Dellepiane-Avellaneda, 2013, p 263): 'The World has turned upside down. A Labour Government is elected and the new Chancellor's first move is to hand over control of macroeconomic policy to the Bank of England.'

The economic socialism of old – which required establishing alternative structures to the free market – could now not be imposed by the state alone (unless Labour was prepared to make a number of U-turns) as the power to do this had been diluted and in many instances ceded to institutions beyond the state's control. As long as the economy continued to grow (or at least not contract), New Labour under Blair and Brown were content to follow and promote their ethical understandings of socialism. This meant accepting inequalities of outcome so long as the absolute position of the poorest in society was improving. This was a continuation of Blair's understanding of the primacy of the equality of opportunity over the equality of outcome and linked to wider notions of individualism.

Blair and Brown were content to draw on the successes of the market economy. One key aspect of the third way discussed in the previous chapter was its attempt to reconcile traditional understandings of capitalism and socialism. Economic growth between 1997 and 2007 allowed New Labour to invest in projects that disproportionately benefited the poorest in society. However, in doing so they implicitly linked the capacities of the state to the fortunes of the market. Such measures left Labour ill-equipped to dramatically change direction following the 2007/2008 crisis, which upon becoming a crisis of the state required large-scale state intervention. The support and belief in the markets that had become economic orthodoxy over the previous 30 years appeared unmovable. Following the crisis, institutions of the state were mobilised to support the capitalist system. The Bank of England (although retaining its independence) emphasised its role as lender of last resort, and through the quantitative easing programme reinflated the economy.

Undoubtedly, allowing the economic system to collapse – which many argue would have resulted from a collapse of the banking system (see for instance Rawnsley, 2010) – would have regressive consequences. The rationale for adopting a more interventionist approach could therefore be defended on the basis of helping the poorest in society despite protecting large bank deposits (by propping up the banks as institutions the government implicitly protected deposits above the statutory allowance of £35,000 that was protected by law in 2007). Important here was that the language (or at least public discourse) of banking collapses centred on deposits – there was no mention of mortgages or loans being cancelled, although of course supporting the banks prevented such scenarios from occurring too.

One problem of failing to offer a new discourse permitting Labour to increase government involvement/spending was that existing economic orthodoxy suggested that all money borrowed needed to be repaid. Such orthodoxy came to the forefront during the coalition government's and later Conservative government's austerity agenda. Labour's failure to offer a defence of the Keynesian approach it undertook, or to create a new paradigm, left the party unable to effectively question or oppose the broader austerity agenda without being blamed for overspending.

Labour and the trade unions

Labour returned to government in 1997 following a period of 18 years of Conservative rule. During this time, many European parties that held institutional links with trade union movements had weakened them. Processes such as globalisation, economic restructuring and a reduction in the size of the traditional working class meant that the unions were no longer seen to be as important electorally and weakening these ties allowed social democratic parties to canvas middle-class voters (Quinn, 2010; see also the previous chapter).

In addition to these electoral considerations, renouncing the links with the unions was important in promoting the 'New' element in New Labour; Blair (1997) was keen to stress that the return of a Labour government would not mean the return to the scenes of industrial unrest in the 1970s. Amid rumours (dismissed by Blair as 'lies') of secretive deals between the Labour Party and the TUC, granting the unions greater power, Blair outlined in *The Times* that there would be 'no return' to the industrial relations of the 1970s and 1980s. Legislation surrounding secondary action and flying pickets would not be reversed and the requirement for secret ballots prior to strike action would remain. 'The changes that we do propose would leave British law the most restrictive on trade unions in the Western world. The scenes from Grunwick, Wapping or the miners' strike could no more happen under our proposals than under the existing laws.' Speaking about the wider relationship between the unions and the Labour Party, Blair was keen to dispel notions of union influence within the party, something that it had been accused of in the 1970s. Blair argued that the Labour Party had been 'transformed in structure and politics from those days. All MPs are now selected by a party membership which has doubled in the past three years. There are no small committees or pressure groups in charge. Those days are gone.'

The redrafting of Clause IV shifted emphasis on the relationship between the party and the trade unions. 'New Labour promised to give the trade unions "fairness, not favours"' (Moran, Johal and Williams, 2010). If Thatcher's reforms of the 1980s were a response to what was framed as the trade union crisis of the 1970s (see Kirkland, 2017), then Labour, upon returning to office, did little to reverse the relationship between organised labour, capital and the government/state.

This led to increased pessimism among some commentators. Ludlam's (2001, p 129) prediction that the '100 year-old labour alliance, in its historic, constitutionally united form, is unlikely to last long into its second century' was not atypical. Although such a prediction is yet to materialise (and in some respects these trends were reversed in the 2010s – see the next chapter), there was a clear trend, which can be seen as a continuation/legacy of the crisis in 1970s. However, this is not to say that there were not periods of agreement between the parties; while Labour did not overturn many of the Conservative policies 'restricting union core activities, Labour passed legislation supporting innovative union practices' (Coderre-LaPalme and Greer, 2018, p 265).

One reason preventing the severing of ties between the unions and the Labour Party was the latter's reliance on the financing of the former. This strengthened the union position within the party. The unions' alienation within the party and their 'inability to influence policy led them temporarily to reduce funding, as exchange models would predict, but in contradiction to the conventional wisdom among academic observers of the Labour Party' (Quinn, 2010, p 358).

The so-called Warwick agreement of 2004 provided a 're-linkage' between the party and the trade unions. It enabled the unions to exchange donations for policy pledges and offered 'Labour stronger incentives to honour its promises and the unions an incentive to continue supplying funds' (Quinn, 2010, p 358). The set of policies was explicitly mentioned in Labour's 2005 manifesto (Labour Party, 2005), which stated that this amounted to 'an agreed set of policies for the workplace'.

This agreement, however, was set firmly within the backdrop of a monetarist understanding of the economy; the Labour Party continued with the economic orthodoxies it inherited, including accepting the primacy of inflation, rather than unemployment, as the key macroeconomic indicator. Unemployment – or rises in unemployment – inevitably weaken trade unions that derive their members from those who are employed. Unemployment stood at 7.07 per cent in 1997 before falling for four years in succession. UK unemployment troughed at 4.59 per cent in 2004 before rising to 5.26 per cent in 2007 but by 2011 the figure had risen to 8.04 per cent (World Bank, 2021).

The UK labour market following the global financial crisis recovered quicker than in previous crises, and increases in unemployment were lower than first feared, although effects were felt unequally across different sectors of the population (for example younger workers). Such, relative, indicators meant that the UK government avoided some of the problems seen in the US and elsewhere. It also meant that the commitments to existing orthodoxies remained largely intact as the UK 'did not introduce a major countercyclical package of discretionary fiscal measures. And unlike countries such as Germany, it did not bring forward labour market policies specifically designed to moderate the effects of the recession on the labour market' (Bell and Blanchflower, 2014, p R3).

In many respects, Labour's approach to unemployment was to try to resolve the issue within the existing paradigm or framework. Trade unions that had been marginalised under Blair, to the point of 'impotence' (Morgan, 2004, p 47), were not included in debates over reshaping policy or able to engage in such debates. Labour's responses to the crisis were arguably more significant for trade unionists than the crisis itself. Unemployment during the crisis 'increased only slightly and was half a decade later almost back at pre-crisis levels'. However, the austerity measures undertaken by the coalition government saw a 10 per cent decrease in public sector employment. Public sector unions, which had suffered long-term declines in membership, were increasingly unable to stop outsourcing and staff reductions (Schmidt, Muller, Ramos-Vielba, Thornqvist and Thornqvist, 2019, p 138).

Where debates about wages, or wage inequality, did exist, they were confined to the excessive amounts of money certain agents, such as Fred Goodwin (chief executive at RBS at the time of its collapse) were paid (Kirkland, 2017). Although Labour had, in 1997, at least implicitly, acknowledged that the free market was unable to effectively distribute income through its implementation of a minimum wage, there was no appetite to explore further inequalities or desire to impose a corresponding maximum wage, or support for such measures. New Labour did not want to be seen as anti-wealth; the same reasons underpinned Gordon Brown's initial reluctance to increase the top rate of taxation above 40 per cent.

Conclusion

Although defining itself as 'New Labour', once in government Blair and Brown demonstrated significant continuity with previous Labour governments. As the previous chapter highlighted, the transition from Labour to New Labour helped the party to overcome the legacy of the governments of the 1970s and make some important changes to the organisation of the party; for example over OMOV and Clause IV.

Blair and Brown drew on links with previous traditions and understandings and developed their understanding of socialism from the ethical tradition within the party. This enabled them in government to utilise the free market to achieve the ultimate aim of greater equality.

The 2007/2008 crisis, however, demonstrated the limitations of this approach. The response to the crisis rested on extending the powers of the state – for example, instructing the Bank of England to embark on quantitative easing measures. Labour's continued defence of the capitalist model – for instance, Brown's 'scientific' assertions relating to the 'end of boom and bust' – left it unable to convincingly shift the discourse away from notions of a spending crisis, which in turn allowed opponents to link the policies of the government back to those associated with Old Labour.

Upon the realisation of the potential effects of the crisis, the government opted to nationalise the costs of the crisis, bailing out financial institutions and offering liquidity to other banks. Just as in 1931, the party opted to defend the existing economic model and institutions, in part due to its rhetoric over the previous decade, but also in part due to a lack of established alternatives. Just as previous governments, New Labour saw (its version of ethical) socialism as stemming from strong economic foundations – the use of tax receipts to fund social spending was testimony to this. The role of government, once the effects of the crisis became apparent, was not to set about establishing new frameworks (although these could be erected later under the guise of protecting depositors etcetera) but rather to ensure that the day-to-day running of the economy and people's lives were not disrupted. Brown's slip in the House of Commons where he argued that the actions of his government 'had saved the world' (before correcting himself to state that the government had 'worked with other countries to save the world's banking system') reflected this lack of desire to create or impose a new economic model, at least in the short term (Duckworth, 2008).

8

Electoral Revision

Introduction

Electoral defeats force political parties to consider their policy programmes. Rejection by the electorate raises questions about the viability of such programmes and can lead to calls for changes in either policy or leadership (between 1992 and 2019, Jeremy Corbyn was the only leader of either the Labour Party or the Conservative Party to remain in post after failing to form a government after an election). It can also lead to tensions between diverse groups within the party.

The elections of Ed Miliband in 2010 and Jeremy Corbyn in 2015 both pitted the PLP against other branches of the broad Labour Party. Miliband relied on the trade unions to overcome his brother in the leadership ballot (Jobson and Wickham-Jones, 2011) and Corbyn, having relied on nominations from parliamentary colleagues who had no intention of voting for him to even appear on the ballot (see for instance BBC News, 2015), owed his position to party members and registered supporters, who were typically more left-wing than Labour MPs. Corbyn was also supported by Momentum, a group not formally affiliated to the Labour Party but established following his decision to stand for Labour leadership. Despite the differences in the formation of the two groups, Momentum was likened to the 'extremist' Militant Tendency of the 1970s and 1980s, and moderates argued that it represented 'a party within a party', and was encouraging Corbyn to move the party away from the centre ground of British politics (Roe-Crines, 2016; Denis, 2020). Many Labour MPs who had former experience in either government or shadow government refused to serve under Corbyn (Goes, 2018, p 61). This tension was further borne out in 2016 when Owen Smith – unsuccessfully – launched a leadership bid against Corbyn (Watts and Bale, 2019).

Throughout this period, the Labour Party struggled to form an electoral coalition in the wake of the 2007/2008 economic crisis, its election defeat in 2010 and the Conservative-led coalition government's policies of austerity. Questions over the role and nature of government debt, state spending capacities and globalisation contributed to the party's defeats in 2010 and 2015.

Additional tensions were seen in terms of the changing electoral support offered to the Labour Party, and divisions over Brexit. Corbyn's premiership challenged the pro-European policies established by Kinnock and Blair, and continued under New Labour. The Brexit referendum, and in particular the closeness of the decision to leave the EU, highlighted divisions between Corbyn, who traditionally held anti-European positions, and the pro-European stance of much of the PLP. The debates surrounding Brexit further highlighted questions over the role of Parliament, especially in relation to what the right-wing media defined as the blocking of legislation aimed at implementing the 'will of the people'.

This chapter ends with the 2019 general election and Corbyn's announcement that he would resign as leader of the Labour Party in 2020. It therefore differs from other chapters, since it ends before the party had fully formulated its resolution to the crisis described.

(More) wilderness years

In reporting the 2010 election night, Kavanagh and Cowley (2010, pp 192–202) highlight the initial optimism within Labour's ranks. The first results in Sunderland all returned Labour MPs – as expected – and offered little evidence of a Liberal Democrat surge. Two large swings to the Conservatives in Houghton and Sunderland South and Washington and Sunderland West, if replicated elsewhere, would have produced a Conservative majority; however, the swing of just 4.8 per cent in Sunderland Central suggested that 'Labour may be able to hold off the Conservatives where it mattered'. In Scotland, Brown's own majority increased by 6.4 per cent compared with 2005, Labour regained Glasgow East – a seat it had lost to the Scottish National Party (SNP) in a by-election in 2008 – and held off a challenge by the Liberal Democrats in Edinburgh South by 316 votes. During his journey back to London, Brown spoke about his plans to remain as Prime Minister, buoyed by the fact that Labour retained Rochdale – home of Gillian Duffy and the scene for 'biogate', where Brown was recorded describing a lifelong Labour member as a bigoted woman following a discussion surrounding immigration (Kavanagh and Cowley, 2010, pp 173–5). London also retained enough Labour MPs to ensure that the Conservatives would be denied a majority – Labour held the seats of Westminster North and Hammersmith against Conservative 'A-list' candidates, including future London mayoral candidate, Shaun Bailey.

Although Labour suffered an electoral defeat in 2010, it had reasons to be optimistic about the decade ahead. Despite the 2007/2008 crisis, the

Conservatives were unable to form a majority government, gaining just 4 per cent from 2005, and had to rely on the support of Liberal Democrat MPs (Dunleavy, 2010). Many Labour members had feared a far worse election result (Fielding, 2010). They also felt that the coalition government would be unpopular with a public that was seen to be supportive of Britain's 'winner takes all' electoral system. This feeling was confirmed by a 2011 referendum, offered as part of Conservatives' concessions to their coalition partners, which rejected changing the electoral system from a 'first past the post' system to the more proportional 'alternative vote' system. Labour also believed that austerity would demonstrate that the Conservative Party had not – despite the rhetoric of its new leader and now Prime Minister, David Cameron – significantly changed since the 1980s.

Defeat in 2015 was significantly different from that of 2010. Despite Labour's optimism throughout the coalition government, Cameron became the first 'Prime Minister since Margaret Thatcher in 1983 to increase the party's number of Conservative MPs from one election to the next and the first Tory PM since Anthony Eden in 1955 to increase the party's share of the vote'. Furthermore, anticipated boundary reforms suggested that Labour would need 'a swing as big as those achieved by Herbert Asquith in 1906 and Clement Attlee in 1945 to win an overall majority next time around' (Bale and Webb, 2015, pp 41–42).

Electoral defeats in 2010 and 2015 saw the party needing to build a new electoral coalition. Just as in the 1980s, it needed to broaden its appeal. The party's return of just 30.4 per cent (down 5 per cent on 2010) in 2015 was compounded by the fact that support seemed to be shifting away in traditional seats. Although it 'increased its majorities in London seats and in university towns, the party was under pressure from UKIP in the Midlands and the North East of England and lost all its seats but one in Scotland'. Developing policies to appeal across such varied groups 'would not be an easy task' (Goes, 2018, p 60).

As in 1955 and 1979, defeat in 2015 encouraged the Labour Party to adapt and change. The optimism of a quick return to government that existed after 1951 or 2010 had evaporated. Following Miliband's resignation after the election, the debate about party ideology transcended beyond the leadership to the broader party. The MPs tasked with nominating candidates spoke of the need to offer a plurality of views to the membership. In practice this allowed the left-wing candidate Jeremy Corbyn to be included on the ballot paper after he received the bare minimum of parliamentary nominations. Much to the surprise of his colleagues, he won the election, owing most of his support to registered supporters, a new category in the electorate, designed to make leadership elections more inclusive. This reversed the assumptions about broadening Labour's democratic processes that were made in previous decades, when groups such as the Campaign for Labour Victory argued that a wider franchise would lead to more moderate outcomes. It also led to a tension between different sections of the electorate, with some MPs asking whether such supporters shared the aims and values of the Labour Party (Wintour, 2015b).

Corbyn's perceived unpopularity with the wider electorate was a motivation for the decision of new Conservative Prime Minister, Theresa May, who had replaced Cameron following the Brexit referendum, to call an early election on 8 June 2017. May's assumptions of obtaining a large majority were not unfounded. Labour lost the Copeland by-election in February 2017 – the first government gain in a by-election election since 1982 – and narrowly held the previously safe seat of Stoke on Trent Central. 'In May, the party lost 382 seats at the local elections while the Conservatives managed the rare feat for a party of government of winning 563 new seats' (Goes, 2018, p 63). Opinion polls at the start of the campaign gave the Conservatives leads of up to 20 per cent.

Yet the 2017 election was seen as a success for Corbyn, who was able to recover ground throughout the campaign. Despite losing the election, Labour polled 40 per cent of the vote – a higher percentage than any party had achieved since Blair in 2001. Labour's increase in the vote share between 2015 and 2017 was the largest since 1945. Corbyn was able to turn a Conservative majority government into a minority one, reliant on a confidence and supply agreement with the Democratic Unionist Party (DUP) (Byrne, 2019, p 251). Labour's gains were seats that the party would normally only win if it was winning the election.

> Bellwether constituencies like Enfield Southgate, Warwick and Leamington, Reading East, Ipswich and Peterborough, went Labour. Mountainous SNP majorities fell. Supposed London marginals such as Ealing Central, Tooting and Hampstead and Kilburn became safe seats. Canterbury, having been Conservative since the Great War, was won by Labour. Kensington, including the richest residents in the country, was swallowed in a vengeful blood-red wave across London as its forgotten working-class constituencies took revenge on an atrocious Tory MP. (Seymour, 2017, p x)

Labour managed to form an electoral coalition in 2017 by arguing against the proposals set out by the Conservative government while simultaneously convincing enough Brexit supporters that it was at least as committed to the notion of Brexit as the Conservative Party. As with his internal leadership campaign, Corbyn also managed to attract 'radical' voters of various persuasions to associate with Labour. By doing so, he managed to polarise support on the two main parties.

The relative success of an electoral approach that looked to radicals and the left, instead of the centre ground, could be seen as shifting the goal posts by both Labour and Conservative supporters, to the extent that 'arguments the Tories thought they had won over the free market and the role of the state were suddenly contested again' (Hannah, 2018, p 241). However, it did not remove the fears of some on the left that more radical measures would still be needed. Hannah argues that the 'socialist left' were unable to use existing institutions to make progress and criticised Corbyn's project of 'moderate tax and spend proposals with the hope that the economy doesn't crash upon the arrival of a left government'. Hannah offers a cautious reading of the left's success even with Corbyn in power, arguing that if 'there is capital flight, currency speculation or establishment resistance to left policies, then Labour will be faced with a challenge it has rarely taken on before in directly confronting the power of capitalism'.

Polarisation at the 2017 election was also aided by the relative collapse of UKIP, whose primary focus was to advocate withdrawal from the EU. UKIP fought just 378 constituencies, having fought 614 two years earlier, when it gained 12.6 per cent. Its decline left other parties – including the Conservatives and Labour – to compete for UKIP's 3.8 million Euro-sceptic votes. Curtice, Fisher, Ford and English (2018, pp 450, 453) demonstrate that Labour's gains in areas that had the highest percentage of Leave voters in 2016 (60 per cent+) were 1.6 per cent points lower than the corresponding Conservative gains. Incumbent Labour MPs were able to hold off a Conservative challenge in a number of seats due to the large majorities they were defending, but an important trend was emerging.

Labour gained seats such as Canterbury (for the first time ever), Sheffield Hallam (defeating former Deputy Prime Minister and Liberal Democrat leader, Nick Clegg) and Peterborough (for the first time since 2001), suggesting it was appealing beyond traditional voters. Although Labour's gains in 2017 were more numerous than its losses the party lost seats to the Conservatives in its traditional heartlands, suggesting a weakening of ties with its traditional base. Conservatives gained Copeland (which had been a Labour seat from 1983 until the by-election in 2017), Mansfield (Labour held since 1923), Middlesbrough South and Cleveland East (held since its interception in 1997) and Walsall North (which the Conservatives had only held previously between 1976 and 1979 and Labour had won at every general election since 1955) (Cowley and Kavanagh, 2018, p 528).

Such trends were to continue at the 2019 election, where Labour lost many seats in the so-called 'Red Wall', a stretch of seats spanning the breadth of England (and parts of Wales) in traditional working-class areas of the North and Midlands, such as Bolsover, Bury North, Darlington, Great Grimsby, Lincoln, Wolverhampton North East and Wrexham, leading to Labour's worst polling since 1935 (Mitchell and Jump, 2020). Goes (2020, pp 85–87) highlights two factors in understanding Labour's dramatic electoral decline from 2017 to 2019. The first was 'Labour's anti-Semitism crisis', in particular the failure of the party to adopt the International Holocaust Remembrance Alliance's definition of anti-Semitism into the party's code. The second was a failure to develop a more succinct Brexit position following the 2017 general election.

The 2016 Brexit referendum

The Brexit referendum, like the 1975 referendum on membership of the-then European Economic Community (EEC), was not fought along party lines. On both occasions, coalitions representing pro- and anti-European integration were formed comprising of senior politicians (and others) from across the left–right spectrum. However, unlike 1975, when such membership was relatively new, the 2016 result challenged a deeply engrained status quo. The issue of how Brexit could be implemented produced enduring divisions both between and within the political parties.

The 2016 result reflected wider social changes. Much literature on referendums demonstrates that they are often used by voters, not only as a means of having a say on a specific policy area, but also as a protest against the incumbent government. Franklin, van der Eijk and Marsh (1994) make this point regarding previous referendums on European integration/policy. Ed Miliband (2017, p 8) argued that a belief that the referendum was simply about the issue of European integration was to 'misunderstand Brexit fundamentally'. For Miliband, the referendum offered voters the chance to vote on wider (domestic) policy issues. Economic factors as much as political ideas were responsible for encouraging people to vote the way they did. 'Brexit was, in the words of my constituents, a vote for "a new beginning for my grandchildren", "a chance to get industry back", "a future for young people", or simply "worth a try".'

The Brexit vote highlighted the fact that feelings of being left behind were no longer confined to economic understandings. Rather, they symbolised dividing lines in terms of identity politics. The class system that was highlighted as being in decline in the 1980s continued to decline into the 21st century. Labour's success in the elections of 1997, 2001 and 2005 helped to overshadow these gradual changes. Sobolewska and Ford (2020, p 21) note that there was nothing unusual about these changes per se, but the continuation of macroeconomic policy between Thatcherism and New Labour meant they were not picked up until 2016.

The authors note that societal changes are often gradual and only become apparent when highlighted by a 'watershed moment'. The result of the referendum provided such a moment. 'What people saw in the wake of the "Leave" victory was a land suddenly divided, at odds with itself and locked into intractable conflicts: Brexitland. But the divides Brexit exposed were not new. They had been building in the electorate for years.' Such changes were a result of the expansion of university education beyond the 'preserve of a privileged minority' and 'mass migration' particularly beyond Britain's largest cities, both of which helped drive a 'slow but relentless transformation of the electorate, with the youngest generations dramatically more highly qualified and ethnically diverse than the oldest' (Sobolewska and Ford, 2020, p 22).

These new dividing lines cut across Labour's traditional base; Labour's support for multiculturalism and immigration was received very differently outside of the largest urban areas and the increase in the number of university graduates signified a shift in economic opportunities away from older voters who had not had the opportunity of a university education. Sobolewska and Ford (2020, p 22) highlight this divide in terms of ethnocentrism, which is defined as the 'view of things in which one's own group is the centre of everything'. The authors outline the two sides of the debate, based on their identities. The first are 'identity conservatives', 'white voters with lower levels of formal education who most frequently hold ethnocentric worldviews, making them more strongly attached to in-group identities like national identity and more threatened by out-groups such as migrants and minorities'. Juxtaposed against this group are 'identity liberals', who are graduates and people from minority ethnic communities who share a rejection of ethnocentrism. Sobolewska and Ford argue that the tensions between these groups 'runs right through the heart of the electorate' and can be seen as a 'major source of the political upheavals and volatility of the past decade'.

This division was particularly serious for Labour, whose coalition of traditional blue-collar workers and liberal, university-educated middle-class voters saw the debate very differently. Labour's commitment to globalisation and a clear pro-European stance, developed under New Labour, not only helped expose Britain to the economic crisis of 2008 but also led to a feeling of exclusion in areas of traditional support. People with such feelings associated integration with a sense of loss of control or ability to change things. Voters who had lost (or perceived themselves to have lost) out from policies of neoliberalism expressed various feelings of 'anger, resentment, discontent and hope, of feeling left behind or left out. These feelings were engendered by, or responding to, decades of growing injustice and inequality' (Cromby, 2018, p 59). The referendum offered voters the first opportunity in a generation to express these concerns explicitly.

Labour's voters in 2016 expressed a clear divergence from the party itself, leaving many pro-EU MPs with large 'Leave' majorities within their constituencies. As the issue of Brexit became increasingly salient, the party's pro-European stance became an increasing liability for the party, which had linked globalisation and neoliberalism to notions of economic credibility. If Labour was (seen to be) less than whole-hearted in implementing the result, it risked further alienating traditional voters, overlooking not only their economic needs/desires but also their political ones.

Brexit thus became a key test of Corbyn's new programme. Prior to the referendum, the issue of Europe was seen as the most important issue facing the country by just 1 per cent of respondents to an Ipsos MORI poll, and debates were confined to traditional Eurosceptics. However, following the referendum, the salience of Britain's relationship with the EU increased dramatically, with 59 per cent of respondents to the same question in April 2019 regarding it as the most important issue (Richards, 2019).

Labour's lack of presence in the EU referendum, partly due to the tensions between Corbyn and others within the PLP (see Cushion and Lewis, 2016) left it on the back foot once the results were declared. The party had offered lukewarm support to the Remain campaign, yet as analysis of the results materialised it became clear that a significant proportion of Labour's working-class voters in northern towns and cities had voted to leave the EU. This created an electoral dilemma: how to appeal to middle-class Remain voters (who were needed to win a majority of seats in a future Westminster election) while at the same time carrying the support of working-class pro-Brexit voters.

As the issue of Brexit gained prominence, Corbyn and the wider Labour Party could no longer simply be united by anti-austerity narratives/arguments. Brexit replaced austerity as the focal point for British politics and thus highlighted tensions between Corbyn and the PLP. To many voters, Labour's policy post-referendum was no clearer than it had been before. Some senior figures supported calls for a 'people's vote' before Brexit was implemented, while, in Parliament, the party was presented by opponents as obstructing Brexit by refusing to support successive governmental proposals/legislation.

The election of Boris Johnson as Conservative leader in 2019 intensified Labour's problem. Johnson, a prominent figure in the Leave campaign, replaced Theresa May who had offered limited support for a 'Remain' vote throughout the campaign. In relation to the December 2019 general election, Johnson's election slogan of 'Get Brexit done' showed a new decisiveness within the Conservative Party that appealed particularly to those who felt frustrated by the lack of commitment to the referendum result, establishing a clearer distinction between the two main political parties. Rayson (2020, p 236) quotes one former teacher and first-time Conservative teacher in Bolsover:

It is no surprise that so many of us held our noses and voted conservative ... I voted for them because of reasonable certainty over Brexit; rejection of unpatriotic left-wing politics and anti-Semitism. I want Brexit complete and a recognition of the views on the working class;

a reinvigoration of the economy outside the metropolitan areas and an improvement in our standing in the world.

Labour's failure to enthusiastically support Brexit was linked to wider questions over who the party now represented – especially in Red Wall seats, although, as Rayson (2020) notes, focusing on Brexit hides longer-term structural changes. Support for Labour had declined for several reasons prior to the Brexit referendum. Once the preserve of economic understandings, notions of 'the left behind' became synonymous with border ideas and ideologies. While one part of this was economic – those who, for a variety of reasons, were unable to benefit from globalisation – a core component was about identity. Rayson (2020, p 234) quotes Labour MP for Leigh, Jo Platt, who advised colleagues 'our party is viewed as entitled and elitist because key figures within the party are entitled and have expressed their "we know best" attitude for far too long'.

The party's commitment to offering a path for remaining in the EU broadened its appeal to middle-class voters and university graduates at the expense of working-class communities. This decline challenged traditional economic understandings – something that the party's anti-austerity agenda alone was insufficient in responding to. Brexit had demonstrated that people were willing to prioritise non-economic factors over economic ones. The Remain campaign was criticised for focusing too heavily on the economic impact of Brexit (particularly among voters who had little to lose) and ignoring wider questions and divisions over identity.

Labour's ideology

Labour's vote between 2005 and 2015 fractured across the political spectrum, from other left-wing parties such as the Greens to the right-wing UKIP. Two main ideological strands were developed under Ed Miliband to try to reverse this trend: 'Blue Labour', which stemmed from the work of Maurice Glasman; and the ideology stemming from *The Purple Book* (Philpot, 2011a), which Beech and Hickson (2014) label 'Purple Labour'.

Glasman (2010) argues that Labour's traditions are rooted in Aristotelian notions of the good life and a tradition of the 'rights of freeborn Englishmen' stemming from resistance to the Norman Conquest of 1066. Commitments to natural law from part of Britain's political history and institutions such as Parliament and the church were used to 'constrain the domination of the monarchy'. At the turn of the 20th century, Labour was founded as a marriage between working-class groups of the trade unions, the cooperative movement and the 'building society and mutuals ... built ... out of the materials available to hand' and the middle-class institutions of the Fabian Society, Hyndman's Social Democratic Federation, the Anglican Church and 'the strong tradition of ruling-class public service and the architects, scientists and writers who were deeply connected to the development of the labour movement and developed ambitious plans for government'.

Glasman (2010) sees 1945 as a defining point in Labour's history, but rather than see it as the success that most – including many within the New Labour tradition do – he sees it as a 'rupture' that 'was the trigger for [Labour's] long-term decline'. For Glasman (2010, p 29) following this victory:

> In the name of abstract justice, the movement was sacrificed. The democratic responsibility and practice that formed the labour movement, and that had built up over a hundred years, was severed from the idea of the Common Good and left without a role. This has intensified over the last fifty years. The trade unions became antagonistic forces within the economy, nationalisation placed managerial prerogative as the fundamental principle of organisation, and universal benefit replaced mutual responsibility as the basic principle of welfare.

Glasman (2011, p 31) extends this understanding, noting that 'Labour's commitment to the state as the exclusive instrument of economic regulation had to fail. It was too blunt, too big, too small, and generally inappropriate'. For Blue Labour the answer lay in giving greater autonomy to citizens and promoting a much more local democratic system of cooperation and mutuality.

Lawrence (2013, p 11) criticised Glasman and Blue Labour for simplifying the history of the Labour Party, in particular through ignoring the role of liberalism within its creation, and overlooking Labour's inability to form an electoral coalition capable of winning an election until 1945. Lawrence argues that Labour's victory in 1945 owed much to the wartime propaganda surrounding notions of the 'people's war'. Labour used this to 'construct a political appeal which was explicitly inclusive and national, yet placed the eradication of poverty and its evils centre stage'. The party did this, not through explicitly socialist claims, but by invoking notions of '"security" rather than "welfare" when they spoke about social reform, and placed great emphasis on the importance of universal rather than means-tested benefits and services'.

Economically, Blue Labour was influenced by Karl Polanyi's critiques of the marketisation of social realities. This saw a 'a fundamental contradiction between ethical community and the market; the latter commodifies life, labour and nature, pulling things out of the particular, communal contexts within which they have meaning or value and subordinating them to the abstract measure of price' (Finlayson, 2013, p 76).

Davis (2015, p 197) argues that Labour has a 'conservative tradition' although she notes that this is not a term that the party likes to use. Blue

Labour, according to Davis, 'reminds us that our history is more radical and more conservative than anything many of us want to imagine'. Blue Labour links to Miliband's core theme of responsibility and the arguments of Rachel Reeves (who served as Shadow Secretary of State for Work and Pensions and Shadow Chief Secretary to the Treasury between 2010 and 2015) surrounding fiscal discipline. Davis argues that the last Labour government saw the potential for using growth within the City of London to fund public services, but failed to think 'enough about how dependent this left us on the banks'. Once the bubble burst, as it did in 2007, there was little safeguarding for the state or public finances. 'Failing to challenge the market was one reason why the last Labour government put so much emphasis on the state ... when you can't challenge free market orthodoxy, the state becomes your only lever for change, so you overuse it.'

Davis (2015, p 198) and Blue Labour argued that Labour should achieve social aims by reforming the supply side of the economy, rather than increase spending on the demand side. This offered a new understanding of Labour's policies: advocating prudence, reducing waste and noting that the party thought too much about public sector workers at the expense of 'brothers and sisters in the private sector' but seeks to combine these with an 'alternative that the Conservative Party can't understand' – a living wage, an end to corporate monopolies and 'growth that delivers increased wages as well as increased profits'.

In contrast, Purple Labour, named after *The Purple Book* (Philpot, 2011a) published by the Blairite Progress think-tank, focused on how Labour could build a winning coalition within the electorate. Purple Labour aimed to 'revive Labour's decentralising tradition of participation, self-government and "moral reform"' (Philpot, 2011b, pp 11, 12). Purple Labour drew inspiration from social democratic revisionists, arguing that without revisionism 'the Labour Party would have clung to outdated policies and [been] weighed down by dusty ideology. It would be a political sect, not a governing party.'

Both blue and purple iterations saw a common problem: namely how can Labour build a new coalition of voters? Both saw New Labour as their starting base for this. Blue Labour attempted to offer a socially conservative but economically left-leaning agenda, but two controversies surrounding Glasman, who suggested opening dialogue with the supporters of the far-right English Defence League (EDL) and advocated a temporary suspension to immigration, discredited the ideas behind Blue Labour (Beech and Hickson, 2014, p 80) and prompted a shift in emphasis. Purple Labour argued that the starting point for the revival could not be 1994 but had to be 2011. Philpot (2011b) argues that four aspects would be important in this revival. The first was a willingness 'to escape the "false choices around Labour's electoral strategy"', and presenting, typically northern, traditional working-class and new, principally southern, middle-class voters not as a binary choice but offering a programme that could appeal to both groups. The second was 'an honest account of New Labour's period in office and its lessons. Third, a willingness to confront the division within the left on the role of the state. And finally, the development of new policies – guided by the principle of redistributing power.'

Corbyn's election challenged the understanding of a non-statist approach to the economy, and the idea that the starting point for Labour's revival should be seen as 2011, instead focusing on the lessons of the 2007/2008 crisis. However, as Batrouni (2021, pp 123–127) notes, Shadow Chancellor, John McDonnell, rather than Corbyn, led on economic policy, offering solutions to questions such as: What would replace neoliberalism? This reflected a wider tradition within the Labour Party that leaders have often left economic understandings to those tasked with overseeing the economy (see Chapters 4 and 7). As in the case of the 1930s and 1950s, Labour looked beyond the party for scholars to offer 'intellectual weight' to what became known as Corbynomics, and 'enlisted celebrated economists Joseph Stiglitz and Thomas Piketty' (Crines, 2015). McDonnell created the Economic Advisory Committee including those thinkers as well as 'Mariana Mazzucato, Simon Wren-Lewis, Ann Pettifor and Danny Blanchflower'. This suggested that 'there would be no return to "Old" Labour ideas ... and [that] Corbynism drew on new ideas for a new century'. The new structure did not resolve differences between the economists and Labour's leadership; two members, Piketty and Blanchflower, resigned the following year, with the latter calling for Corbyn to quit (Batroini, 2021, pp 124–125).

McDonnell (2018) introduced the central ideas of Corbynomics in an edited collection *Economics for the Many*, with a critique of neoliberalism in the aftermath of the 2007/2008 crisis. McDonnell notes that the crisis dispelled the central notions of neoliberalism; that the market is the best possible means of organising the economy, that wealth would simply 'trickle down' and that the state should have a minimal role (if any) in moderating the will of the free market.

Wren-Lewis (2018, p 13) notes the existence of a large degree of consensus, even between Keynesians and monetarists, as both groups agreed that the booms and troughs of the economic cycle should be regulated, although importantly they differed on how this could best be achieved. For Wren-Lewis the 1980s ushered in a new consensus, where it was agreed that 'independent central banks should control inflation and aggregate demand by varying short-term interest rates [and] [g]overnments were charged with using fiscal policy to manage the amount of government debt'. Wren-Lewis (2018, pp 18–19) advocated modern macroeconomic theory, which has at its starting point a recognition that the UK has its own currency and central bank and the government is always able to 'fund spending by creating its own currency'. The government does not have to borrow from the markets, meaning that the markets have no power of veto over the size of the government's deficit.

Such understanding distinguishes the UK's economy from that of Eurozone members who suffered problems precisely because they did not have their own currencies or central banks from which they could borrow money. This linked to Corbyn's notion of using quantitative easing to fund social projects. However, this was not a licence to print money and there was still a recognition that doing so would increase inflation. Just as Gordon Brown deployed economic 'rules' to demonstrate Labour's economic credibility, the Economic Advisory Committee recommended a new Fiscal Credibility Rule, which offered a target for reducing the deficit, while containing a 'crucial "knockout"'. If interest rates hit their lower bound, or if the central bank says this is likely to happen, the goal of fiscal policy changes from meeting a deficit target to stimulating the economy.' The idea behind this is to avoid cutting and deepening any recession, even 'if this leads to an increase in government debt', which can be dealt with over the long term once the problems of recession have been conquered. This rule also avoids the mistake whereby 'dealing with the deficit stops you helping the recovery, and indeed can make a recession worse' (Wren-Lewis, 2018, p 17).

Ann Pettifor (2018, p 46), another member of the Economic Advisory Committee, contributed a chapter in McDonnell's book. She argues that the 2007/2008 crisis was not the only crisis that should feed into economic arguments/planning. This is linked to the 'knockout' in the Fiscal Credibility Rule as she also notes that overcoming the debt associated with 2007/2008 means not spending money elsewhere in the economy and could lead to wider problems. Pettifor argues in favour of a Green New Deal. She contends that traditional understandings that 'the expansion of economic growth can be, and is, limitless, [and] that it will move relentlessly in an upward trajectory' were irreconcilable with the environmental challenge/crisis. In order to rebalance the economy – and incorporate into economic planning the environmental issues that big businesses were apathetic towards – Pettifor (2018, pp 54–55) argues for a 'carbon-army' of skilled, well-paid workers that 'help substitute labour for carbon and that through [green] employment will generate income'. Such a change in emphasis offered by the Green New Deal will 'ensure a more stable, more sustainable economy – one that will generate the finance and income needed to transform the economy away from fossil fuels'. Important here is that Labour sought to question existing macroeconomic indicators, and argued that more emphasis should be placed on environmental issues. The crisis of 2007/2008 demonstrated the limitations of using existing measures such as GDP growth to assess the health of the UK economy.

Labour's responses to the crisis

Previous chapters have shown that, following large election defeats (1931, 1979), Labour has tended to embark on a period of recrimination. This encouraged the party to adopt a more ideological position – critiquing the previous government for not being socialist enough or not adhering rigidly to socialism. The election results of 2010 were not seen as a defeat that challenged the prevailing party's ideology on this scale.

In many respects, 2010 can be seen alongside 1951 – where Labour gained more votes (but not seats) than the Conservatives – and 1970. On both of these occasions the leader (Attlee and Wilson, respectively) remained in post, and the party believed that it would win the following election – which Wilson did in 1974. Although Miliband replaced Brown in 2010 he was careful not to drift too far from New Labour and keen to highlight its successes.

Miliband's leadership was not revisionist in the same way as Gaitskell's became in the late 1950s or Kinnock's in the 1980s. Certainly compared with Kinnock's there were no factions within the party that the leadership sought to remove or fundamental ideology to be replaced. Miliband's early leadership was 'something of a slow burner. He did not immediately put forward a clear vision for Labour' (Crines, 2014, p 189), meaning that he had to spend a significant amount of time responding to narratives of his leadership given by his political opponents, for example notions of 'Red Ed' or his likeness to Wallace from the cartoon Wallace and Gromit (Gaffney and Lahel, 2013; Crines, 2014). Indeed, Miliband's desire to break from New Labour was ambiguous; the 2015 manifesto 'hardly marked a fundamental departure from the 2010 government's policies'. Rather than explore the reasons for electoral defeat in 2010, Miliband's rhetoric 'provide[d] legitimacy for critics to attack the Blair/Brown legacy indiscriminately' (Diamond, 2021, p 332).

Miliband relied on scholars, London think-tanks and technocratic knowledge and language to appeal to voters. His economic policies rested upon attempts to challenge 'established thinking', but were still couched within the existing framework of repaying debts and existing understandings of the 2007/2008 financial crisis as one of debt/excessive spending; this was not meant to be utopian thinking. Such policies were designed within the expected financial constraints a future Labour government would face. Discussions were 'often prefaced with a "reforms for when there is less money around" or "big reforms, not big spending" type of caveat'. Such ideas reflected not only the legacy of the crisis but 'a particular perception about how voters and, crucially, relevant actors would react to them' (Goes, 2016, p 178). The expectation was that Labour could not shift the debate away from notions of spending and debt and therefore worked within such parameters rather than seek to develop a new paradigm/narrative.

Labour's inability to effectively counter the narrative that excessive spending led to the crisis limited its capacity to attack the coalition and later Conservative governments when they missed their spending reduction targets. Goes (2016, p 63) further notes that 'ultimately Labour reluctantly succumbed to the prevailing neoliberal views – on the grounds that it was the only way to regain economic credibility – by accepting public spending cuts as the only acceptable recipe to eliminate the public deficit and public debt'. As part of this need to regain economic credibility, Labour's 2015 manifesto (Labour Party, 2015) stated on its first page that: 'Every policy in this manifesto is paid for. Not one commitment requires additional borrowing. We are the first party to make that pledge and with this manifesto it is delivered.'

Defeat in the 2015 election, however, was viewed markedly different from 2010. Miliband, who had been the Secretary of State for Energy and Climate Change in Gordon Brown's government, continued to view the economy through the same lens as Brown following the 2007/2008 crisis and was weary of straying too far from New Labour's ideology. Defeat encouraged the party to reassess the legacy of New Labour and in particular the narratives surrounding the crisis.

Corbyn, unlike Miliband, was not tied to New Labour's period in office. He was not a member of the executive under New Labour, but instead a constant rebel. Corbyn was more willing to embrace new, ideological, approaches. Corbyn's 'central pitch' rested on a rejection of the 'overarching framework of austerity', freeing Labour from the criticisms of its role in the crisis of 2007/2008. Austerity was not accepted as being bound by scientific understanding of how the economy operates (or at least how it should operate) but understood as 'a political choice' (McDonnell, 2015). By utilising such discourse, Corbyn sought to shift the economic debate further than Miliband, principally through the idea of '[p]eople's quantitative easing' balanced against the idea of 'matching current expenditure with tax revenues, but continuing to borrow for capital expenditure' (Shipman, 2015). In doing so, Corbyn emulated what Thatcher and Blair were able to do – albeit without their electoral success – and offer his name to a distinctive (economic) ideology (Corbynomics).

These ideas did not reach the forefront of the party's 2017 and 2019 manifestos, both of which, as in 2015, were presented as being 'fully costed'. Although such claims were debated (see for example Lee, 2019; Rentoul, 2019), Labour's arguments remained couched in the same overarching framework as in 2010 and the more it emphasised such costings the less scope it had for rejecting the simplified links between overspending under New Labour and Britain's economic problems.

Although on the same scale as 1983 and 1935, the 2019 election defeat displayed some differences. The 2019 election was the third election since

2010, and the second Labour fought (and lost) under Corbyn. Both 1935 and 1983 can historically be viewed as turning points. They were seen as respective nadirs of Labour's fortunes in the periods 1931–1945 and 1979–1997. Although it is too early to confirm/refute such understandings of seeing 2019 in this vein, it is worth noting that it took Labour 14 years following 1983 to win an election, and ten years after 1935, a process sped up due to the (effects of the) Second World War.

Labour's understanding of socialism

Few argued that the crisis of 2007/2008 represented a fundamental change in the economy, leaving much of the discussion within the shadow of New Labour. As highlighted earlier, the 2010 election did not prove to be a conclusive defeat for the Labour Party, and some warned of departing too far from the successes of the New Labour project. The outcomes of the 2007/2008 crisis – in particular its redefinition as a debt crisis following the 2010 general election – did not generate a paradigm shift in British politics in the same way the 1980s did (Kirkland, 2017). The debates of the 2010s were fundamentally a continuation of the debates of 2008–2010; there was no Crosland nor at least a Crosland-like figure to argue that capitalism had transformed itself and the Labour Party needed to do so too. According to former Cabinet minister, Peter Hain (2015, p 77): 'Frankly, nothing fundamental changed after the crisis, except the stakes kept rising every year because the banks still acted irresponsibly. They continued speculating with other people's money, still practising casino banking.'

Miliband offered an apology for Labour's role in the financial crisis, but as *The Economist* and others argued, this was only half-hearted. Miliband's apology centred on the banking crisis and ignored/overlooked narratives of the debt crisis popularised by political opponents. The central claim of Miliband's argument, according to *The Economist*, was that the deficit alone was not the problem, and only became problematic when combined with the banking crisis, which required large government spending on bank bailouts and other interventionist policies. *The Economist* (2011) presented Miliband's rejection of notions of overspending as a clear misunderstanding of the economic cycle, akin to Brown's much-chastised prediction of 'no more boom and bust'. Here Miliband's argument was criticised for failing to accept and plan for downturns in the economy. *The Economist* claimed that such downturns are not things that can 'be transcended, [but] rather ... a cold reality that governments must make preparations and provisions for'.

Miliband criticised predatory capitalism and employed the rhetoric of transformational socialism, but ultimately his approach to economic policy was one of caution. Although the leader 'disavowed neo-liberalism, Labour's safety-first mindset still prevailed' (Diamond, 2021, p 337). While Miliband may have been keen to move on from New Labour's economic legacy, changing the party's emphasis on campaigning and electioneering, reverting to more ideological positions on key issues proved significantly harder.

Labour's association with blame for the 2007/2008 crisis offered the Conservatives an easy rebuttal when any of their own shortcomings were highlighted. Between 2010 and 2015, the Conservatives used terms such as 'deficit' and 'debt' interchangeably, for which David Cameron was publicly corrected by the chair of the UK Statistics Authority, Andrew Dilnot (*The Guardian*, 2013), missed deficit reduction targets, borrowed more than Labour's 'disastrously high targets' (Hain, 2015, p 320) and saw a downgrade of Britain's prized AAA credit rating – something Cameron and the Chancellor, George Osborne, had previously seen as a hallmark of a government's credibility (Treanor and Syal, 2013). Yet Labour was unable to capitalise on any of these events, which in turn had no significant long-lasting impact on their fortunes in the polls. Wintour (2015a) later noted that Miliband's failure to challenge the premise for the deficit meant that Labour lost control of the economic agenda, unable to effectively criticise Conservative austerity plans that were still seen/presented as being necessary or scientific. Wintour quotes one of Miliband's top advisers as saying: 'At the start of the parliament, we had an immediate challenge … The question was whether you confront the Tory spin that Labour had overspent, causing the crash, or whether you concede the point. But we neither confronted nor conceded.' Such plans to 'simply move on' backfired and left Labour unable to regain economic credibility or to shift the discourse away from the language of debts and deficits.

Corbyn was more content to be portrayed in ideological terms. He did not refute such accusations as Miliband had done, but (quoted by Panitch and Leys, 2020, p 218) defined Labour's 2017 manifesto as 'the programme of a modern, progressive socialist party that has rediscovered its roots and its purpose', although 'conflating Corbyn's own political philosophy with the party's tend[ed] to obscure the wider institutional framework involved in devising the party's policy platform'. Others argued that Labour's manifesto of 2017 did not share the same radicalism as its leader (see for instance Manwaring and Smith, 2020, p 45). Alongside the commitments that manifesto pledges were 'fully costed' (see earlier), the 2017 commitments to renationalisation did not seek to overturn all the privatisations of the 1980s (the manifesto mentioned only the railways, water, energy and Royal Mail and removing privatisation from the NHS) nor did the 'reintroduction of the 50 per cent rate of tax' mark a return to the 'punitive tax rates of the 1970s' (Dorey, 2017, p 313; Labour Party, 2017).

Although Labour has traditionally embarked on periods of recrimination, which have encouraged the party to shift leftwards, its return to government has historically been through generating new coalitions based around central ideas: Attlee and reconstruction, Wilson and technological change, Blair and the notion of the third way.

Rather than shifting towards the centre in order to find a new coalition, Corbyn sought to create a new coalition by appealing to those broadly on the left of the political spectrum. Unlike Blair especially, Corbyn sought to appeal not directly to Conservative voters but to disgruntled Green, Liberal Democrat and SNP voters. This was reflected in the expansion of Labour Party membership under Corbyn and his increase in the vote share between the 2015 and 2016 leadership contests. In 2016, facing a challenge for the leadership, Corbyn increased his vote share despite opposition from within the PLP. Corbyn's success was due to the increase in Labour Party members, many of whom joined because of Corbyn or the chance to vote for him in the election, and the registered supporters able to vote in the election. Such members and registered supporters were attracted by 'seemingly new, radical, politics he promoted, a variant of Left-wing populism. This, though, had established an ideological disjuncture between Corbyn and his grass-roots supporters on the one hand, and most of the Parliamentary Labour Party on the other' (Dorey, 2017, pp 309–310).

The expansion was not, however, equally spread across socioeconomic groups, and re-enforced the perception that Labour was shifting attention from its traditional working-class voter base. New members did not share the same experiences as those who had been in the party under previous leaders. They were seen as (or at least perceived to be) more middle class. Such changes in membership affected the wider views of the party. Labour, under Corbyn, became defined as the party of the 'Waitrose liberals' and as one focus group participant said, the images associated with Labour under Corbyn had also changed: 'the traditional pint of beer had been replaced by the wholegrain food, quinoa. The working-class past times of bingo and dog racing were supplanted by student protests and anti-austerity demonstrations in the left's iconography alongside music festivals and Glastonbury' (Diamond, 2021, p 371).

Since the 1920s, Labour has committed itself to parliamentary means. This is to say that it worked within British democracy and institutions to achieve its aims. The Brexit referendum challenged this link between Parliament and democracy. Labour's 2019 policy of supporting a second referendum, based on newly negotiated terms for exiting the EU (Labour Party, 2019), when juxtaposed against Johnson's slogan 'get Brexit done', lost many working-class voters in the so-called Red Wall, leading to large-scale losses in places that returned Labour MPs even in 1983.

Brexit led to tensions. The perception that Parliament itself was delaying implementation of the referendum result raised questions about the relationship between Parliament and democracy (previously Labour saw these as interchangeable terms) and where sovereignty resides. The result of the referendum was particularly difficult for Labour: 'while some 80 per cent of Labour members were for Remain, two-thirds of Labour MPs represented constituencies where an often large majority had voted to leave' (Panitch and Leys, 2020, p 188).

This highlighted questions over the role of MPs, as representatives of their constituents or broader ideas of their party. Given overwhelming evidence suggesting that the effects of Brexit would be regressive, decisions relating to Labour's Brexit policy also linked to wider relationships between supporting Brexit and the anti-austerity measures and tensions between the party's traditional working-class voters and the ideological coalition Corbyn was seeking to build.

The Conservatives played on this relationship and in so doing attracted voters in seats that were not traditionally regarded as swing or marginal seats but were seats that Labour had held for almost a century. Such seats possessed three common characteristics. 'Firstly, they had voted to leave the EU in 2016. Second, large proportions of each constituency identified as English rather than British or any other nationality. Finally, these seats were culturally conservative according to polling by Lord Ashcroft' (Rayson, 2020, p 5).

The Labour Party and the trade unions

The trade unions were crucial in the election of Ed Miliband over his brother David in 2010. Miliband was dubbed 'Red Ed' in part due to such associations. For the first time in Labour's history, however, the leader had been elected demonstrably due to trade union support. The unions were the only one of the three electoral categories (MPs/MEPs, Labour Party members and affiliated members) in which he led his brother.

Miliband's inability to shift the economic debate away from notions of debt and overspending left the unions and wider population susceptible to the Conservatives' regressive, austerity agenda. However, the biggest change in the relationship between the trade unions and the Labour leadership came following alleged actions of the Unite union in Falkirk, facilitating its members to both join the Labour Party and participate in the vote that chose the candidate to stand in the next election (see French and Hodder, 2016).

Such concerns led Miliband to commission the Collins Review in 2013 and Labour to adopt a new system of trade union affiliation, put to a special conference of the party in 2014. One crucial change was that the leader should be elected by a simple vote of eligible members, from a list of candidates who had demonstrated a minimum level of support from all the parliamentary party, constituencies and unions. Members of affiliated unions were eligible to vote, but had to register their interest to do so. The change had unanticipated effects when first used, in the 2015 election of Jeremy Corbyn.

The period of opposition from 2015 further condensed some longer-term trends within the Labour Party – the party–trade union relationship. First, the working class alone were no longer able to provide sufficient support for Labour to form a majority, a trend that was first identified in the 1970s (see Chapters 5 and 6). Corbyn's solution to this problem lay in his desire to transcend class lines and pursue a coalition on ideological grounds. Second, the trade unions were unable to significantly influence their members' political choices or the wider working classes. Again this was not new in the 2010s but had huge implications for the party under Corbyn; despite warning of the dangers of Brexit, such as job losses and threats to workers' rights (see TUC, 2016), many working-class voters voted for something that was not seen to be in their economic interest.

The 2015 leadership election, however, signified that Labour's membership was willing to pursue policies significantly to the left of the PLP. Here greater democratisation – for example allowing the introduction of registered supporters to vote for Miliband's replacement – facilitated the election of Jeremy Corbyn. Corbyn further looked beyond the Labour Party to help mobilise his support – both in his leadership elections but also in general elections. Corbyn worked with the group Momentum, which was not affiliated to the Labour Party, to promote his policies on an ideological basis. Links between Momentum and left-wing groups in the 1980s were well publicised, especially by Corbyn's opponents, but used to attract new members to both Momentum and the Labour Party. Corbyn legitimised his ideas within the grassroots movement of the party and in doing so presented himself as a 'populist' against the PLP, which was seen as a part of the 'establishment elite' (Watts and Bale, 2019, p 111).

Corbyn's leadership saw the reversal of many of the understandings that had emerged in the 1970s and 1980s. Previously, in order to dispel trade union influence, the party moved towards enhancing the powers of individual members. This was seen as a safeguard against Labour shifting decisively to the left. It diluted the power away from those who attended Constituency Labour Party meetings and instead equalised the powers held by all of those who paid subscription fees, through for instance OMOV.

Conclusion

Labour's return to opposition after the 2010 general election mirrored that of 1979 and even 1931. The party was blamed for an economic crisis that it failed to both prevent and contain. However, Labour did not suffer the same weaknesses as it had done in 1979. There was no evidence to suggest that Labour would spend the decade (and more) in exile from the government's benches and this led to relatively fewer calls to radically alter the policies offered by the party. As O'Hara (2018) notes, Labour between 2010 and

2015 managed to avoid the civil wars that formed in the 1950s, 1970s and 1980s. In part this was due to the optimism of a quick return to government; the Liberal Democrats' declining popularity after forming a coalition with the Conservatives appeared to present Labour with 'an easy way back to power' and 'for almost that entire period Labour was indeed ahead in the polls. At the mid-point of the 2010–2015 Parliament, for instance, they led the Conservatives on average by between ten and eleven percentage points.'

Miliband's emphasis on party unity delayed a radical lurch to the left, as seen in the election of Michael Foot in 1980. Miliband was keen to adhere to economic orthodoxy and couched his economic arguments within the context of government debt and austerity. Labour's optimism that it would see a swift return to government, akin to its period in opposition between 1970 and 1974, when Wilson offered stability by maintaining the party leadership, was dashed in the 2015 general election.

Panitch and Leys (2020, p 1) argue that the economic crises faced by Labour governments, those in 1931, the late 1970s and after 2007/2008, led to corresponding crises within the party. Each 'crisis posed fundamental questions of ideology, organisation and unity, and ended up by propelling into the leadership a radical socialist MP from the party's left wing', while Labour's right reacted to each crisis by attempting to block 'whatever potential the crisis had for taking the party in a new democratic-socialist direction'.

Although broadly correct, this analysis ignores a fundamental difference, that Ed Miliband, despite being from the party's left wing, did not generate the same shifts as Corbyn would later do. The 2010 general election result was not seen by the Labour Party as a defeat on the same scale as 1931 or 1979. Defeat in 2015 changed such understandings. In many respects the post-mortem identified by Panitch and Leys occurred only after 2015. That the Conservatives, after heading a coalition government, were able to gain a majority in 2015 led Labour to search for a new platform/policy agenda. The election of Corbyn and the vast number of registered supporters joining to vote for him encouraged Corbyn and his allies to forge a different path to power than Wilson or Blair had done. Rather than trying to build an electoral coalition that would move Labour towards the centre ground, Corbyn sought to appeal to those on the political left, based around an anti-austerity programme.

Defeat in 2015 encouraged the party to reassess the legacy of New Labour. The election of Corbyn allowed the tensions that Miliband had effectively navigated to surface and openly pitted branches of the Labour Party against one another. Corbyn derived his legitimacy from the party's membership and grassroots and drew on movements such as Momentum. However, he was unable to effectively establish a new economic ideology for the party, he was unable to present a programme that was economically credible in the eyes of voters or he was unable to extend Labour's electoral support, with much of the gains coming at the expense of traditional voters in working-class constituencies, particularly in response to Labour's Brexit strategy/plans.

Labour's fourth successive electoral defeat in 2019 demonstrates that the party has not overcome the electability crisis highlighted in this chapter. Previous chapters suggest that in order to do so it will need to create a new coalition, around a big theme or crisis and demonstrate that the contemporary Labour Party is markedly different from the Labour government that was removed from office in 2010.

9

Conclusion

This book has, at its core, argued three distinct points. First, that crises have shaped Labour's economic ideology. They have encouraged the party to think more holistically about economic questions (see Chapter 3 on the Great Slump) and in opposition (for example, in the 1950s and 1980s; see Chapters 4 and 6) forced the party to shift towards the right, accepting much of the capitalist model. Second, that distinctions between Labour's responses cannot be fully appreciated within the distinction between 'Old' and 'New' Labour. Rather than seeing 1994 or 1997 as marking a significant shift in the party's ideology, a more nuanced understanding would explore similarities and differences between Labour in government and the party in opposition. And finally, in opposition, the party has focused more on ideological battles, often criticising previous leaders/governments for being too conservative and not going far enough in implementing socialist policies.

Understanding Labour's crises in a historical context

This book has covered multiple crises, chosen for their impact on Labour's economic policy. This is not meant to represent an exhaustive list, nor should it be seen as an attempt to explain wider, non–economic, policies. Other policies have been developed out of other crises, for example foreign policy and terrorist threats.

The crises covered in this book are by no means equal in their scope or in terms of their impact, either on British politics or on the Labour Party. Both the split of 1931 and the prolonged opposition between 1979 and 1997 encouraged Labour to think more systematically about its economic ideology and to offer a radically different programme than the previous Labour government. In contrast, the General Strike of 1926 reinforced Labour's existing commitments to parliamentary socialism and the Second World War affirmed Labour's commitments to state planning and much of the programme the party developed in the previous decade. Equally, some of the responses to the crises had more significant effects than others;

for example, the nationalisation and welfare programmes of the late 1940s set the foundations for British politics until the 1970s. Compared with this, the party's response to the Taff Vale judgment was limited in its scope, not least as Labour was not yet Britain's second party, and was reliant on agreements with the Liberals in order to win parliamentary representation. Differences also existed between the Labour governments' responses to the crises. The effects of the 2007/2008 economic crisis, which ultimately led to the election defeat in 2010 and left Labour in opposition for more than a decade, had more impact on the party than the sterling crisis of 1947, which did not remove a Labour government or even prevent Labour from winning the next election.

The impacts of the crises covered also extend beyond the Labour Party. Many crises that can be seen as enabling were so as they adversely affected other parties or structures. The First World War enabled Labour to better position itself as the main challenger to the Conservative Party due to the splits created within the Liberal Party and the 1992 ERM crisis eroded perceptions within the electorate that the Conservative Party was best able to manage the economy.

Nor is this to suggest that each crisis represents a self-contained entity; for example, New Labour's understanding of the relationship between the party and the trade unions stemmed from the experiences of the 1970s, and the crisis of 2007/2008 overshadowed not just the-then Prime Minister, Gordon Brown, but also his successor, Ed Miliband.

Labour's socialism

Crises can, and do, provide opportunities to pursue radically different alternatives; they can lead to social learning and even paradigm shifts (Hall, 1993) depending on who or what is blamed for the events that have unfolded. Such transitions are by no means inevitable. Labour presided over no less than three crises of capitalism – in 1931, the 1970s and 2007/2008 – but in each instance favoured pursuing policies that upheld the existing capitalist system, due to wider considerations (for example, electability). Here commitments to socialism focused on ethical socialism (for example, equality of opportunity). This allowed Labour politicians from across the party to argue that their socialism was consistent with existing traditions drawing upon thinkers such as Tawney. Yet at the same time, such discourses offered a means of rejecting broader (revolutionary) understandings of socialism, derived from Marx, as proposals for speedy transitions to an alternative economic system were abandoned in what became termed 'parliamentary socialism'.

The Labour Party does not have a monopoly on the ideology of socialism. It is one of several parties within British politics that advocates for socialism, each with their own interpretation of the term. This book does not represent a history of socialism, but simply Labour's interpretations of an ideology that has been revised on numerous occasions. Socialism itself has a much longer history than the Labour Party (the most famous publication of socialist thought, *The Communist Manifesto* (Marx and Engles, 1848 [1888]) was published in 1848, some 52 years before the first meeting of the Labour Representation Committee). Socialism has traditionally been conceived as a critique of the (worst excesses of the) capitalist model of production, and one that requires wholesale changes to economic and political institutions. The state (or government) has a key role to play in creating new institutions and norms to facilitate this.

This book has sought to develop some of these ideas, defining the different interpretations or inspirations for socialism and by doing so showing continuity and change over the party's 120-year history. Through doing so I have sought to highlight not just the differences in what the Labour Party, or at least its leaders, have understood by the term 'socialism' and how socialism could be achieved, but also how such differences have been shaped by historic events.

Socialist ideology within the Labour Party can be both constraining and enabling. It can force advocates of particular ideological strands to defend their positions not only in terms of contemporary policies but also in terms of party history or tradition, and conversely criticise opponents through the same methods. The history of the Labour Party, however, is more complex than a single ideology can accommodate. Labour's divisions are not simply about policy or contemporary understandings, between left and right wings or factions within the party, but rather about reinterpreting the party's history. The main example of this was the advent of New Labour in 1994, which sought to create not only a 'new' party under the stewardship of Blair and Brown, but also to define what could then be termed 'Old Labour'. However, this was not the first such (re)writing of the party's history; for example, debates over Clause IV were not confined to the 1990s, but existed in the 1950s.

Ralph Miliband (quoted in Coates, 2003, p 7) talked about 'an older generation of Labour leaders [who] always set very definitive limits, in their programmes and policies, to Labour's socialism'. Even Crosland (2006, p 408) linked the future of socialism to the history and future of the Labour Party, arguing that socialist agendas needed to be rooted in contemporary problems rather than subscribing to fixed ideologies. He contended that Labour should extend planning to the City of London, arguing that this was of greater importance than 'planning the chemical industry'. Labour, according to Crosland, was well positioned to take up the socialist causes due to its 'long-standing belief in social as opposed to private values, and the tender, respectful feeling for culture that characterises the educated working class'. Labour equally had the opportunity in the 1950s to advance such causes, as material needs were increasingly met to the extent that governments were able to 'spare more energy, and more resources, for beauty and culture' (on this point see also Inglehart's arguments about post-materialism: Inglehart, 1977).

Labour leaders – including Blair and Brown – have been keen to highlight their commitment to socialism or a socialist cause – although this is not to say that understandings of what this entails have remained static. As this book demonstrates, Labour's vision of socialism, at least as an economic ideology, remained imprecise until at least the 1930s, and since then revisionist thinkers have argued that socialism should not be seen as a static entity, but one that can and does adapt to wider economic changes. Rather, as capitalism changes, so too must the critiques of the prevailing economic system and alternative options.

The transition to socialism, then, posed a paradox for the Labour Party, especially in times of government. One of the key criticisms that socialist thinkers have of the capitalist model is that it is prone to crises, yet opinions differ as to how to respond to such crises. At numerous times in its history, the Labour Party has been in power amid economic crises, in 1929–1931, 1967, 1976 and 2007/2008. These were arguably not crises of Labour's own making, but rather of what Marx and later socialists identify as inherent flaws in capitalism. Yet these crises became associated with the party. Although Francis (1996, p 41) talks specifically about the experiences of the Attlee post-war administration, his analysis is typical of Labour governments' experiences. Francis argues that Labour, when in government, frequently undertook decisions for pragmatic or administrative reasons, rather than based on ideology; the 'relationship between government policy and socialist ideas was consistently framed, and occasionally circumscribed, by a number of structural constraints. The most obvious of these constraints was Britain's precarious economic situation.'

Socialism, for much of the Labour Party, was never designed to be instigated from a crisis of capitalism but orchestrated from a position of economic strength. The problem, however, was that this meant Labour, alongside introducing socialism, simultaneously saw its objective as upholding and strengthening capitalism. Labour in power, according to Coates (2003, p 141), drew heavily on private business to help guide its planning, which had the effect not of challenging the relationship between the state and the capitalist order, but strengthening the interconnections that existed between the two.

Of those who have set out blueprints of how to transition towards a socialist society, few have offered detailed time frames for such developments. Governments do not have the luxury of time to implement or develop their ideology as scholars and, to a lesser extent, as opposition parties do. Crises by definition demand immediate responses and resolutions (see Chapter 1). Governments are scrutinised in real time by opposition parties, the media and populations. Regular elections mean governments must continually deliver for the voters. The devaluation crisis of 1967 and the financial crisis of 2007/2008 occurred part way through the government term, limiting the time available to find a solution to the problems. Sometimes, as in the case of the Winter of Discontent, crises can expedite the date of the next general election, further increasing pressure on incumbent governments.

This is exemplified by the MP Tony Wright (1999, p 193), who notes that Labour's understanding of socialism has always needed to adapt. Wright argues that we should take Crosland's advice that 'it is surely time to stop searching for fresh inspiration in the old orthodoxies, and thumbing over the classic texts as though they could give ocular guidance for the future'. Wright suggests that 'Crosland's advice in the 1950s should be applied to his own work now. The future of socialism is not to be found in *The Future of Socialism* and it would be absurd if it was. He was grappling with his world and we have to grapple with ours.'

This builds on Kinnock's warning of the dangers of sticking too rigidly to ideology when this runs against the day-to-day needs of society (see Chapter 6). This, along with the party's ability to redefine more durable key indicators, such as equality (see Chapters 6 and 7), diminishes the role and importance of ideology. In turn, if it is accepted that ideology – or ideological commitments – have not monopolised or even shaped Labour's programmes, then it is important to explore what structural factors have been important.

Although the Labour Party has been keen to promote its commitment to socialism, not all of those who align themselves with the aims of the Labour Party would define themselves as socialist; the party has never seen itself as exclusively a socialist party and remains a broad church. One theme that successive crises (especially after the General Strike of 1926) have demonstrated is that the trade union movement has often been less concerned with wider social change or revolution than supporting their members. This distinguishes the trade unions from the Labour Party, and although the unions were important in the creation of the Labour Party prior to the First World War, the two groups were never ideologically homogenous (see Chapter 2). Despite narratives emerging of over-zealous or over-powerful trade unions in the 1970s, purported by the New Right and building on notions of an overloaded state, the trade unions were never ideologically wedded to the aims and goals of the Labour Party, even in the tripartite relationship of the post-war settlement (King, 1975; Kirkland, 2017). The debates over the processes of nationalisation in the 1930s and 1940s (see Chapters 3 and 4) and opposition to government-prescribed wage increases in the 1970s led to increasing industrial action to defend the principles of collective bargaining.

This broad-church understanding of the party can also help explain its pragmatism. Party policies and platforms have been subject to fluctuations within Labour's leadership. This has been seen in periods of opposition where tensions between the left and right of the party have come to the forefront and different leaders have advocated different solutions (see for example the differences between Labour leaders between 1979 and 1997 and more recent differences in the 2010s).

Labour in government and opposition

Labour's greatest economic achievements have coincided with periods of economic growth/confidence. It is in this regard that the capitalist system has enabled the party's (self-defined) socialist measures to be enacted. While such programmes were not without their critics, an important relationship emerges here: that (expectations of) increases in absolute positions can be used to justify reducing relative inequalities.

As McAnulla (2006, p 122) notes, the Labour government on taking office significantly increased government spending only to reverse these measures when economic problems emerges. Such U-turns were further compounded by 'financial markets [that have] tended to lack faith in Labour governments and its perceived economic failure disillusioned voters, usually helping precipitate a quick exit from government'. McAnulla's understanding challenges conventional assumptions made by those who argue that the contradictions and crises within capitalism will eventually lead to its downfall. Rather, the experiences of the Labour Party in government suggest that crises of capitalism encourage governments to ensure a quick return to 'normal' or 'normality' often defined in the context of the pre-crisis period, rather than advocate new economic structures entirely. The Labour Party in 1931, 1951 and the late 1960s opted to respond to different crises through implementing budget cuts, as short-term pressures such as public opinion trumped any ideological desires to create a new economic model.

It would, however, be a mistake to argue that Labour's commitments in government have only been ideological. Socialism, however defined, is not the only goal of the party. Economic crises are inherently regressive, disproportionately affecting the poorest members of society. At each of those occasions when a Labour government has had to choose between orchestrating the widespread economic change required for socialism to advance or minimising uncertainty and economic hardship, it has sought to uphold the existing economic system, partly for fear of the short-term effects that changes may entail for the population, and partly due to short-term electoral considerations. Here lies the key problem of implementing radical reform: to what extent can a Labour government accept medium-term (or even short-term) disruption (for example, high unemployment, high inflation) in order to create a new socialist model? Crises may offer political opportunities to change the status quo, but pursuing such changes is not without risk.

If crises in government have led the Labour Party to adopt pragmatic, rather than ideological, responses then so too have crises in opposition. Opposition parties play a different role from governing parties within the political system; however, many of the structural constraints faced by governments also apply to oppositions (for example, regular elections). During prolonged periods of opposition (as occurred in the 1950s and the 1980s), those who were effectively able to influence policy directions argued that socialism or particular understandings of socialism needed to be adapted to meet the relevant needs of the population (or at least a significant proportion of the electorate).

The need to maintain electoral blocs and voters is an important structural constraint on any government, irrespective of political desire to instigate a new economic paradigm. Although the experience of the 1970s (and accompanying revisionist accounts in the 1980s) often presents the unions as provocateurs, making excessive demands and willing to bring down the government if these are not met, such relationships between the Labour Party and workers (organised labour) can also generate stability. These relationships force Labour to focus on tangible metrics such as employment and the cost of living rather than pursue ideological goals. Labour's historic close links to the trade union and ideological/rhetorical commitments to the working class(es) further encourage short-term thinking.

Labour in opposition did not simply adopt revisionist or social democratic positions. The examples of the early 1980s and the latter half of the 2010s demonstrate that Labour's ideology in opposition is more fluid or nuanced than such arguments would allow. The meanings of electoral defeats were contested within the party and have, on occasion, allowed/facilitated the left of the party to control the political agenda, although this has not translated into electoral success. Opposition prior to the Second World War forced the party to think more deeply about its economic policy, something that was exacerbated by the split of 1931. Labour's two governments prior to 1945 were short lived and lacked a holistic understanding of the role of the economy. Partly this was due to the heterogenous groups that found homes within the early Labour Party, but it made Labour susceptible to external events.

Arguably, Labour lost elections in 1931, 1951, 1979 and 2010 due to its handling of crises. These electoral defeats prompted ideological debates about what kind of party the Labour Party should be. Diamond (2004, pp 2–3) points to four historic phases in revisionist thought, which correspond to the elections that defeated incumbent Labour governments and led to prolonged periods in opposition. The first three of these occurred or became more prominent after defeats in 1931, 1951 and 1979. The final 'process of ideological change' identified by Diamond stems from the electoral nadir of 1983. The experience of the party post 2015 can also be seen in this light, with (revisionist) debates about the economic record of the previous government taking centre stage. Such debates were conducted in ideological terminology, with those involved often explicitly using (different definitions of) 'socialism' to argue which policies should be implemented.

Following each of these crises, the left of the party blamed the previous leadership for failing to adhere to socialist principles. Bevan established this critique of MacDonald (see Chapter 3), Crossman of Attlee (see Chapter 4) and Castle (1995, p 43) summarises Labours failings, citing examples from 1929 and 1976, noting that the 'Labour government failed to the extent that they were hypnotised by the monetarist dictums of the City and the Treasury'. Yet, almost paradoxically, the Labour Party, certainly since the General Strike of 1926, has committed to work within the institutions of the British tradition by adopting parliamentary, rather than revolutionary, socialism.

Such ideological debates, in and of themselves, are no guarantees of returning to power. It took Labour three elections to return to power after defeats in 1951 and four in 1979. The party has lost three successive elections since 2010. The exception was between 1970 and 1974 when Wilson remained leader and was returned to government fewer than four years after leaving Downing Street, although even here Labour obtained fewer votes than the Conservatives, and its victory was aided by the Conservative weaknesses in handling industrial relations disputes in the early 1970s.

(How) can Labour win again?

One lesson to be drawn from the crises highlighted in this book is that Labour can overcome crises, and in doing so it can offer a version of socialism. Although, as Chapter 8 noted, Labour has not yet overcome its latest crisis, this is not the same as saying that it will not do so.

Labour has traditionally overcome crises by asking not 'why did Labour lose the previous election?', a question that traditionally follows elections that remove incumbent Labour Prime Ministers, but 'how can Labour win again?'. Leaders as diverse as Attlee, Wilson and Blair have led Labour to election victories by offering contemporary ideas and understandings of socialism. Attlee built a coalition around the theme of reconstruction, Wilson around technological innovation and Blair the ideas of the third way.

Today, the COVID-19 pandemic has dominated the political agenda for almost two years and, although still two years from the timetabled date of the next general election, may prove a crisis that could enable Labour to offer a new economic paradigm that re-examines the economics of work (as significant numbers of people have experience of working remotely) or the relationship between the economy and individuals (health). Linked to this are debates surrounding other longer-term crises, such as climate change, that have not traditionally made it to the forefront of British politics for a sustained period of time. Equally, there may be further crises that emerge ahead of the next general election.

The responses to the pandemic will also underpin Britain's economy over the next decade or so. Throughout the crisis the government has pursued quantitative easing to allow it to expand – albeit temporarily – the role of the state through programmes such as the furlough scheme (IMF, 2021). How these programmes are both wound down and ultimately paid for will be politically contested, especially if the Conservatives pursue further austerity measures.

Labour must also broaden its appeal beyond those who previously voted for the party. As election results over the past decade have demonstrated, there has been a polarisation of debates. The two-party vote share increased from just under two thirds of voters (65.1 per cent) in 2010 to more than three quarters (75.7 per cent) in 2019, having hit a high of 82.4 per cent in 2017. The working class alone have been insufficient to bring about a Labour majority for more than half a century, partly due to weakening trade union power, meaning new voters need to be canvassed. More recently, as Chapter 8 demonstrated, the relationship between Labour and the working class has been further fractured by debates over Brexit and identity.

This does not necessarily mean that Labour needs to shift to the right. Although this is how Blair secured his landslide victory in 1997, he understood the need to offer socialist foundations for much of his programme (see Chapter 6). Corbyn, by contrast, in 2017 gained just 3.2 per cent fewer votes than Labour's landslide of 1997, by mobilising new supporters through offering what was presented as a radical left-wing programme that appealed to voters who felt unrepresented or left behind. Indeed, with social cleavages changing fast in response to events of the 2010s, such as Brexit, traditional left–right understandings may be insufficient to build coalitions upon.

Any coalition must also acknowledge changes in the relationship between the Labour Party and external groups, such as the trade unions. Although the two were never ideologically homogenous, the period since 1979 has seen a decline not only in the number of union members but also in the ability of trade unions to mobilise their members for political ends. Linked to this is the relationship between individual party members and activists who campaign for Labour come general elections. Although inactive party members were traditionally seen as being located more on the right of the party, compared with those who regularly attend constituency meetings or campaign at election times, the changes to membership rules and the accommodation of registered supporters' involvement in leadership campaigns (in part designed to reduce the power of the trade unions within the party; see Chapters 6 and 8) has led to a shift in the ideological balance of party members. This means that individual members may not be able to balance trade union power in the way they have previously and may in turn reduce the willingness of the right of the party, who are typically overrepresented within the PLP, to extend party democracy. One example of this is the decision in 2020 not to allow registered supporters to vote in Labour's leadership election.

Undoubtedly, any further transitions will be heavily contested, just as previous ones have been. They will also be subject to wider constraints, for example the changing fortunes of the Conservative Party and wider economic indicators post COVID-19. Other, unseen, factors may also impact on any future transitions.

References

Abrams, M., Rose, R. and Hinden, R. (1960). *Must Labour Lose?* Harmondsworth: Penguin.

Acharya, V.V., Drechsler, I. and Schnabl, P. (2011). A Pyrrhic Victory? Bank Bailouts and Sovereign Credit Risks. Retrieved 11 August 2013 from: http://archive.nyu.edu/fda/bitstream/2451/31331/2/ADS_Paper_Aug2011.pdf

Addison, P. (1977). *The Road to 1945: British Politics and the Second World War.* London: Quartet Books.

Adelman, P. (2014). *The Rise of the Labour Party 1880–1945.* London: Routledge.

Aldcroft, D.H. and Oliver, M.J. (2000). *Trade Unions and the Economy: 1870–2000.* Aldershot: Ashgate.

Alderman, K. and Carter, N. (1994). The Labour Party and the Trade Unions: Loosening the Ties. *Parliamentary Affairs*, 47(3), 321–337.

Alderman, K. and Carter, N. (1995). The Labour Party Leadership and Deputy Leadership Elections of 1994. *Parliamentary Affairs*, 48(3), 438–455.

Allen, W.A. (2014). *Monetary Policy and Financial Repression in Britain 1951–59.* London: Palgrave Macmillan.

Artis, M. and Cobham, D. (1991). *Labour's Economic Policies 1974–79.* Manchester: Manchester University Press.

Artus, J.A. (1975). The 1967 Devaluation of the Pound Sterling. *Staff Papers (International Monetary Fund)*, 22(3), 595–640.

Attlee, C. (1937). *The Labour Party in Perspective.* London: Victor Gollancz.

Attlee, C. (2019). *As It Happened.* London: Sharpe Books.

Bale, T. and Webb, P. (2015). The Conservatives: Their Sweetest Victory? In A. Geddes and J. Tonge (eds) *Britain Votes 2015* (pp 41–53). Oxford: Oxford University Press.

Ball, S. (1988). *Baldwin and the Conservative Party.* London: Yale University Press.

Balls, E. and O'Donnell, G. (2002). *Reforming Britain's Economic and Financial Policy: Towards Greater Economic Stability.* Basingstoke: Palgrave Macmillan.

Bank of England. (2020). Bank of England. Retrieved 17 June 2021 from: https://www.bankofengland.co.uk/-/media/boe/files/monetary-pol icy-report/2020/august/monetary-policy-report-august-2020

Bank of England. (2021). What Is Quantitative Easing? Retrieved 14 July 2022 from: https://www.bankofengland.co.uk/monetary-policy/quant itative-easing

Banks, R.F. (1969). The Reform of British Industrial Relations: The Donovan Report and the Labour Government's Policy Proposals. *Industrial Relations, 24*(2), 333–382.

Barberis, P. (2006). The Labour Party and Mr Keynes in the 1930s: A Partial Keynesian Revolution without Mr Keynes. *Labour History Review, 71*(2), 145–166.

Barker, R. (1976). Political Myth: Ramsay MacDonald and the Labour Party. *History, 61*(201), 46–56.

Bartley, P. (2019). *Labour Women in Power: Cabinet Ministers in the Twentieth Century*. Cham: Springer International.

Batroini, D. (2021). *The Battle of Ideas in the Labour Party: From Attlee to Corbyn and Brexit*. Bristol: Bristol University Press.

BBC News. (1998, 5 October). Brown Pushes for IMF Reform. Retrieved 14 June 2021 from: http://news.bbc.co.uk/1/hi/special_report/1998/10/98/imf/184918.stm

BBC News. (2014, 3 December). Government to Pay off WW1 Debt. Retrieved 29 June 2021 from: https://www.bbc.co.uk/news/business-3030657

BBC News. (2015, 22 July). Margaret Beckett: I was Moron to Nominate Jeremy Corbyn. Retrieved 11 April 2022 from: https://www.bbc.co.uk/news/uk-politics-33625612

Beech, M. and Hickson, K. (2007). *Labour's Thinkers: The Intellectual Roots of Labour from Tawney to Gordon Brown*. London: Tauris Academic Studies.

Beech, M. and Hickson, K. (2014). Blue or Purple? Reflection on the Future of the Labour Party. *Political Studies Review, 12*, 75–87.

Beech, M. and Page, R.M. (2015). Blue and Purple Labour Challenges to the Welfare State: How Should 'Statist' Social Democrats Respond? *Social Policy and Society, 14*(3), 341–356.

Beer, S. (1965). *Modern British Politics*. London: Faber & Faber.

Beers, L. (2008). Book Review: Matt Beech and Kevin Hickson Labour's Thinkers: The Intellectual Roots of Labour from Tawney to Gordon Brown. *Journal of British Studies, 47*(3), 727–728.

Bell, D.N. and Blanchflower, D.G. (2014). UK Unemployment in the Great Recession. *National Institute Economic Review, 214*, R3–R25.

Bell, P. (2004). *The Labour Party in Opposition 1970–1974*. London: Routledge.

Benn, T. (1996). *The Benn Diaries 1940–1990*. London: Arrow Books.

Bevan, A. (2008). *In Place of Fear*. Weybridge: The Aneurin Bevan Society.

Beveridge, W. (1942). *Social Insurance and Allied Services*. London: HMSO.

Blaazer, D. (1999). 'Devalued and Dejected Britons': The Pound in Public Discourse in the Mid 1960s. *History Workshop Journal*, *47*(1), 121–140.

Blair, T. (1994a). *Socialism Fabian Pamphlet 565*. Retrieved 11 April 2022 from: https://digital.library.lse.ac.uk/objects/lse:har787wav

Blair, T. (1994b). Leader's Speech, Blackpool 1994. Retrieved 11 April 2022 from: http://www.britishpoliticalspeech.org/speech-archive.htm?speech=200

Blair, T. (1997, 31 March). We Won't Look Back to the 1970s. *The Times*, p 20.

Blair, T. (1998, 21 September). New Politics for the New Century. Retrieved 10 May 2022 from: https://www.independent.co.uk/arts-entertainment/new-politics-for-the-new-century-1199625.html

Blair, T. (2004). Foreword. In P. Diamond, *New Labour's Old Roots* (p v). Exeter: Imprint Academic.

Blewett, N. (1972). *The Peers, the Parties and the People: The General Elections of 1910*. London: Macmillan.

Blick, A. (2006). Harold Wilson, Labour and the Machinery of Government. *Contemporary British History*, *20*(3), 343–362.

Blyth, M. (1997). 'Any More Bright Ideas?' The Ideational Turn of Comparative Political Economy. *Comparative Politics*, *29*(2), 229–250.

Blyth, M. (2013). *Austerity: The History of a Dangerous Idea*. Oxford: Oxford University Press.

Bogdanor, V. (2015, 10 March). The General Election 1979. Retrieved 8 July 2021 from: https://webcache.googleusercontent.com/search?q=cache:Bhhttps://www.gresham.ac.uk/lecture/transcript/download/the-general-election-1979/

Bogdanor, V. (2016). The IMF Crisis of 1976. Retrieved 23 August 2021 from: https://www.gresham.ac.uk/lectures-and-events/the-imf-crisis-1976

Booth, A. (1996). How Long are Light Years in British Politics? The Labour Party's Economic Ideas in the 1930s. *Twentieth Century British History*, *7*(1), 1–26.

Brittan, S. (1977). *The Economic Consequences of Democracy*. London: Temple Smith.

Brooke, S. (1991). Problems of 'Socialist Planning': Evan Durbin and the Labour Government of 1945. *The Historical Journal*, *34*(3), 687–702.

Brooke, S. (1992). *Labour's War: The Labour Party and the Second World War*. Oxford: Oxford University Press.

Brookes, R. (1985). The Little Man and the Slump: Sidney Strube's Cartoons and the Politics of Unemployment 1929–1931. *Oxford Art Journal*, *8*(1), 49–61.

Brown, G. (1966). Letter to Harold Wilson. Retrieved 7 October 2020 from: https://www.nationalarchives.gov.uk/education/resources/sixties-britain/failure-national-plan/

Brown, G. (1999). Equality – Then and Now. In D. Leonard (ed) *Crosland and New Labour* (pp 35–48). Basingstoke: Palgrave Macmillan.

Brown, G. (2001). The Conditions for High and Stable Growth and Employment. *The Economic Journal*, *111*(471), C30–C44.

Brown, G. (2003). State and Market: Towards a Public Interest. *The Political Quarterly*, *74*(3), 266–284.

Brown, G. (2010). *Beyond the Crash: Overcoming the First Crisis of Globalization.* New York: Simon and Schuster.

Brown, G. (2017). *My Life, Our Times.* London: The Bodley Head.

Bull, P. (2000). New Labour, New Rhetoric? An Analysis of the Rhetoric of Tony Blair. In C. De Landtsheer and O. Feldman (eds) *Beyond Public Speech and Symbols: Explorations in the Rhetoric of Politicians and the Media* (pp 3–16). Westport: Praeger.

Burk, K. and Cairncross, A. (1992). *Goodbye, Great Britain: The 1976 IMF Crisis.* London: Yale University Press.

Butler, D. and Freeman, J. (1969). *British Political Facts 1900–1968.* London: Macmillan.

Butler, D. and Kavanagh, D. (1974). *The British General Election of February 1974.* Basingstoke: Macmillan.

Butler, D. and Kavanagh, D. (1980). *The British General Election of 1979.* London: Macmillan.

Butler, D. and Kavanagh, D. (1992). *The British General Election of 1992.* London: Macmillan.

Butler, D. and Kavanagh, D. (1997). *The British General Election of 1997.* London: Palgrave Macmillan.

Byrne, L. (2019). How Jeremy Corbyn Brought Labour Back to the Future: Visions of the Future and Concrete Utopia in Labour's 2017 General Election Campaign. *British Politics*, *14*(3), 250–268.

Caincross, A. and Eichengreen, B. (2003). *Sterling in Decline: The Devaluations of 1931, 1949 and 1967.* Basingstoke: Palgrave Macmillan.

Callaghan, J. (1976). Leader's Speech Blackpool, 1976. Retrieved 24 July 2020 from: http://www.britishpoliticalspeech.org/speech-archive.htm?speech=174

Campbell, A. and McIlroy, J. (2018). 'The Trojan Horse': Communist Entrism in the British Labour Party, 1933–43. *Labor History*, *59*(5), 513–554.

Cannan, E. (1910). Review: Socialism and Government by J. Ramsay MacDonald. *The Economic Journal*, *77*, 63–66.

Carter, M. (2003). *T.H. Green and the Development of Ethical Socialism.* Exeter: Imprint Academic.

Castle, B. (1969). In Place of Strife. Retrieved 7 August 2020 from: https://www.nationalarchives.gov.uk/education/resources/sixties-britain/place-strife/

Castle, B. (1993). *Fighting all the Way*. London: Macmillan.

Castle, B. (1995). Lessons for Labour. *Soundings*, 1, 35–45.

Catterall, P. (2017). Winston Churchill and the General Strike. Retrieved 18 August 2021 from: https://westminsterresearch.westminster.ac.uk/downl oad/b25bb295b59526f3c0abf21f66702a6f67711a69295fe310a379034da 2380925/157467/CHURCHILL%20AND%20THE%20GENERAL%20 STRIKE%20copyedited.pdf

Clarke, H.D., Stewart, M. and Whiteley, P.F. (1998). New Models for New Labour: The Political Economy of Labour Party Support January 1992– April 1997. *The American Political Science Review*, *92*(3), 559–575.

Clarke, H.D., Sanders, D., Stewart, M.C. and Whiteley, P. (2004). *Political Choice in Britain*. Oxford: Oxford University Press.

Clegg, H.A. (1985). *A History of British Trade Unions since 1889: Volume II: 1911–33*. Oxford: Clarendon Press.

Clegg, H.A. (1994). *A History of British Trade Unions Since 1889: Volume III: 1934–1951*. Oxford: Oxford University Press.

Clegg, H.A., Fox, A. and Thompson, A.F. (1977). *A History of British Trade Unions since 1889 Vol I 1899–1910*. Oxford: Oxford University Press.

Cliff, B. and Tomlinson, J. (2002). Tawney and the Third Way. *Journal of Political Ideologies*, 7(3), 315–331.

Clifford, C. (1997). The Rise and Fall of the Department of Economic Affairs: British Government and Indicative Planning. *Contemporary British History*, *11*(2), 94–116.

Coates, D. (2003). The Failure of the Socialist Promise. In D. Coates, *Paving the Third Way: The Critique of Parliamentary Socialism* (pp 137–156). London: The Merlin Press.

Coates, D. (2005). *Prolonged Labour: The Slow Birth of New Labour in Britain*. Basingstoke: Palgrave Macmillan.

Coates, D. (2008). 'Darling, It Is Entirely My Fault!' Gordon Brown's Legacy to Alistair and Himself. *British Politics*, *3*, 3–21.

Coates, D. (2013). Labour after New Labour: Escaping the Debt. *British Journal of Politics and International Relations*, *15*, 38–52.

Cobham, D. (1997). Inevitable Disappointment? The ERM as the Framework for UK Monetary Policy 1990–92. *International Review of Applied Economics*, *11*(2), 213–228.

Coderre-LaPalme, G. and Greer, I. (2018). Dependence on a Hostile State: UK Trade Unions before and after Brexit. In S. Lehndorff, H. Dribbusch and T. Schulten (eds) *Rough Waters: European Trade Unions in a Time of Crises* (pp 259–284). Brussels: ETUI Printshop.

Cohen, S. (2012). Equal Pay – or What? Economics, Politics and the 1968 Ford Sewing Machinists Strike. *Labor History*, *53*(1), 51–68.

Cole, G.D.H. (1929). *The Next Ten Years in British Social and Economic History*. London: Macmillan.

Cole, G.D.H. (1948). *A History of the Labour Party from 1914*. New York: Routledge.

Cole, G.D.H. (2011). *Self-Government in Industry*. London: Routledge

Conservative Party. (1918). The Manifesto of Lloyd George and Bonar Law. Retrieved 30 June 2021 from: Conservative Party Manifestos: http://www.conservativemanifesto.com/1918/1918-conservative-manifesto.shtml

Cowley, P. and Kavanagh, D. (2018). *The British General Election of 2017*. Cham: Palgrave Macmillan.

Crafts, N.F.R. (1995). 'You've Never Had It so Good?' British Economic Policy and Performance, 1945–60. In B. Eichengreen (ed) *Europe's Post-war Recovery* (pp 246–270). Cambridge: Cambridge University Press.

Crafts, N.F.R. (1998). The British Economy: Missing Out or Catching Up? In B. Foley (ed) *European Economies since the Second World War* (pp 1–24). Basingstoke: Macmillan.

Cribb, J. (2013). Income Equality in the UK. Retrieved 17 June 2021 from: https://ifs.org.uk/docs/ER_JC_2013.pdf

Crines, A. (2014). The Oratory of Ed Miliband. In A. Crines and R. Hayton (eds) *Labour's Orators from Bevan to Miliband* (pp 187–199). Manchester: Manchester University Press.

Crines, A. (2015). Reforming Labour: The Leadership of Jeremy Corbyn. *Political Insight*, *6*(3), 4–7.

Cromby, J. (2018). The Myths of Brexit. *Journal of Community and Applied Social Psychology*, *29*(1), 56–66.

Crosland, A. (1975a). Socialism Now. In D. Leonard (ed) *Socialism Now and Other Essays* (pp 15–58). London: Jonathan Cape.

Crosland, A. (1975b). Government and Industry. In D. Leonard (ed) *Socialism Now and Other Essays* (pp 246–256). London: Jonathan Cape.

Crosland, A. (2006). *The Future of Socialism*. London: Constable.

Crossman, R. (1977). *The Diaries of a Cabinet Minister: Volume Three: Secretary of State for Social Services 1968–70*. London: Hamish Hamilton.

Crouch, C. (2011). *The Strange Non-Death of Neoliberalism*. Cambridge: Polity.

Crowcroft, R. and Theakston, K. (2013). The Fall of the Attlee Government, 1951. In T. Heppell and K. Theakston (eds) *How Labour Governments Fall* (pp 61–82). Basingstoke: Palgrave Macmillan.

Curtice, J., Fisher, S., Ford, S. and English, P. (2018). The Results Analysed. In P. Cowley and D. Kavanagh (eds) *The British General Election of 2017* (pp 449–496). Basingstoke: Palgrave Macmillan.

Cushion, S. and Lewis, J. (2016). Scrutinising Statistical Claims and Constructing Balance: Television News Coverage of the 2016 EU Referendum. In D. Jackson, E. Thorsen and D. Wring (eds) *EU Referendum Analysis 2016: Early Reflections from Leading UK Academics* (pp 40–41). Poole: Bournemouth University.

Dalton, H. (1945). *Practical Socialism*. London: George Routledge and Sons.

Daniels, P. (1998). From Hostility to 'Constructive Engagement' to Europeanisation of the Labour Party. *West European Politics*, *21*(1), 72–96.

Darling, A. (2012). *Back from the Brink*. London: Atlantic Books.

Davis, M. (2003). 'Labourism' and the New Left. In J. Callaghan, S. Fielding and S. Ludlam (eds) *Interpreting the Labour Party* (pp 39–56). Manchester: Manchester University Press.

Davis, R. (2015). Labour's Conservative Tradition. In I. Geary and A. Pabst (eds) *Blue Labour: Forging a New Politics* (pp 195–202). London: I.B. Tauris.

Dellepiane-Avellaneda, S. (2013). Gordon Unbound: The Heresthetic of Central Bank Independence in Britain. *British Journal of Political Science*, *43*(2), 263–293.

Denis, J. (2020). A Party Within a Party Posing as a Movement? Momentum as a Movement Faction. *Journal of Information Technology and Politics*, *17*(2), 97–113.

Department of Economic Affairs. (1965). Labour's National Plan. Retrieved 10 July 2020 from: https://www.nationalarchives.gov.uk/education/resources/sixties-britain/national-plan/

Diamond, P. (2004). *New Labour's Old Roots*. Exeter: Imprint Academic.

Diamond, P. (2021). *The British Labour Party in Opposition and Power 1979–2019: Forward March of Labour Halted*. Abingdon: Routledge.

Dolphin, T. (2011). *Debts and Deficit: How Much Is Labour to Blame?* London: Institute for Public Policy Research.

Dorey, P. (1999). The Blairite Betrayal: New Labour and the Trade Unions. In G.R. Taylor (ed) *The Impact of New Labour* (pp 190–207). Basingstoke: Macmillan.

Dorey, P. (2017). Jeremy Corbyn Confounds His Critics: Explaining the Labour Party's Remarkable Resurgence in the 2017 Election. *British Politics*, *12*, 308–334.

Dorey, P. and Denham, A. (2016). 'The Longest Suicide Vote in History': The Labour Party Leadership Election of 2015. *British Politics*, *11*, 259–282.

Downs, A. (1957). *An Economic Theory of Democracy*. New York: Harper.

Dowse, R.E. (1974). Introduction. In R.E. Dowse (ed) *From Serfdom to Socialism, James Keir Hardie; Labour and the Empire, James Ramsay MacDonald; The Socialist's Budget, Philip Snowden*. Hassocks: Harvester Press.

Duca, J.V., Muellbauer, J. and Murphy, A. (2010). Housing Markets and the Financial Crisis of 2007–2009: Lessons for the Future. *Journal of Financial Stability*, *6*(4), 203–217.

Duckworth, A. (2008, 10 December). Gordon Brown 'We not only saved the world …'. Retrieved 23 July 2021 from: https://www.theguardian.com/politics/audio/2008/dec/10/gordon-brown-saves-the-world

Dunleavy, P. (2010, 7 May). 2010 Election Analysis – Nobody has Won in Terms of Votes, But the Last-Minute Momentum was to Labour. Retrieved 11 April 2022 from: https://blogs.lse.ac.uk/politicsandpolicy/2010-elect ion-analysis-%E2%80%93-nobody-has-won-in-terms-of-votes-but-the-last-minute-momentum-was-to-labour/

Durbin, E. (1933). *Purchasing Power and Trade Depression: A Critique of Under-Consumption Theories*. London: Jonathan Cape.

Durbin, E. (1940). *Politics of Democratic Socialism*. London: Routledge.

Durbin, E. (1985). *New Jerusalems: Labour Party and the Economics of Democratic Socialism*. London: Routledge.

Eatwell, R. and Wright, A. (1978). Labour and the Lessons of 1931. *History*, *63*(207), 38–53.

Edgerton, D. (2002). Public Ownership and the British Arms Industry 1920–50. In R. Millward and J. Singleton (eds) *The Political Economy of Nationalisation in Britain 1920–50* (pp 164–188). Cambridge: Cambridge University Press.

Ellison, N. (1996). Consensus Here, Consensus There ... But not Consensus Everywhere: The Labour Party, Equality and Social Policy in the 1950s. In H. Jones and M. Kandiah (eds) *The Myth of Consensus: New Views on British History* (pp 17–39). Basingstoke: Macmillan.

Engelen, E., Ertuk, I., Froud, J., Johal, S., Moran, M., Nilddon, A. and Williams, K. (2011). *After the Great Complacence: Financial Crisis and the Politics of Reform*. Oxford: Oxford University Press.

Fairman, C. (1942). The Law of Martial Rule and the National Emergency. *Harvard Law Review*, *55*(8), 1253–1302.

Favretoo, I. (2000). 'Wilsonism' Reconsidered: Labour Party Revisionism 1952–64. *Contemporary British History*, *14*(4), 54–80.

Fielding, S. (1992). Labourism in the 1940s. *Twentieth Century British History*, *3*(2), 138–153.

Fielding, S. (1994). Neil Kinnock: An Overview of the Labour Party. *Contemporary Record*, *8*(3), 589–601.

Fielding, S. (2003). *The Labour Party: Continuity and Change in the Making of 'New Labour'*. Basingstoke: Palgrave.

Fielding, S. (2010). Labour's Campaign: Things Can Only Get ... Worse? *Parliamentary Affairs*, *63*(4), 653–666.

Finlayson, A. (2013). From Blue to Green and Everything in Between: Ideational Change and Left Political Economy after New Labour. *British Journal of Politics and International Relations*, *15*, 70–88.

Foot, M. (1973). *Aneurin Bevin, 1945–1960*. London: Davis-Poynter.

Foot, M. (1977). Book Review: Ramsay MacDonald by David Marquand. *Bulletin - Society for the Study of Labour History*, *35*, 67–71.

Foote, G. (1997). *The Labour Party's Political Thought: A History*. Basingstoke: Macmillan.

Francis, M. (1996). 'Not Reformed but … Democratic Socialism': The Ideology of the Labour Leadership, 1945–51. In H. Jones and M. Kandiah (eds) *The Myth of Consensus: New Views on British History 1945–64* (pp 40–57). Basingstoke: Macmillan.

Francis, M. (1997). *Ideas and Policies under Labour, 1945–51: Building a New Britain*. Manchester: Manchester University Press.

Franklin, M., van der Eijk, C. and Marsh, M. (1994). Referendum Outcomes and Trust in Government: Public Support for Europe in the Wake of Maastricht. *Western European Politics*, *18*(3), 101–118.

French, S. and Hodder, A. (2016). Plus ca Change: The Coalition Government and the Trade Unions. In S. Williams and P. Scott (eds) *Employment Relations under Coalition Government: The UK Experience, 2010–15* (pp 165–184). Abingdon: Routledge

French, S.L. and Thrift, N. (2009). A Very Geographical Crisis: The Making and Breaking of the 2007–2008 Financial Crisis. *Cambridge Journal of Regions, Economy and Society*, *2*(2), 287–302.

Froud, J., Moran, M., Nilsson, A. and Williams, K. (2010). Wasting a Crisis? Democracy and Markets in Britain After 2007. *The Political Quarterly*, *81*(1), 25–38.

Gaffney, J. and Lahel, A. (2013). Political Performance and Leadership Persona: The UK Labour Party Conference of 2012. *Government and Opposition*, *48*(4), 481–505.

Gaitskell, H. (1956). *Socialism and Nationalism Fabian Tract 300*. London: Fabian Society.

Gamble, A. (2005). The Meaning of the Third Way. In A. Seldon and D. Kavanagh (eds) *The Blair Effect 2001–2005* (pp 430–438). Cambridge: Cambridge University Press.

Gamble, A. (2009). *The Spectre at the Feast: Capitalist Crisis and the Politics of Recession*. Basingstoke: Palgrave.

Gamble, A. (2010). New Labour and Political Change. *Parliamentary Affairs*, *63*(4), 639–652.

Gano, A. (2015). Clause IV: A Brief History. Retrieved 24 August 2021 from: https://www.theguardian.com/politics/2015/aug/09/clause-iv-of-labour-party-constitution-what-is-all-the-fuss-about-reinstating-it

Giddens, A. (1994). *Beyond Left and Right: The Future of Radical Politics*. Cambridge: Polity.

Glasman, M. (2010). Labour as a Radical Tradition: Labour's Renewal Lies in its Traditions of Mutualism, Reciprocity and the Common Good. *Soundings: A Journal of Politics and Culture, 46*.

Glasman, M. (2011). Labour as a Radical Tradition. In M. Glasman, J. Rutherford, M. Stears and S. White (eds) *The Labour Tradition and the Politics of Paradox* (pp 14–34). London: The Oxford–London Seminars/Soundings.

Goes, E. (2016). *The Labour Party under Ed Miliband: Trying but Failing to Renew Social Democracy*. Manchester: Manchester University Press.

Goes, E. (2018). 'Jez, We Can!' Labour's Campaign: Defeat with a Taste of Victory. *Parliamentary Affairs*, 71(S1), 59–71.

Goes, E. (2020). Labour's 2019 Campaign: Defeat of Epic Proportions. In J. Tonge, S. Wilks-Heeg and L. Thompson (eds) *Britain Votes: The 2019 General Election* (pp 84–102). Oxford: Oxford University Press.

Goldstein, M. and Veron, N. (2011) Too Big to Fail: The Transatlantic Debate Peterson Institute for International Economics Working Paper No. 11-2, SSRN: https://ssrn.com/abstract=1746982

Goodhart, A.L. (1927). The Legality of the General Strike in England. *The Yale Law Journal*, 36(4), 464–485.

Goodhart, C. (2008). The Background to the 2007 Financial Crisis. *International Economics and Economic Policy*, 4(4), 331–346.

Gouge, E. (2012). Michael Foot 1980–3. In T. Heppell (ed) *Leaders of the Opposition: From Churchill to Cameron* (pp 126–141). Basingstoke: Palgrave Macmillan.

Graham, A. and Beckerman, W. (1972). Introduction: Economic Performance and the Foreign Balance. In W. Beckerman (ed) *The Labour Government's Economic Record 1964–70* (pp 11–28). London: Gerald Duckworth and Company.

Greenwood, A. (1945, 17 August). Debate on the Address. Retrieved 6 July 2021 from: https://hansard.parliament.uk/Commons/1945-08-17/debates/4a890d2a-b263-4872-a93d-d57799e38924/DebateOnTheAddress?highlight=socialism#contribution-bd31de68-cf83-466e-8c8d-30e2241ece38

Griffiths, S. (2009). The Public Services under Gordon Brown – Similar Reforms, Less Money. *Policy Studies*, 30(1), 53–67.

Griffiths, S. (2012). Neil Kinnock 1983–92. In T. Heppell (ed) *Leaders of the Opposition* (pp 142–154). London: Palgrave.

Hain, P. (2015). *Back to the Future of Socialism*. Bristol: Policy Press.

Hall, P. (1993). Policy Paradigms, Social Learning, and the State: The Case of Economic Policymaking in Britain. *Comparative Politics*, 25(3), 275–296.

Hancke, B. (2009). *Debating Varieties of Capitalism: A Reader*. Oxford: Oxford University Press.

Hannah, S. (2018). *A Party with Socialists in It: A History of the Labour Left*. London: Pluto Press.

Hardie, J.K. (1974). From Serfdom to Socialism. In R.K. Dowse (ed) *From Serfdom to Socialism, James Keir Hardie; Labour and the Empire, James Ramsay MacDonald; The Socialist's Budget, Philip Snowden* (pp 1–130). Hassocks, Nr Brighton: The Harvester Press.

Harrison, R. (1971). The War Emergency Workers' National Committee, 1914–1920. In A. Briggs and J. Saville (eds) *Essays in Labour History 1886–1923*. London: Macmillan.

Harrop, M. and Shaw, A. (1989). *Can Labour Win?* London: HarperCollins.

Harvey, C. and Press, J. (2000). Management and the Taff Vale Strike of 1900. *Business History*, *42*(2), 63–86.

Haseler, S. (1969). *The Gaitskellites: Revisionism in the British Labour Party, 1951–64*. London: Macmillan.

Hay, C. (1994). Labour's Thatcherite Revision: Playing the 'Politics of Catch-up'. *Political Studies*, *42*(4), 700–707.

Hay, C. (1996). Narrating Crisis: The Discursive Construction of the 'Winter of Discontent'. *Sociology*, *30*(2), 253–277.

Hay, C. (1999). *The Political Economy of New Labour: Labouring under False Pretences?* Manchester: Manchester University Press.

Hay, C. (2010). Chronicles of a Death Foretold: The Winter of Discontent and Construction of the Crisis of British Keynesianism. *Parliamentary Affairs*, *63*(3), 446–470.

Hay, C. (2011). Pathology without Crisis? The Strange Demise of the Anglo-Liberal Growth Model. *Government and Opposition*, *46*(1), 1–31.

Hay, C. (2013). Treating the Symptom Not the Condition: Crisis Definition, Deficit Reduction and the Search for a New British Growth Model. *The British Journal of Politics and International Relations*, *15*(1), 23–37.

Hayter, D. (2005). *Fightback! Labour's Traditional Right in the 1970s and 1980s*. Manchester: Manchester University Press.

HC Deb (1978, 12 13). HC Deb, 13 December 1978, vol 960, cc673-810. Retrieved 28 January 2013 from: http://hansard.millbanksystems.com/commons/1978/dec/13/counter-inflation-policy

Heath, A., Jowell, R. and Curtice, J. (1994). *Labour's Last Chance? The 1992 Election and Beyond*. Aldershot: Dartmouth.

Heffernan, R. and Marqusee, M. (1992). *Defeat from the Jaws of Victory: Inside Neil Kinnock's Labour Party*. London: Verso.

Hennessey, P. (2000). *The Prime Minister: The Office and Its Holders since 1945*. London: Allen Lane.

Hindmoor, A. and McConnell, A. (2013). 'Why Didn't They See It Coming?' *Political Studies, Warning Signs, Acceptable Risks and the Global Financial Crisis*, *61*(3), 543–560.

HM Government (1944). *Employment Policy*. London: HMSO.

Hobsbawm, E. (1978). The Forward March of Labour Halted. *Marxism Today*, 279–286.

Hodson, D. and Mabbett, D. (2008). UK Economic Policy and the Global Financial Crisis: Paradigm Lost? *Journal of Common Market Studies*, *47*(5), 1041–1061.

Holden, R. (1999). Labour's Transformation: Searching for the Point of Origin – The European Dynamic. *Politics, 19*(2), 103–108.

Holland, S. (1975). *The Socialist Challenge.* London: Quartet Books.

Holland, S. (1976). *Regional Problem.* Basingstoke: Macmillan.

Holland, S. (1987). *The Global Economy: From Meso to Macroeconomics.* London: Weidenfeld and Nicolson.

Holton, R.J. (1985). Revolutionary Syndicalism and the British Labour Movement. In W.J. Mommsen and H. Husung (eds) *The Development of Trade Unionism in Great Britain and Germany 1880–1914.* London: Routledge.

House of Lords (2021). Economic Affairs Committee: 1st Report of Session 2021–22 Quantitative Easing: A Dangerous Addiction. Retrieved 9 October 2021 from: https://publications.parliament.uk/pa/ld5802/ldsel ect/ldeconaf/42/42.pdf

Howell, D. (1980). *British Social Democracy: A Study in Development and Decay.* London: Croom Helm.

Howell, C. (2005). *Trade Unions and the State.* Princeton: Princeton University Press.

Howell, C. (2007a). *Trade Unions and the State: The Construction of Industrial Relations Institutions in Britain 1890–2000.* Princeton: Princeton University Press.

Howell, C. (2007b). The British Variety of Capitalism: Institutional Change, Industrial Relations and British Politics. *British Politics, 2,* 239–263.

Hutton, G. and Shalchi, A. (2021). Financial Services: Contribution to the UK Economy. Retrieved 10 May 2022 from: https://researchbriefings. files.parliament.uk/documents/SN06193/SN06193.pdf

Inglehart, R. (1977). *The Silent Revolution: Changing Values and Political Styles Among Western Publics.* Princeton: Princeton University Press.

Inman, P. (2012). Black Wednesday 20 Years on: How the Day Unfolded. Retrieved 25 March 2020 from: https://www.theguardian.com/business/ 2012/sep/13/black-wednesday-20-years-pound-erm

Institute for Fiscal Studies (2010). Public Spending under Labour: 2010 Election Briefing Note No. 5. Retrieved 25 August 2021 from: https:// ifs.org.uk/bns/bn92.pdf

International Monetary Fund (2021). Policy Responses to COVID-19: United Kingdom. Retrieved 31 August 2021 from: https://www.imf. org/en/Topics/imf-and-covid19/Policy-Responses-to-COVID-19#top

Jackson, B. (2007). *Equality and the British Left: A Study in Progressive Political Thought 1900–64.* Manchester: Manchester University Press.

Jessop, B. (2018). Valid Construals and/or Correct Readings? On the Symptomatology of Crises. In B. Jessop and K. Kino (eds) *The Pedagogy of Economic, Political and Social Crises* (pp 49–72). London: Routledge.

Jobson, R. (2013). 'Waving the Banners of a Bygone Age': Nostalgia and Labour's Clause IV Controversy, 1959–60. *Contemporary British History*, 27(2), 123–144.

Jobson, R. and Wickham-Jones, M. (2011). Reinventing the Block Vote? Trade Unions and the 2010 Labour Party Leadership Election. *British Politics*, 6, 317–344.

Jones, B. and Keating, M. (1985). *Labour and the British State*. Oxford: Clarendon Press.

Jones, T. (1994). Neil Kinnock's Socialist Journey: From Clause Four to the Policy Review. *Contemporary Record*, 8(3), 567–588.

Jones, T. (1996). *Remaking the Labour Party: From Gaitskell to Blair*. London: Routledge.

Jones, T. (1997). 'Taking Genesis out of the Bible': Hugh Gaitskell, Clause IV and Labour's Socialist Myth. *Contemporary British History*, 11(2), 1–23.

Joyce, P. (1999). *Realignment of the Left? A History of the Relationship between the Liberal Democrat and Labour Parties*. London: Palgrave Macmillan.

Jupe, R. (2011). 'A Poll Tax on Wheels': Might the Move to Privatise Rail in Britain Have Failed? *Business History*, 53(3), 324–343.

Kavanagh, D. and Cowley, P. (2010). *The British General Election of 2010*. Basingstoke: Palgrave.

Kenny, M. and Smith, M.J. (1997). (Mis)understanding Blair. *Political Quarterly*, 68(3), 220–230.

King, A. (1975). Overload: Problems of Governing in the 1970s. *Political Studies*, 23(2–3), 284–296.

Kinnock, N. (1984). Leader's Speech, Blackpool 1984. Retrieved 16 June 2021 from: http://www.britishpoliticalspeech.org/speech-archive.htm?speech=190

Kinnock, N. (1985a). The Future of Socialism: Fabian Tract 509. Retrieved 2 July 2020 from: https://digital.library.lse.ac.uk/objects/lse:yek232haj

Kinnock, N. (1985b). Leader's Speech, Bournemouth 1985. Retrieved 23 June 2020 from: http://www.britishpoliticalspeech.org/speech-archive.htm?speech=191

Kinnock, N. (1988). *Statement of Democratic Socialist Aims and Values*. London: Labour Party.

Kinnock, N. (1994). Reforming the Labour Party. *Contemporary Record*, 8(3), 535–554.

Kirkland, C. (2015). Thatcherism and the Origins of the 2007 Crisis. *British Politics*, 10(4), 514–535.

Kirkland, C. (2017). *The Political Economy of Britain in Crisis: The Trade Unions and the Banking Sector*. Basingstoke: Palgrave Macmillan.

Klarman, M.J. (1989). Parliamentary Reversal of the Osborne Judgement. *The Historical Journal*, 32(4), 893–924.

Kollewe, J. (2016, 4 August). UK Interest Rate Moves Since 2007 – Timeline. Retrieved 16 June 2021 from: https://www.theguardian.com/business/2016/jul/14/uk-interest-rates-timeline-bank-of-england-uk-economy

Labour Party. (1900). 1900 Labour Party General Election Manifesto. Retrieved 27 August 2021 from: http://labourmanifesto.com/1900/1900-labour-manifesto.shtml

Labour Party. (1910). January 1910 Labour Party General Election Manifesto. Retrieved 27 August 2021 from: http://www.labour-party.org.uk/manifestos/1910/jan/1910-jan-labour-manifesto.shtml

Labour Party. (1918). 1918 Labour Party General Election Manifesto: Labour's Call to the People. Retrieved 25 June 2021 from: http://www.labour-party.org.uk/manifestos/1918/1918-labour-manifesto.shtml

Labour Party. (1928). *Labour and the Nation*. London: Labour Party.

Labour Party. (1934). *For Socialism and Peace*. London: Labour Party.

Labour Party. (1935). 1935 Labour Party General Election Manifesto. Retrieved 23 August 2021 from: http://www.labour-party.org.uk/manifestos/1935/1935-labour-manifesto.shtml

Labour Party. (1945). Let Us Face the Future: A Declaration of Labour Policy for the Consideration of the Nation. Retrieved 19 August 2020 from: http://www.labour-party.org.uk/manifestos/1945/1945-labour-manifesto.shtml

Labour Party. (1950). Let Us Win through Together. Retrieved 6 July 2021 from: http://www.labour-party.org.uk/manifestos/1950/1950-labour-manifesto.shtml

Labour Party. (1959). 1959 Labour Party Election Manifesto. Retrieved 6 July 2021 from: http://www.labour-party.org.uk/manifestos/1959/1959-labour-manifesto.shtml

Labour Party. (1964). The New Britain: 1964 Labour Party Election Manifesto. Retrieved 14 July 2021 from: http://labour-party.org.uk/manifestos/1964/1964-labour-manifesto.shtml

Labour Party. (1970). Now Britain Is Strong – Let's Make It Great to Live In: 1970 Labour Party Manifesto. Retrieved 8 July 2021 from: http://www.labour-party.org.uk/manifestos/1970/1970-labour-manifesto.shtml

Labour Party. (1974). *Labour's Programme: Campaign Document 1974*. London: Labour Party.

Labour Party. (1979). The Labour Way Is the Better Way: 1979 Labour Party Manifesto. Retrieved 8 July 2021 from: http://www.labour-party.org.uk/manifestos/1979/1979-labour-manifesto.shtml

Labour Party. (1983). *The New Hope for Britain: Labour's Manifesto 1983*. London: Labour Party.

Labour Party. (1987). 1987 Labour Party Manifesto: Britain Will Win with Labour. Retrieved 25 June 2021 from: http://www.labour-party.org.uk/manifestos/1987/1987-labour-manifesto.shtml

Labour Party. (1992). It's Time to Get Britain Working Again: The 1992 Labour Party Manifesto. Retrieved 27 July 2021 from: http://www.labour-party.org.uk/manifestos/1992/1992-labour-manifesto.shtml#dem

Labour Party. (1997). New Labour: Because Britain Deserves Better. Retrieved 8 July 08 2021 from: http://www.labour-party.org.uk/manifestos/1997/1997-labour-manifesto.shtml

Labour Party. (2005). Britain Forward Not Back: The Labour Party Manifesto 2005. Retrieved 8 July 2021 from: http://newsimg.bbc.co.uk/1/shared/bsp/hi/pdfs/LAB_uk_manifesto.pdf

Labour Party. (2010). *A Future Fair for All: The Labour Party Manifesto 2010*. London: Labour Party.

Labour Party. (2015). Britain Can Be Better: The Labour Party Manifesto 2015. Retrieved 20 July 2021 from: https://b.3cdn.net/labouruk/e1d45da42456423b8c_vwm6brbvb.pdf

Labour Party. (2017). For the Many Not the Few: The Labour Party 2017 Manifesto. Retrieved 11 April 2022 from: https://labour.org.uk/wp-content/uploads/2017/10/labour-manifesto-2017.pdf

Labour Party. (2019). It's Time for Real Change. Retrieved 17 August 2021 from: https://labour.org.uk/wp-content/uploads/2019/11/Real-Change-Labour-Manifesto-2019.pdf

Lamb, P. (2004). *Harold Laski: Problems of Democracy, the Sovereign State, and International Society*. Basingstoke: Palgrave Macmillan.

Laski, H. (1933). *Democracy in Crisis*. Chapel Hill: The University of North Carolina Press.

Lawrence, J. (2013). Blue Labour, One Nation Labour and the Lessons of History. *Renewal*, *21*(2), 6–13.

Lee, G. (2019, 25 November). The Gaps in Labour's Spending Plans. Retrieved 11 June 2021 from: https://www.channel4.com/news/factcheck/factcheck-the-gaps-in-labours-spending-plans

Leonard, D. (1975). Foreword. In D. Leonard, *Socialism Now and Other Essays* (pp 7–12). London: Jonathan Cape.

Leopold, D. (2007). Socialism and (the Rejection of) Utopia. *Journal of Political Ideologies*, *12*(3), 219–237.

Lovell, J. (1986). *British Trade Unions 1875–1933*. Basingstoke: Macmillan.

Ludlam, S. (2001). New Labour and the Unions: The End of the Contentious Alliance? In S. Ludlam and M. Smith (eds) *New Labour in Government*. Basingstoke: Palgrave Macmillan.

MacKenzie, N. and MacKenzie, J. (1979). *The First Fabians*. London: Quartet Press.

Manwaring, R. and Smith, E. (2020). Corbyn, British Labour and Policy Change. *British Politics*, *15*(1), 25–47.

Marquand, D. (1977). *Ramsay MacDonald*. London: Jonathan Cape.

Martin, C. and Milas, C. (2013). Financial Crises and Monetary Policy: Evidence from the UK. *Journal of Financial Stability*, *9*(4), 654–661.

Martin, D. (1985). Ideology and Composition. In K.D. Brown (ed) *The First Labour Party 1906–1914* (pp 17–37). Beckenham: Croom Helm.

Marx, K. and Engles, F. (1848 [1888]). *The Communist Manifesto, authorized English translation edited by Friedrich Engels*. New York: New York Labor News, 1888.

Mason, A. (1969). The Government and the General Strike of 1926. *International Review of Social History*, *14*(1), 1–21.

McAnulla, S. (2006). *British Politics: A Critical Introduction*. London: Continuum.

McAnulla, S. (2012). Tony Blair, 1994–7. In T. Heppell (ed) *Leaders of the Opposition: From Churchill to Cameron* (pp 168–183). Basingstoke: Palgrave Macmillan.

McCafferty, I. (2017, 5 October). Speech: Twenty Years of Bank of England Independence: The Evolution of Monetary Policy. Retrieved 16 June 2021 from: https://www.bankofengland.co.uk/-/media/boe/files/speech/2017/twenty-years-of-boe-independence-the-evolution-of-monetary-policy.pdf

McCord, N. (1993). Taff Vale Revisited. *History*, *78*(253), 243–260.

McDonnell, J. (2015, 11 December). John McDonnell – 2015 Speech to Labour Party Conference. Retrieved 7 July 2021 from: https://www.ukpol.co.uk/john-mcdonnell-2015-speech-to-labour-party-conference/

McDonnell, J. (2018). Introduction. In J. McDonnell, *Economics for the Many*. London: Verso.

McIlory, J. (1998). The Enduring Alliance? Trade Unions and the Making of New Labour 1994–1997. *British Journal of Industrial Relations*, *36*(4), 537–564.

McKenzie, R. and Silver, A. (1968). *Angels in Marble: Working Class Conservatives in Urban England*. London: University of Chicago Press.

McKibbin, R. (1970). James Ramsay MacDonald and the Problem of the Independence of the Labour Party 1910–1914. *Journal of Modern History*, *42*(2), 216–235.

McKibbin, R. (1984). Why Was There No Marxism in Great Britain? *The English Historical Review*, *99*(391), 297–331.

McSmith, A. (1996). *New Labour: The Inside Story*. London: Verso.

Miliband, E. (2017). Inequality and Left Politics. *Renewal*, *25*(2), 6–11.

Miliband, R. (1961). *Parliamentary Socialism*. London: George Allen & Unwin.

Miliband, R. (1969). *The State in Capitalist Society*. London: Weidenfeld and Nicolson.

Miliband, R. (1994). *Socialism for a Sceptical Age*. Cambridge: Polity.

Miliband, R. (2003). The Climax of Labourism. In D. Coates (ed) *Paving the Third Way: The Critique of Parliamentary Socialism* (pp 12–45). London: The Merlin Press.

Miliband, R. (2009). *Parliamentary Socialism*. Pontypool: The Merlin Press.

Millward, R. (1997). The 1940s Nationalizations in Britain: Means to an End or the Means of Production. *Economic History Review*, *2*, 209–234.

Millward, R. and Singleton, J. (1995). The Ownership of British Industry in the Post-War Era: An Explanation. In R. Millward and J. Singleton (eds) *The Political Economy of Nationalisation in Britain 1920–1950* (pp 309–320). Cambridge: Cambridge University Press.

Minkin, L. (1974). British Labour Party and the Trade Unions: Crisis and Compact. *Industrial and Labour Relations Review*, *28*(1), 7–37.

Minkin, L. (1991). *The Contentious Alliance: Trade Unions and the Labour Party*. Edinburgh: Edinburgh University Press.

Mitchell, A. (1979). *Can Labour Win Again? Fabian Tract 463*. London: Fabian Society.

Mitchell, J. and Jump, R.C. (2020). Labour, the 'Red Wall' and the Vicissitudes of Britain's Voting System. Retrieved 31 August 2021 from: https://www.opendemocracy.net/en/oureconomy/labour-red-wall-and-vicissitudes-britains-voting-system/

Moher, J.G. (2009). The Osborne Judgement of 1909: Trade Union Funding of Political Parties in Historical Perspective. Retrieved 5 August 2021 from: https://www.historyandpolicy.org/policy-papers/papers/the-osbo rne-judgement-of-1909-trade-union-funding-of-political-parties-in-h

Moran, M., Johal, S. and Williams, K. (2010). The Financial Crisis and Its Consequences. In N. Allen and J. Bartle (eds) *Britain at the Polls* (pp 89–119). London: Sage.

Morgan, K.O. (1985). *Labour in Power, 1945–51*. Oxford: Oxford University Press.

Morgan, K.O. (1997). *Callaghan: A Life*. Oxford: Oxford University Press.

Morgan, K.O. (2004). United Kingdom: A Comparative Case Study of Labour Prime Ministers Attlee, Wilson, Callaghan and Blair. *The Journal of Legislative Studies*, *10*(2–3), 38–52.

Morgan, K.O. (2011). The New Liberal Party from Dawn to Downfall 1906–1924. Retrieved 30 June 2021 from: https://journals.openedition.org/mimmoc/671?lang=fr

Morrison, H. (1933). *Socialisation and Transport*. London: Constable.

Morrison, H. (1940). Economic Organisation HC Debate, vol 356, cc1309–438. Retrieved 2 August 2021 from: https://api.parliament.uk/historic-hansard/commons/1940/feb/01/economic-organisation

Murray, B.K. (1973). *The People's Budget 1909/10: Lloyd George and Liberal Politics*. New York: Clarendon Press.

Nairn, T. (1964). The Nature of the Labour Party (Part I). *New Left Review*, *1*(27).

Nason, J.M. and Vahey, S.P. (2007). The McKenna Rule and UK World War I Finance. *The American Economic Review*, *97*(2), 290–294.

National Archives. (nd). The First World War: Aftermath. Retrieved 29 June 2021 from: http://www.nationalarchives.gov.uk/pathways/firstworld war/aftermath/brit_after_war.htm

National Archives. (2020). Sterling Devalued and the IMF loan. Retrieved 11 March 2021 from: https://www.nationalarchives.gov.uk/cabinetpap ers/themes/sterling-devalued-imf-loan.htm

National Audit Office. (2020). Tax Payer Support for UK Banks. Retrieved 25 August 2021 from: https://www.nao.org.uk/highlights/taxpayer-supp ort-for-uk-banks-faqs/

Neef, F. and Holland, R. (1967). Comparative Unemployment Rates, 1964–66. *Monthly Labor Review, 90*(4), 18–20.

Newton, C.C. (1984). The Sterling Crisis of 1947 and the British Response to the Marshall Plan. *The Economic History Review, 37*(3), 391–408.

Nijhuis, D.O. (2009). Rethinking the Beveridge Strait-Jacket: The Labour Party, the TUC and the Introduction of Superannuation. *Twentieth Century British History, 20*(3), 370–395.

Nordlinger, E.A. (1967). *The Working Class Tories: Authority, Deference and Stable Democracy.* London: MacGibbon and Kee.

O'Connor, J. (1987). *The Meaning of Crisis: A Theoretical Introduction.* New York: Basil Blackwell.

O'Hara, G. (2018, 26 November). How Did New Labour Become 'Neoliberal'? Ed Miliband's Efforts to Break with the Party's Past. Retrieved 11 April 2022 from: https://blogs.lse.ac.uk/politicsandpolicy/ed-milib and-new-labour/

Office for National Statistics. (2015, 6 July). Mid-1851 to Mid-2014 Population Estimates for United Kingdom. Retrieved 30 June 2021 from: https://www.ons.gov.uk/peoplepopulationandcommunity/populat ionandmigration/populationestimates/adhocs/004356ukpopulationesti mates1851to2014

Office for National Statistics. (2019a). Long-Term Trends in UK Employment: 1861 to 2018. Retrieved 26 August 2021 from: https:// www.ons.gov.uk/economy/nationalaccounts/uksectoraccounts/compend ium/economicreview/april2019/longtermtrendsinukemployment1861to2 018#public-and-private-sector-employment

Office for National Statistics. (2019b). Changes in the Economy since the 1970s. Retrieved 23 August 2021 from: https://www.ons.gov.uk/econ omy/economicoutputandproductivity/output/articles/changesintheecono mysincethe1970s/2019-09-02

Panitch, L. (2003). Socialists and the Labour Party: A Reappraisal. In D. Coates (ed) *Paving the Third Way: The Critique of Parliamentary Socialism* (pp 159–180). London: Merlin Press.

Panitch, L. and Leys, C. (2020). *Searching for Socialism: The Project of the Labour New Left from Benn to Corbyn.* London: Verso.

Parish, J. (1999, 1 January). It Was Tax What Lost It for Labour. Retrieved 28 July 2021 from: https://web.archive.org/web/20110606022117/http://www.newstatesman.com/199901010027

Parkin, F. (1967). Working-class Conservatives: A Theory of Political Defiance. *The British Journal of Sociology*, *18*, 278–290.

Partington, R. (2019, 8 March). The Verdict on 10 years of Quantitative Easing. Retrieved 6 June 2021 from: https://www.theguardian.com/business/2019/mar/08/the-verdict-on-10-years-of-quantitative-easing

Payne, S. (2015). Yvette Cooper and Liz Kendall Put In Strong Performances at Fabian Hustings. Retrieved 17 May 2021 from: https://www.spectator.co.uk/article/yvette-cooper-and-liz-kendall-put-in-strong-performances-at-fabian-hustings

Pelling, H. (1982). The Politics of the Osborne Judgement. *The Historical Journal*, *25*(4), 889–909.

Pelling, H. (1984). *The Labour Governments, 1945–51*. London: Palgrave Macmillan.

Pelling, H. and Reid, J.A. (1996). *A Short History of the Labour Party*. Basingstoke: Macmillan.

Pettifor, A. (2018). To Secure a Future Britain Needs a Green New Deal. In J. McDonnell (ed) *Economics for the Many* (pp 43–55). London: Verso.

Philpot, R. (2011a) *The Purple Book: A Progressive Future for Labour*. London: Biteback Publishing.

Philpot, R. (2011b). Introduction: Todays Choice Before Labour. In R. Philpot, *The Purple Book: A Progressive Future for Labour*. London: Biteback Publishing.

Pigou, A.C. (1918). A Special Levy to Discharge War Debt. *The Economic Journal*, *28*(110), 135–156.

Pimlott, B. (1971). The Socialist League: Intellectuals and the Labour Left in the 1930s. *Journal of Contemporary History*, *6*(3), 12–38.

Pimlott, B. (1985). *Hugh Dalton*. London: Jonathan Cape.

Pimlott, B. (1993). *Harold Wilson*. London: HarperCollins.

Porritt, E. (1910). The British Labour Party in 1910. *Political Science Quarterly*, *25*(10), 297–316.

Pym, H. and Kocham, N. (1998). *Gordon Brown: The First Year in Power*. London: Bloomsbury.

Quinn, T. (2010). New Labour and the Trade Unions in Britain. *Journal of Elections, Public Opinion and Parties*, *20*(3), 357–380.

Radice, G. (1978). *The Industrial Democrats: Trade Unions in an Uncertain World*. London: George Allen & Unwin.

Rawnsley, A. (2010, 21 February). The Weekend Gordon Brown Saved the Banks from the Abyss. Retrieved 17 June 2021 from: https://www.theguardian.com/politics/2010/feb/21/gordon-brown-saved-banks

Rayson, S. (2020). *The Fall of the Red Wall*. Self-published.

Rentoul, J. (2019, 12 November). Now We Know What We Already Suspected: Labour's Fully Costed Plans Were Full of Holes. Retrieved 11 April 2022 from: https://www.independent.co.uk/voices/jeremy-cor byn-labour-2017-election-campaign-nhs-spending-plans-a8555621.html

Richards, B. (2019, 9 October). British People Hardly Ever Thought about the EU before Brexit, Now It Dominates Their Lives. Retrieved 19 August 2021 from: https://theconversation.com/british-people-hardly-ever-thou ght-about-the-eu-before-brexit-now-it-dominates-their-lives-123784

Riddell, N. (1995). 'The Age of Cole?' G.D.H. Cole and the British Labour Movement 1929–1933. *The Historical Journal, 38*(4), 933–957.

Riddell, N. (1999). *Labour in Crisis: The Second Labour Government.* Manchester: Manchester University Press.

Robertson, A. (1987). *The Bleak Midwinter, 1947.* Manchester: Manchester University Press.

Rodgers, W. (1984). Government under Stress: Britain's Winter of Discontent 1979. *The Political Quarterly, 55*(2), 171–179.

Roe-Crines, A. (2016). Explainer: What Is Momentum and What Does It Want? Retrieved 19 August 2021 from: https://theconversation.com/ explainer-what-is-momentum-and-what-does-it-want-56408

Rogan, T. (2017). *The Moral Economists: R.H. Tawney, Karl Polanyi, E.P. Thompson and the Critique of Capitalism.* Princeton: Princeton University Press.

Rogers, C. (2009). From Social Contract to 'Social Contrick': The Depoliticisation of Economic Policy-Making under Harold Wilson, 1974–75. *British Journal of Politics and International Relations, 11*(4), 634–651.

Ross, T., Dominiczak, P. and Riley-Smith, B. (2015). Death of New Labour as Jeremy Corbyn's Party Begins a Period of Civil War. Retrieved 26 March 2021 from: https://www.telegraph.co.uk/politics/2015/09/12/ death-new-labour-jeremy-corbyns-socialist-party-begins-period/

Runciman, W.G. (1966). *Relative Deprivation and Social Justice.* London: Routledge.

Sandbrooke, D. (2012). *Seasons in the Sun: The Battle for Britain 1974–79.* London: Allen Lane.

Sanders, D. (2004). Vote Functions and Popularity Functions in British Politics. *Electoral Studies, 23*(2), 307–313.

Saville, J. (1967). Labourism and the Labour Government. *The Socialist Register, 4,* 43–71.

Schmidt, W., Muller, A., Ramos-Vielba, I., Thornqvist, A. and Thornqvist, C. (2019). Austerity and Public Sector Trade Union Power: Before and After the Crisis. *European Journal of Industrial Relations, 25*(2), 129–145.

Seaman, L.C. (1993). *Post-Victorian Britain 1902–1951.* London: Routledge.

Seyd, P. and Whiteley, P. (1992). *Labour's Grassroots: The Politics of Party Membership.* Oxford: Clarendon Press.

Seymour, R. (2017). *Corbyn: The Strange Rebirth of Radical Politics*. London: Verso.

Shaw, E. (1988). *Discipline and Discord in the Labour Party: The Politics of Managerial Control*. Manchester: Manchester University Press.

Shinwell, E. (1944). *When the Men Come Home*. London: Victor Gollancz.

Shipman, A. (2015, 21 August). Explainer: Would Jeremy Corbyn's Quantitative Easing for the People Work? Retrieved 11 June 2021 from: https://theconversation.com/explainer-would-jeremy-corbyns-quantitative-easing-for-the-people-work-46368

Simpson, B. (1973). *Labour the Unions and the Party*. London: George Allen & Unwin.

Singleton, J. (1995). Labour, the Conservatives and Nationalisation. In R. Millward and J. Singleton (eds) *The Political Economy of Nationalisation in Britain, 1920–1950* (pp 13–33). Cambridge: Cambridge University Press.

Skelton, D. (2013). Margaret Thatcher: Friend of the Unions? Retrieved 24 August 2021 from: https://www.spectator.co.uk/article/margaret-thatcher-friend-of-the-unions-

Snowden, P. (1934). *An Autobiography Volume Two 1919–1934*. London: Ivor Nicholson and Watson.

Snowden, P. (1974). The Socialist's Budget. In R.E. Dowse (ed) *From Serfdom to Socialism James Keir Hardie; Labour and the Empire, James Ramsay MacDonald; The Socialist's Budget, Philip Snowden*. Hassocks: The Harvester Press.

Sobolewska, M. and Ford, R. (2020). *Brexitland: Identity, Diversity and the Reshaping of British Politics*. Cambridge: Cambridge University Press.

Stears, M. (1998). Guild Socialism and Ideological Diversity on the British Left, 1914–1926. *Journal of Political Ideologies*, *3*(3), 289–306.

Steele, G.R. (2008). Harold Wilson's Devaluation: A Salutary Lesson. *Economic Affairs*, *28*(3), 68–69.

Stewart, H. and Allegretti, A. (2021). Cooper, Lammy and Nandy among Beneficiaries of Starmer's Reshuffle. Retrieved 6 December 2021 from: https://www.theguardian.com/politics/2021/nov/29/keir-starmer-to-reshuffle-labour-frontbench-for-second-time-in-a-year

Stewart, M. (1974). *Protest or Power? A Study of the Labour Party*. London: George Allen & Unwin.

Stewart, M. (1977). *The Jekyll and Hyde Years: Politics and Economic Policy Since 1964*. London: J.M. Dent and Sons.

Stuart, M. (2012). John Smith 1992–4. In T. Heppell (ed) *Leaders of the Opposition: From Churchill to Cameron* (pp 155–167). Basingstoke: Palgrave.

Tanner, D. (1990). *Political Change and the Labour Party 1900–1918*. Cambridge: Cambridge University Press.

Tawney, R.H. (1921). *The Acquisitive Society*. New York: Harcourt, Brace and Co.

Taylor, A. (2001). The Stepping Stones Programme: Conservative Party Thinking on Trade Unions, 1975–9. *Historical Studies in Industrial Relations*, *11*, 109–133.

The Economist. (2011, 16 January). Ed Miliband Says Sorry for Everything Apart from Spending too Much. Retrieved 12 February 2021 from: https://www.economist.com/blighty/2011/01/16/ed-miliband-says-sorry-for-everything-apart-from-spending-too-much

The Guardian. (2013, 1 February). David Cameron Rebuked by Statistics Watchdog over Debt Claims. Retrieved 11 June 2021 from: https://www.theguardian.com/politics/2013/feb/01/david-cameron-rebuked-over-debt-claims

The Times. (1909, 17 November). Mr. Pease and the Labour Party. *The Times*, p 10.

The Times (2021). The Times' View on Sir Keir Starmer's Reshuffle. Retrieved 6 December 2021 from: https://www.thetimes.co.uk/article/the-times-view-on-sir-keir-starmers-reshuffle-new-labour-76tkj3k82

The World Bank. (2021, 29 January). Unemployment, Total (% of Total Labour) (Modeled ILO Estimate) – United Kingdom. Retrieved 11 April 2022 from: https://data.worldbank.org/indicator/SL.UEM.TOTL.ZS?locations=GB

Thatcher, M. (1993). *The Downing Street Years*. London: HarperCollins.

Thatcher, M. (1995). *The Path to Power*. London: HarperCollins.

Thomas, J. (2007). Bound by History: The Winter of Discontent in British Politics 1979–2004. *Media, Culture and Society*, *29*(2), 263–283.

Thompson, E.P. (1980). *The Making of the English Working Class*. London: Penguin.

Thompson, G., Hawkins, O., Dar, A. and Taylor, M. (2012). Olympic Britain: Social and Economic Changes since the 1908 and 1948 London Games. Retrieved 30 June 2021 from: https://www.parliament.uk/contentassets/3e62059d076142959d5190e1711451d1/olympicbritain.pdf#page=111

Thompson, H. (2013). Austerity as Ideology: The Bait and Switch of the Banking Crisis. *Comparative European Politics*, *11*(6), 729–736.

Thompson, J. (2011). The Liberal Party, Liberalism and Trade Unions 1906–1924. *Cercles*, *21*, 27–38.

Thorpe, A. (1991). *The British General Election of 1931*. Oxford: Oxford University Press.

Thorpe, A. (1999). The Labour Party and the Trade Unions. Retrieved 24 July 2020 from: https://eric.exeter.ac.uk/repository/bitstream/handle/10036/20752/Final%20unions%20article.pdf?sequence=1

Thorpe, A. (2015). *A History of the British Labour Party*. Basingstoke: Palgrave Macmillan.

Tidey, A. (2019, 24 November). The Death of the Left? UK's Labour Fights for Survival after Election Drubbing. Retrieved 11 April 2022 from: https://www.euronews.com/2019/12/21/uk-s-labour-descends-into-civil-war-can-it-survive-its-election-drubbing

Tomlinson, J. (1993). Mr Attlee's Supply Side Socialism. *The Economic History Review*, *46*(1), 1–22.

Tomlinson, J. (1996). *Democratic Socialism and Economic Policy: The Attlee Years 1945–51*. Cambridge: Cambridge University Press.

Tomlinson, J. (2002). The Limits of Tawney's Ethical Socialism: A Historical Perspective on the Labour Party and the Market. *Contemporary British History*, *16*(4), 1–16.

Toye, R. (2002). 'The Gentleman in Whitehall' Reconsidered: The Evolution of Douglas Jay's Views on Economic Planning and Consumer Choice, 1937–1947. *Labour History Review*, *67*(2), 187–204.

Toye, R. (2013). *The Labour Party and the Planned Economy, 1931–1951*. Cambridge: Cambridge University Press.

Treanor, J. and Syal, R. (2013). George Osborne under Pressure as Britain Loses AAA Rating for First Time. Retrieved 14 August 2021 from: https://www.theguardian.com/business/2013/feb/23/george-osborne-britain-aaa

TUC (2016). Our Brexit Campaign. Retrieved 6 July 2021 from: https://www.tuc.org.uk/campaigns/our-brexit-campaign

Turner, H.A. (1969). The Donovan Report. *The Economic Journal*, *79*(313), 1–10.

Tyler, R. (2006). 'Victims of Our History?' Barbara Castle and *In Place of Strife*. *Contemporary British History*, *20*(3), 461–476.

Vaitilngam, R. (2009). *Recession Britain: Findings from Economic and Social Research*. Swindon: Economic and Social Research Council.

Ward, A. and Oakley, D. (2009, 27 August). Bankers Watch as Sweden goes Negative. Retrieved 17 June 2021 from: https://www.ft.com/content/5d3f0692-9334-11de-b146-00144feabdc0

Ward, M. (2020). UK Trade, 1948–2019: Statistics, House of Commons Briefing Paper CBP 8261. Retrieved 12 January 2021 from: https://researchbriefings.files.parliament.uk/documents/CBP-8261/CBP-8261.pdf

Watts, J. and Bale, T. (2019). Populism as an Intra-party Phenomenon: The British Labour Party under Jeremy Corbyn. *British Journal of Politics and International Relations*, *21*(1), 99–115.

Webb, S. (1918a). Labour and the New Social Order. Retrieved 15 July 2021 from: http://webbs.library.lse.ac.uk/563/

Webb, S. (1918b). New Constitution of the Labour Party. Retrieved 7 September 2020 from: webbs.library.lse.ac.uk/124/1/NewConstitutionOfTheLabourParty1918.pdf

Webb, S. (1931). What Happened in 1931: A Record. Retrieved 12 July 2021 from: https://digital.library.lse.ac.uk/objects/lse:fik817jel/read/single#page/6/mode/2up

Wickman-Jones, M. (1996). *Economic Strategy and the Labour Party 1970–1983*. Basingstoke: Palgrave Macmillan.

Wickman-Jones, M. (2014). Introducing OMOV: The Labour Party–Trade Union Review Group and the 1994 Leadership Contest. *British Journal of Industrial Relations, 52*(1), 33–56.

Williams, G.L. and Williams, A.L. (1989). *Labour's Decline and the Social Democrats' Fall*. Basingstoke: Palgrave.

Williams, M. (1975). *Inside Number 10*. London: New English Library.

Wilson, T. (1964). The Coupon and the British General Election of 1918. *The Journal of Modern History, 36*(1), 28–42.

Wintour, P. (2015a, 3 June). The Undoing of Ed Miliband – and How Labour Lost the Election. Retrieved 11 June 2021 from: https://www.theguardian.com/politics/2015/jun/03/undoing-of-ed-miliband-and-how-labour-lost-election

Wintour, P. (2015b). Jeremy Corbyn's late Nomination Shakes up Labour Leadership Contest. Retrieved 30 August 2021 from: https://www.theguardian.com/politics/2015/jun/15/labour-leadership-contest-jeremy-corbyn

Wootton, B. (1945). *Freedom under Planning*. London: Forgotten Books.

Wren-Lewis, S. (2018). Labour's Fiscal Credibility Rule in Context. In J. McDonnell (ed) *Economics for the Many* (pp 12–22). London: Verso.

Wright, A. (1987). *R.H. Tawney*. Manchester: Manchester University Press.

Wright, T. (1999). New Labour, Old Crosland? In D. Leonard (ed) *Crosland and New Labour* (pp 193–202). Basingstoke: Macmillan.

Wyatt, W. (1977). *What's Left of the Labour Party*. London: Sidgwick and Jackson Limited.

Zeigler, P. (1993). *Wilson*. London: Weidenfeld and Nicolson.

Index

A

adult education 24–25
Amalgamated Society of Railway
    Servants 15, 16, 18–19, 20
anti-Semitism crisis 143–144
Asquith, H. 22, 29, 33, 141
Attlee, C.
    nationalisation 71
    New Fabian Research Bureau (NFRB) 46
    resignation 63
    Second World War 60–61
    socialism 7, 28, 30, 73
Attlee government 47, 61–62
    ideology 64–65
    National Health Service (NHS) 70
    nationalisation 5, 6
    socialism 72
    sterling crisis 62–63
austerity 87, 153

B

Bailey v. Pye 17–18
Balls, E. 128, 133
Bank of England
    ERM crisis 107
    financial crisis 2007/2008 131, 133,
        134, 137
    Great Slump of 1931 41–42
    nationalisation 46, 62
    New Labour 122
banking 46
banking crisis 1931 41
banking crisis 2007/2008 12, 124
    see also financial crisis 2007/2008
banking system 69
Banks, T. 104
Barker, R. 23, 33
Barnes, G. 22
Beckerman, W. 83
Beckett, M. 108
Bell, R. 16
Benn, T. 87, 90, 103, 104, 111, 112, 118
Bevan, A. 44, 70
Bevan, N. 52, 60
Beveridge, W. 4

Beveridge Report 64, 77
Bevin, E. 36, 43, 45, 53, 60, 61, 68, 76
Black Wednesday 121
Blair, T.
    equality of opportunity 115
    general election 1997 5, 169
    New Labour 1, 101, 107, 110–111
    party reform 113
    post-war years 125
    socialism 2, 7, 108–109, 116, 119
    trade unions 135
blame 9
Blanchflower, D. 131
Blue Labour 147, 148–149
Blunkett, D. 113
Bonar Law, A. 22
bread rationing 62
Brexit referendum 142, 144–147, 156–157
British Electricity Authority 62
British European Airways 62
British Transport Commission 62
Brittan, S. 93
Brown, B. 95
Brown, George
    devaluation 82, 94
Brown, Gordon
    Bank of England 133
    economic competence 110
    financial crisis 2007/2008 122, 124,
        131, 138
    general election 2010 140
    ideology 125–127, 128–129
    socialism 3, 132
Burns, Sir T. 128

C

Callaghan, J.
    devaluation 82
    electoral defeat 102
    Finance Group 61
    ideology 91
    Party Conference 1976 87, 93
    trade unions 98
    Wilson government 94, 97
Callaghan government 5, 88, 92, 100

Cameron, D. 141, 155
capitalism 24, 25, 44, 71, 91, 134, 164, 166
Castle, B. 4, 84, 85, 87, 94, 97, 100
Chamberlain, N. 60
Change UK 8
Churchill, W. 60
coal industry 37, 48
coalition governments 34, 60–61, 68–69, 78, 134, 139, 141
Coates, D. 62, 65, 122, 164
Cole, G.D.H.
  economic policy 45
  ideology 42, 50
  May Committee 40
  Second World War 60
  socialism 30
  sterling crisis 62
  trade unions 38–39, 52, 55
Conservative and Unionist Party 14
Conservative governments 38, 70, 74, 142
Conservative Party
  coalition governments 34, 134, 139, 141
  financial crisis 2007/2008 10–11, 125, 155
  First World War 22
  general election 1959 66
  general election 1983 101
  Great Slump of 1931 40
  ideology 90
  Labour's electoral defeats 12
  reputation 108, 110
  sterling crisis 63
Conservative voters 117
Cooper, Y. 3
Corbyn, J. 2, 141–143
  Brexit referendum 146
  economic policy 150, 151, 153
  Old Labour 1, 3
  socialism 7, 155–156
  supporters 4, 139, 159, 169
  trade unions 157, 158
Corbynomics 4
Cousins, F. 97
COVID-19 pandemic 168–169
credibility 126
Cribb, J. 129
Crick, B. 113
Cripps, S. 46, 58
crises 9–12
  in historical context 161–162
  Labour's responses to 166
    1964 to 1979 92–94
    1979 onwards 111–113
    2010 to 2019 152–154
    early years 26–27
    inter-war years 49–51
    New Labour 113–114, 129–132, 137
    post-war years 69–70
    Second World War 68–69

Crosland, A.
  austerity 87
  capitalism 71
  economic policy 93
  nationalisation 66–67
  socialism 72–73, 90–91, 95, 132, 163, 165

D
Daily Express 41
Dalton, H. 51–52, 54, 64, 70
Darling, A. 130
Davis, R. 148–149
Deakin, A. 76
debt repayments 21–22, 62–63
democratic socialism 43–44
devaluation 81–85, 107, 165
Diamond, P. 25, 36, 66, 113, 114, 116, 126–127, 167
Dilnot, A. 155
Donovan Commission 83–84
Durbin, Elizabeth 47
Durbin, Evan 43–45, 46, 61, 64, 77

E
Eatwell, J. 121
Echo, The 29
Economic Advisory Committee 150, 151
economic crises 9, 159
  see also banking crisis 1931; banking crisis 2007/2008; financial crisis 2007/2008
economic growth 134
economic performance 80
economic policy 45, 47–48, 51
  see also devaluation
economic reforms 128–129
economic socialism 2, 133–134
Economist 72, 154
education 24–25
electoral defeats 6, 101, 102–108, 139–144, 167, 168
  Labour's responses 111–114, 152–154
Electricity Board 70, 75
equality 91, 115
equality of opportunity 66, 115, 134
ethical socialism 2, 24, 27–28, 51, 65, 100, 127, 134
ethnocentrism 145
European Economic Community (EEC) 80, 107
European Exchange Rate Mechanism (ERM) crisis 107, 125, 162
European Union (EU) 8
  see also Brexit referendum
Eurozone 151

F
Fabian Society 15, 42
feminism 3
finance 46
Finance Group 61

financial crisis 2007/2008 9, 10–11,
      123–125, 134, 151, 162, 165
   Labour's ideology 127
   Labour's response to 129–132, 137
   unemployment 137
   see also banking crisis 2007/2008
financial sector 127–128
First World War 20–23, 26, 33, 36–37, 162
Fiscal Credibility Rule 151
Foot, M. 2, 25, 50, 102, 103, 111, 112
For Socialism and Peace (Labour Party) 48–49
Ford (company) 88, 100
franchise 14, 27, 30–31
full employment 66, 98, 109

G
Gaitskell, H. 46, 61, 66, 67–68, 77–78, 79,
      106
Gas Council 62
general election 1910 29, 32
general election 1918 30, 34
general election 1929 39
general election 1931 47
general election 1935 47
general election 1945 59, 148
general election 1951 63, 70
general election 1955 63, 66, 70
general election 1959 66
general election 1964 90
general election 1966 82
general election 1970 85
general election 1974 90, 103
general election 1979 99, 101, 102
general election 1983 103
general election 1992 105–106
general election 1997 111, 121
general election 2010 140–141, 152, 154
general election 2015 141, 153
general election 2017 142–143
general election 2019 143–144, 153–154
general elections 96
   see also electoral defeats
General Strike of 1926 36–39, 49–51, 52,
      55, 56, 161
Giddens, A. 3, 7, 109–110, 113–114
Glasman, M. 147–148, 149
gold standard 42
government spending 41
Great Depression 43
Great Slump of 1931 9, 39–42, 49–51
Green New Deal 151
Greenwood, A. 61
guild socialism 38, 45, 46, 56

H
Hain, P. 154
Hardie, K. 3, 16
Hattersley, R. 88, 104, 113
Healy, D. 87, 88, 90, 91, 98, 112
Heath, E. 5, 85, 97

Henderson, A. 22, 30
Hewitt, P. 112
Hobson, J.A. 43
Hodge, J. 22
Holland, S. 91, 104
house building programme 75
House of Lords 19–20
House of Lords reform 29, 53

I
ideological pluralism 17
ideology 1–6, 7–8
   1964 to 1979 90–92
   1979 onwards 112
   2005–2015 147–151
   early years 23–26
   inter-war years 42–49
   New Labour 108–111, 113–114, 125–129
   post-war years 64–68
   Second World War 64
   see also socialism
illegal strikes 56
income tax 16, 124
Independent Group 8
Independent Labour Party 8, 23, 42, 60
individualism 25
industrial policy 83–85
Industrial Relations Act 1971 85
industrialism 25
Industry and Society (Labour Party) 67
inequality 129
inflation 64, 86, 87, 95, 107, 110, 126
interest rates 131, 133, 151
International Monetary Fund (IMF)
      crisis 86–87, 92, 95, 99
inter-war years 36–58
   General Strike of 1926 36–39
   Great Slump of 1931 39–42
   Labour's ideology 42–49
   Labour's relationship with trade unions 38,
      54–56
   Labour's responses to crises 49–51
   Labour's understanding of socialism 51–54
   nationalisation 46, 48, 61
Iron and Steel Corporation 62
Isaacs, G. 76

J
Jay, D. 61, 65
Jenkins, R. 66, 102
Johnson, B. 5, 146, 156
Jones, J. 97

K
Kaufman, G. 111
Keynes, J.M. 4, 43, 45, 64
King, M. 124, 131
Kinnock, N.
   general election 1979 111
   and Michael Foot 102

miners' strike 118
party leadership 101, 104–107
socialism 7, 112–113, 114–115, 116
trade unions 117–118

L
Labour and the Nation (Labour Party) 52
Labour governments 166
    see also specific governments
Labour Party
    future electoral success 168–170
    in opposition 167–168; *see also*
        electoral defeats
    origins 14–17
Labour Representation Committee
    (LRC) 15–16, 29
Labour's Programme (Labour Party, 1974) 90
Laffer Curve 129
Lammy, D. 3
Lansbury, G. 30, 46
Laski, H. 45, 46, 54
Liberal Party 14, 23
    as challenger to Labour Party 32
    First World War 33
    Great Slump of 1931 40
    Labour's dependency on 28, 29, 30
    trade unions 16, 31
    working-class parliamentary
        representation 15
Lloyd George, D. 22, 33

M
MacDonald, R. 4, 8
    general election 1918 30
    General Strike of 1926 49
    Great Slump of 1931 40, 42, 44, 50, 53, 61
    ideology 23–24
    parliamentary representation 29
    socialism 26, 27–28
MacDonald-Gladstone Agreement 32
Macmillan, H. 63–64, 71
Major, J. 106
Mandelson, P. 124
markets 121
May, T. 142
May Committee 40
McDonnell, J. 150
McKenna Rule 21
meso-economy 91
Miliband, E. 1, 128, 152, 159
    Brexit referendum 144
    financial crisis 2007/2008 154–155
    ideology 147, 149, 153
    resignation 141
    trade unions 8, 118, 139, 157
Miliband, R. 30, 65, 71, 72, 163
Millward, R. 69, 77
Miners' Federation 16
miners' strike 37, 85, 97, 118
mining industry 37, 47

Momentum 139, 158
Morrison, H. 6, 48, 60, 68–69, 71–72, 73
mortgage crisis 123
multinational economy 91

N
National Coal Board 62
national debt 21–22, 62
National Democratic Party 34
National Health Service (NHS) 2, 65, 70,
    71, 82, 155
National Joint Council 47
National Plan 1965 81
nationalisation 162
    banking crisis 2007/2008 124, 130
    inter-war years 46, 48, 61
    post-war years 5, 52, 62, 65, 66–68, 69–70,
        74–75, 76, 77
    Second World War 68–69
negative interest rates 131
neoliberalism 150
New Fabian Research Bureau
    (NFRB) 45–46
New Labour 1, 3–4, 7, 101, 121–122
    financial crisis 2007/2008 123–125
        Labour's response to 129–132, 137
    ideology 108–111, 113–114, 125–127
    relationship with trade unions 135–137
    revisionism 79
    understanding of socialism 115–116,
        132–134, 138, 163
New Left 95
Northern Rock 123, 124

O
Old Labour 1, 3, 163
'one member, one vote' (OMOV) 102, 117,
    118, 158
opposition parties 5, 167
Osborne, G. 155
Osborne judgement 20, 32
Owen, D. 8, 89–90

P
Parliamentary Labour Party (PLP) 30, 39, 76,
    97, 139
parliamentary socialism 7, 42–43
party ideology *see* ideology
pension reform 77
Pettifor, A. 150, 151
Phillips curve 126
Pigou, A.C. 21, 22
Platt, J. 147
Polanyi, K. 148
policy review groups 105
political crises 9
post-war years 78–79
    Labour's ideology 64–68
    Labour's relationship with trade
        unions 75–78

Labour's responses to crises 69–70
Labour's understanding of socialism 70–75
sterling crisis 62–64
practical socialism 68
Prescott, J. 108
privatised Keynesianism 123
public ownership 66–67, 68, 130
see also nationalisation
Purple Labour 147, 149

Q
quantitative easing 131–132, 151, 169

R
Radice, G. 89
railways 47, 48, 69
see also Taff Vale
rationing 62
Red Wall 143, 147, 156
Reeves, R. 149
Reforming Britain's Economic and Financial Policy (Balls and O'Donnell) 128
revisionism 66, 68, 79, 167–168
understanding of socialism 67, 71, 74, 90–91
revolutionary socialism 7
Robinson, W.A. 39
Rodgers, W. 98, 111
Royal Commission on Trade Union and Employers' Associations 83–84

S
Saklatvala, S. 8
Sankey commission 70
Scanlon, H. 86, 97
seamen's strike 92, 96
Second World War 9, 12, 59–62
effect on Labour Party 78
Labour's ideology 64
Labour's response to crisis 68–69, 161
Trades Union Congress (TUC) 76
Shinwell, E. 19, 69
Shore, P. 102
Silkin, J. 102
Smith, J. 107, 108
Snowden, P. 8, 25, 30, 39, 40, 50, 61
social class 110
social contract 85–86, 88
Social Democratic Party (SDP) 102, 103, 106
social investment state 133
social learning 11, 12
socialisation 46, 47
socialism 2, 3
Labour's understanding of 6–8, 162–166
1964 to 1979 90–91, 94–95
1979 onwards 104, 114–115
2010 to 2019 154–157
early years 15, 23–24, 27–30
inter-war years 51–54

New Labour 108–109, 115–116, 132–134, 138
post-war years 64–65, 66, 67, 68, 70–75
stagflation 81
Starmer, K. 3
state socialism 127
sterling crisis 62–64
sterling devaluation see devaluation
strike action 84, 98
General Strike of 1926 36–39, 49–51, 52, 55, 56, 161
miners' strike 37, 85, 97, 118
seamen's strike 92, 96
see also Taff Vale
syndicalism 54–55, 56, 57

T
Taff Vale 17–20, 28–29, 31, 32, 162
Tawney, R. 24–25, 27
tax rises 124
temporary public ownership 130
Thatcher, M. 80, 89, 106, 117
Thatcherism 108
third way 109, 113–114, 116, 134
Times, The 133, 135
Trade Disputes and Trade Union Act 1927 38, 49, 56, 76, 77
trade union crisis 12
trade unions 3, 8–9, 16, 52, 165
Ed Miliband 8, 118, 139, 157
General Strike of 1926 36–39
Labour's relationship with
1964 to 1979 85–86, 88–89, 96–99, 101–102
1979 onwards 112, 117–119
2010 to 2019 157–158
early years 20, 30–34
in the future 169–170
inter-war years 38, 54–56
New Labour 135–137
post-war years 75–78
Royal Commission on Trade Union and Employers' Associations 83–85
Taff Vale 17–20, 28–29, 31, 32
Trades Union Congress (TUC) 20, 37, 47, 60, 76, 84, 97
Transport and General Workers' Union 76

U
UK Independence Party (UKIP) 8, 141, 143
Umuna, C. 8
under-consumption 43
unemployment 39, 87, 88, 126, 136–137
unemployment benefit 40, 41, 50, 53, 82, 95, 110

W
Wall Street Crash 9, 40
war debts 21–22, 62
Warwick agreement 136

Webb, S. 4, 15, 27, 32, 40, 42
welfare state 65
Williams, S. 8, 25, 90
Wilson, H. 106
Wilson governments 81, 82–83, 85–86, 90,
    92–93, 94–95, 96–97
Winter of Discontent 88–89, 94, 101, 165

working-class parliamentary
    representation 15, 28–29, 32–33
working-class politics 14–15
working-class voters 117, 156, 169
Wren-Lewis, S. 150–151
Wyatt, W. 70, 89